ANGLO-AMERICAN RELATIONS SINCE THE SECOND WORLD WAR

SERIES EDITOR: *Ben Whitaker*

published

BRITISH BROADCASTING
Anthony Smith

THE BRITISH PRESS
Anthony Smith

EASTERN EUROPE SINCE STALIN
Jonathan Steele

THE POPULATION PROBLEM
Stanley Johnson

PRIVACY
Mervyn Jones

TRADE UNIONS IN GREAT BRITAIN
John Hughes and Harold Pollins

in preparation

CHILDREN IN SOCIETY
Rosalind Brooke

CIVIL RIGHTS
Tom Harper

THE CIVIL SERVICE
Maurice Kogan and David Shapiro

COMMUNITY ACTION
Peter Morris and Cynthia Cockburn

THE CONTROL OF THE CITY
David C. Thorns

HIGHER EDUCATION
Brian MacArthur

LOCAL GOVERNMENT
Owen A. Hartley

POVERTY
Frank Field

REVOLUTION
Adam Roberts

SOUTH AFRICA
Sir Robert Birley

THE WELFARE STATE
Geoffrey Smith and E. T. Ashton

WESTERN EUROPEAN INTEGRATION
Malcolm Crawford

ANGLO-AMERICAN RELATIONS SINCE THE SECOND WORLD WAR

Compiled and Edited by

Ian S. McDonald

ST. MARTIN'S PRESS/NEW YORK

Contents

Introduction

Britain and the United States, which together had borne the struggle against the Axis powers with equal heroism and dedication, soon found themselves with the coming of peace in situations of widely disproportionate political and economic influence. While the United States economy was booming under the impetus of the greatest sustained effort of industrial production the world had ever seen, Britain—which had been the dominant international power on the world scene in the early years of the century—was staggering under the burden created by widespread destruction at home and a crushing foreign debt.

During the war the common cause which had united the two nations had served to conceal the real disparity in their true strengths. The allies had built up close links under the stress of conflict which were unprecedented. In a very real sense Britain and the United States had become indispensable to each other during the years between the outbreak of fighting and the collapse of Germany. Americans had come to admire the British during the Battle of Britain when they stood alone against the Nazi onslaught. This special feeling led to the Lend-Lease assistance programme and, after Pearl Harbour, to the full commitment of the vast United States resources to the joint war effort.

This far-reaching cooperation became personified by the ties of admiration and respect which Winston Churchill, the British Prime Minister, and Franklin Roosevelt, the American President, swiftly developed for each other. Through their shared naval experience, their personal letters and their close agreement on the major issues of policy—however many disagreements there might be on details—the two leaders built a special relationship that would survive long after their own years in power were over.

It had not always been so. The years before the war had been marked by America's withdrawal into isolationism and the consequent collapse of the League of Nations experiment. As Churchill later said: 'Nor can the United States escape the censure of history. Absorbed in their own affairs and all the abounding interests, activities and accidents of a free community, they simply gaped at the vast changes that were taking place in Europe, and imagined they were no concern of theirs.' At the same time, the attitude of British statesmen towards the United States was not one calculated to bridge the gap. Stanley Baldwin, as Prime Minister, was negative in his attitude towards the United States. Austen Chamberlain, his foreign secretary, showed little friendship towards the United States, and the same was true of Neville Chamberlain. Only Ramsay MacDonald, among British prime ministers in the interwar period, can be said to have had a genuine admiration and friendship for Americans. British suspicions and jealousy of the rising American power and the long-drawn-out debate over the issue of the 1914–18 War Debt did little to promote harmony between the two countries; while American opinion towards Britain was not improved by the abdication of King Edward VIII after he had resolved to marry a divorced woman who was an American citizen.

At the outbreak of war in 1939, therefore, few could have forecast the full extent of the deep and abiding relationship that would develop under the twin leadership of Roosevelt and Churchill. During the early years of the war, Churchill's massive prestige, built up during the two years when Britain stood alone against the German offensive, enabled him to exert a considerable influence on the United States that was quite out of proportion to the two nations' relative size and strength. Churchill was able persistently to argue over allied policy and to participate as an equal partner in strategy. The status that was accorded the British leader is reflected by such a document as the Atlantic Charter. Later, as America slowly took on more and more of the responsibility for the conduct of the war, Churchill was compelled against his will increasingly to take a subsidiary seat, often accepting decisions he disagreed with— especially concerning policy towards Eastern Europe and the ever-advancing Soviet power. With some justice he privately— and to a great extent powerlessly—regarded Roosevelt's policies as dangerously inclined towards accommodation with the Soviets. At the same time, however, with commendable restraint he did not make public his disagreements.

At the war's end the perilous predicament of Britain's finances was all too apparent. The new Labour Government was forced to turn ignominiously, cap in hand, to the United States. The action of the Truman administration in swiftly and, it seemed, arbitrarily cutting off Lend-Lease assistance to Britain once the war in Europe was over only compounded the situation and led to one of the earliest strains in the postwar relationship between the two countries.

Ever since the heady days of inter-allied cooperation during the peak of the war effort Britain has faced the problem of finding her true post-imperial place and role in the world. Her relationship with the United States has always been an invaluable support, but successive British governments have been forced to face the dilemma of having to try and preserve the alliance without allowing Britain to be drawn into the position of a satellite. What has been most remarkable in the postwar period has been the extent to which governments of either party in Britain have adhered to the alliance in spite of repeated strains and conflicts of interest. Although the fringes on both the Conservative right and the Labour left have at times chafed against the transatlantic bonds, each party, whenever it has come to power, has promptly professed its fidelity to the alliance. The Conservatives, after some grumbling, finally accepted an American admiral of the Atlantic. More recently the Labour Party's leadership swallowed its distaste for American policy in Vietnam and loyally supported Washington in the interests of the alliance. None of the recurrent rifts in the alliance has proved fatal, but there have been times when the relationship between the two nations has been severely strained. Indeed the course of the so-called 'special relationship' can best be traced, like the relationships in the average family, through the squabbles that have occurred between the partners. The British public suspected that the American oil companies were conspiring at the time of the Abadan crisis to force British interests out of Iran. Similarly President Kennedy's sudden cancellation of the Skybolt missile was viewed as an attempt to drive the Royal Air Force out of the skies as an effective strike force.

But the biggest confrontation of all—the one which came the closest to rupturing the alliance—was the Suez crisis of 1956. On this issue, the British Government felt, with reason, that the United States had failed to stand by its most loyal ally in a matter vital to that ally's interest and had fallen back in the face of a thinly veiled threat from the Soviet Union. The tensions between the two allies were intensified by the contempt with which Sir Anthony Eden, the British Prime Minister, regarded John Foster Dulles, the American Secretary of State —a dislike which was fully reciprocated by Mr Dulles. In the long run, the American refusal to support the Anglo-French venture probably saved the two nations from becoming entangled in a far worse situation in the Middle East. But the manner in which the United States abandoned its allies rankled deeply. More than any other event, Suez marked a watershed in postwar relations between the United States and Britain. The special relationship survived, but it would never again regain its former intensity.

For her part, however, on several occasions Britain was able to exert a salutary restraining influence on United States policies. One such occasion was when Clement Attlee, the then Prime Minister, flew suddenly to the United States in December 1950 as a gesture of British concern over reports that the Truman administration was contemplating using the atomic bomb in the Korean war. Subsequently Eden was able to restrain the Eisenhower administration from becoming too deeply committed in Indo-China in 1955, while British prime ministers regularly took the lead in pressing for disarmament measures and meetings at the summit.

But, as the Skybolt incident showed, when British defence policies conflicted with America's changing strategic plans, the United States was swift to disregard any claims of the 'special relationship' when it determined to pursue its own interests. To many Britons it appeared at times that the relationship was a one-way street in which Britain received very little in return for her loyalty to the alliance. Movements, such as that of Senator Javits for a North Atlantic Free Trade Area, or Sir George Catlin's concept of an Atlantic Commonwealth, always ran up against the insurmountable block of the great disparity in size, wealth and influence between the two Anglo-Saxon democracies. Any form of closer union, many Britons were afraid, would inevitably result in Britain being swallowed up by the United States and an American way of life which they mistrusted and even feared. In view of this, it was inevitable that, when the time came for Britain to make a choice as to her future, she should opt for the European Economic Community, which appeared to offer the benefits of membership in a wider economic union without—at least in the foreseeable future— the risk of the eclipse of her political and social traditions.

PART ONE

The Antecedents

The Atlantic Charter was the most important product of the meeting between President Franklin Roosevelt and Winston Churchill, the British Prime Minister, on board the cruiser Augusta off Newfoundland in August 1941. The British tried to obtain some commitment from the still officially neutral Americans in the event of the Japanese attacking British possessions in the Far East. In this, as in everything at that stage on the conflict, the Americans refused to make any concrete commitments.

The Atlantic Charter was the product of careful negotiation and recorded Anglo-American agreement on certain common principles on which the two governments based 'their hopes for a better future for the world'. These principles involved a commitment to no territorial aggrandisement, the right of all peoples to choose the form of government under which they wished to live and the right of all peoples to live in peace and freedom from fear, want and aggression.

The terms of the charter alarmed the isolationists in the United States, but was approved by most Americans for its idealistic sentiments. More important, its principles served as a basis for allied cooperation after the United States had entered the war, and influenced the two governments' later approach to the drafting of the United Nations Charter.

1 Franklin D. Roosevelt and Winston Churchill
THE ATLANTIC CHARTER (12 August 1941)

The President of the United States of America and the Prime Minister, Mr Churchill, representing His Majesty's Government in the United Kingdom, being met together, deem it right to make known certain common principles in the national policies of their respective countries on which they base their hopes for a better future for the world.

First, their countries seek no aggrandisement, territorial or other.

Second, they desire to see no territorial changes that do not accord with the freely expressed wishes of the peoples concerned.

Third, they respect the right of all peoples to choose the form of government under which they will live; and they wish to see sovereign rights and self-government restored to those who have been forcibly deprived of them.

Fourth, they will endeavour, with due respect for their existing obligations, to further the enjoyment by all States, great or small, victor or vanquished, of access, on equal terms, to the trade and to the raw materials of the world which are needed for their economic prosperity.

Fifth, they desire to bring about the fullest collaboration between all nations in the economic field, with the object of securing for all improved labour standards, economic advancement, and social security.

Sixth, after the final destruction of the Nazi tyranny they hope to see established a peace which will afford to all nations the means of dwelling in safety within their own boundaries, and which will afford assurance that all the men in all the lands may live out their lives in freedom from fear and want.

Seventh, such a peace should enable all men to traverse the high seas and oceans without hindrance.

Eighth, they believe that all the nations of the world, for realistic as well as spiritual reasons, must come to the abandonment of the use of force. Since no future peace can be maintained if land, sea, or air armaments continue to be employed by nations which threaten, or may threaten, aggression outside of their frontiers, they believe, pending the establishment of a wider and permanent system of general security, that the disarmament of such nations is essential. They will likewise aid and encourage all other practicable measures which will lighten for peace-loving peoples the crushing burden of armaments.

SOURCE: Winston S. Churchill. *The Second World War:* vol 3, *The Grand Alliance*, 443–4

The Yalta meeting was the final conference of the Big Three before the surrender of Germany. While it should have marked the high water point of allied unity, it was marred by the growing signs of dissension that would split the alliance wide open after the war. The United States and Britain went to considerable lengths to coordinate their policies before they gathered at Yalta in early February 1945.

At Yalta every problem—so far as the future of Europe, the Far East and the United Nations were concerned—was discussed. While the West made a number of concessions, especially concerning the future of Poland and the other so-called 'liberated territories', the Western allies also benefited. They secured Soviet agreement to participate in the United Nations, to give France a share in the allied control of defeated Germany and, nominally, to respect the integrity of the peoples of Eastern Europe.

2 Winston Churchill, Franklin D. Roosevelt and Marshal Stalin
THE YALTA PROTOCOL (11 February 1945)

The following statement is made by the Prime Minister of Great Britain, the President of the United States of America, and the Chairman of the Council of People's Commissars of the Union of Soviet Socialist Republics on the results of the Crimean Conference.

The Defeat of Germany

We have considered and determined the military plans of the three Allied Powers for the final defeat of the common enemy. The military staffs of the three Allied Nations have met in daily meetings throughout the conference. These meetings have been most satisfactory from every point of view and have resulted in closer coordination of the military effort of the three Allies than ever before. The fullest information has been interchanged. The timing, scope, and coordination of new and even more powerful blows to be launched by our Armies and Air Forces into the heart of Germany from the east, west, north, and south have been fully agreed and planned in detail.

Our combined military plans will be made known only as we execute them, but we believe that the very close working partnership among the three staffs attained at this conference will result in shortening the war. Meetings of the three staffs will be continued in the future whenever the need arises.

Nazi Germany is doomed. The German people will only make the cost of their defeat heavier to themselves by attempting to continue a hopeless resistance.

We have agreed on common policies and plans for enforcing the unconditional surrender terms which we shall impose together on Nazi Germany after German armed resistance has been finally crushed. These terms will not be made known until the final defeat of Germany has been accomplished. Under the agreed plan, the forces of the three powers will each occupy a separate zone of Germany. Coordinated administration and control has been provided for under the plan through a central Control Commission, consisting of the supreme commanders of the three powers, with headquarters in Berlin. It has been agreed that France should be invited by the three powers, if she should so desire, to take over a zone of occupation, and to participate as a fourth member of the Control Commission. The limits of the French zone will be agreed by the four Governments concerned through their representatives on the European Advisory Commission.

It is our inflexible purpose to destroy German militarism and nazi-ism and to ensure that Germany will never again be able to disturb the peace of the world. We are determined to disarm and disband all German armed forces; break up for all time the German General Staff that has repeatedly contrived the resurgence of German militarism; remove or destroy all German military equipment; eliminate or control all German industry that could be used for military production; bring all war criminals to just and swift punishment and exact reparation in kind for the destruction wrought by the Germans; wipe out the Nazi Party, Nazi laws, organizations, and institutions, remove all Nazi and militarist influences from public office and from the cultural and economic life of the German people; and take in harmony such other measures in Germany as may be necessary to the future peace and safety of the world. It is not our purpose to destroy the people of Germany, but only when nazi-ism and militarism have been extirpated will there be hope for a decent life for Germans, and a place for them in the comity of nations.

Reparation by Germany

We have considered the question of the damage caused by Germany to the Allied Nations in this war and recognized it as just that Germany be obliged to make compensation for this damage in kind to the greatest extent possible. A commission for the compensation of damage will be established. The commission will be instructed to consider the question of the extent and methods for compensating damage caused by Germany to the Allied countries. The commission will work in Moscow.

We are resolved upon the earliest possible establishment with our allies of a general international organization to maintain peace and security. We believe that this is essential, both to prevent aggression and to remove the political, economic, and social causes of war through the close and continuing collaboration of all peace-loving peoples.

The foundations were laid at Dumbarton Oaks. On the important question of voting procedure, however, agreement was not there reached. The present conference has been able to resolve this difficulty.

We have agreed that a conference of United Nations should be called to meet at San Francisco in the United States on April 25, 1945, to prepare the charter of such an organization, along the lines proposed in the informal conversations at Dumbarton Oaks.

The Government of China and the Provisional Government of France will be immediately consulted and invited to sponsor invitations to the conference jointly with the Governments of the United States, Great Britain, and the Union of Soviet Socialist Republics. As soon as the consultation with China and France has been completed, the text of the proposals on voting procedure will be made public.

Declaration on Liberated Europe

The Premier of the Union of Soviet Socialist Republics, the Prime Minister of the United Kingdom, and the President of the United States of America have consulted with each other in the common interests of the peoples of their countries and those of liberated Europe. They jointly declare their mutual agreement to concert during the temporary period of instability in liberated Europe the policies of their three Governments in assisting the peoples liberated from the domination of Nazi Germany and the peoples of the former Axis satellite states of Europe to solve by democratic means their pressing political and economic problems.

The establishment of order in Europe and the rebuilding of national economic life must be achieved by processes which will enable the liberated peoples to destroy the last vestiges of nazi-ism and fascism and to create democratic institutions of their own choice. This is a principle of the Atlantic Charter—the right of all peoples to choose the form of government under which they will live—the restoration of sovereign rights and self-government to those peoples who have been forcibly deprived of them by the aggressor nations.

To foster the conditions in which the liberated peoples may exercise these rights, the three Governments will jointly assist the people in any European liberated state or former Axis satellite state in Europe where in their judgment conditions require (a) to establish conditions of internal peace; (b) to carry out emergency measures for the relief of distressed peoples; (c) to form interim governmental authorities broadly representative of all democratic elements in the population and pledged to the earliest possible establishment through free elections of governments responsible to the will of the people; and (d) to facilitate where necessary the holding of such elections.

The three Governments will consult the other United Nations and provisional authorities or other governments in Europe when matters of direct interest to them are under consideration.

When, in the opinion of the three Governments, conditions in any European liberated state or any former Axis satellite state in Europe make such action necessary, they will immediately consult together on the measures necessary to discharge the joint responsibilities set forth in this declaration.

By this declaration we reaffirm our faith in the principles of the Atlantic Charter, our pledge in the declaration by the United Nations, and our determination to build in cooperation with other peace-loving nations world order under law, dedicated to peace, security, freedom, and general well-being of all mankind.

In issuing this declaration, the three powers express the hope that the Provisional Government of the French Republic may be associated with them in the procedure suggested.

Poland

A new situation has been created in Poland as a result of her complete liberation by the Red Army. This calls for the establishment of a Polish Provisional Government which can be more broadly based than was possible before the recent liberation of western Poland. The Provisional Government which is now functioning in Poland should therefore be reorganized on a broader democratic basis with the inclusion of democratic leaders from Poland itself and from Poles abroad. This new Government should then be called the Polish Provisional Government of National Unity.

M. Molotov, Mr. Harriman, and Sir A. Clark Kerr are authorized as a commission to consult in the first instance in Moscow with members of the present Provisional Government and with other Polish democratic leaders from within Poland and from abroad, with a view to the reorganization of the present Government along the above lines. This Polish Provisional Government of National Unity shall be pledged to the holding of free and unfettered elections as soon as possible, on the basis of universal suffrage and secret ballot. In these elections all democratic and anti-Nazi parties shall have the right to take part and to put forward candidates.

When a Polish Provisional Government of National Unity has been properly formed in conformity with the above, the Government of the Union of Soviet Socialist Republics, which now maintains diplomatic relations with the present Provisional Government of Poland, and the Government of the United Kingdom, and the Government of the United States of America, will establish diplomatic relations with the new Polish Provisional Government of National Unity, and will exchange ambassadors by whose reports the respective governments will be kept informed about the situation in Poland.

The three heads of Government consider that the eastern frontier of Poland should follow the Curzon line with digressions from it in some regions of 5 to 8 kilometers in favor of Poland. They recognized that Poland must receive substantial accessions of territory in the north and west. They feel that the opinion of the new Polish Provisional Government of National Unity should be sought in due course on the extent of these accessions and that the final delimitation of the western frontier of Poland should thereafter await the peace conference.

SOURCE: US Department of State Bulletin, XIV, 282

The holocaust that was unleashed on Hiroshima and Nagasaki came as a shattering demonstration to the world of the unparalleled power of the atomic bomb, which had been developed secretly by the allies during the war.

Faced by the awesome challenge of the bomb, the three nations which had cooperated in its development—the United States, Britain and Canada—saw the urgent need to cooperate to prevent the use of the atom for destruction and instead promote the development of atomic power for peaceful ends.

With this in mind the three nations, on 15 November 1945, agreed to join in setting up a United Nations commission to deal with the threat. The scope of the danger, along with the terms of reference of the proposed commission, were set out in a communiqué signed by the President of the United States and the Prime Ministers of Britain and Canada.

3 Harry S. Truman, Clement Attlee and Mackenzie King
THREE-POWER DECLARATION ON ATOMIC ENERGY (15 November 1945)

Joint Declaration by the President of the United States, the Prime Minister of the United Kingdom, and the Prime Minister of Canada

1. We recognize that the application of recent scientific discoveries to the methods and practice of war has placed at the disposal of mankind means of destruction hitherto unknown, against which there can be no adequate military defence, and in the employment of which no single nation can in fact have a monopoly.

2. We desire to emphasize that the responsibility for devising means to ensure that the new discoveries shall be used for the benefit of mankind, instead of as a means of destruction, rests not on our nations alone, but upon the whole civilized world. Nevertheless, the progress that we have made in the develop-

ment and use of atomic energy demands that we take an initiative in the matter, and we have accordingly met together to consider the possibility of international action:—

(a) To prevent the use of atomic energy for destructive purposes

(b) To promote the use of recent and future advances in scientific knowledge, particularly in the utilization of atomic energy, for peaceful and humanitarian ends.

3. We are aware that the only complete protection for the civilized world from the destructive use of scientific knowledge lies in the prevention of war. No system of safeguards that can be devised will of itself provide an effective guarantee against production of atomic weapons by a nation bent on aggression. Nor can we ignore the possibility of the development of other weapons, or of new methods of warfare, which may constitute as great a threat to civilization as the military use of atomic energy.

4. Representing as we do, the three countries which possess the knowledge essential to the use of atomic energy, we declare at the outset our willingness, as a first contribution, to proceed with the exchange of fundamental scientific information and the interchange of scientists and scientific literature for peaceful ends with any nation that will fully reciprocate.

5. We believe that the fruits of scientific research should be made available to all nations, and that freedom of investigation and free interchange of ideas are essential to the progress of knowledge. In pursuance of this policy, the basic scientific information essential to the development of atomic energy for peaceful purposes has already been made available to the world. It is our intention that all further information of this character that may become available from time to time shall be similarly treated. We trust that other nations will adopt the same policy, thereby creating an atmosphere of reciprocal confidence in which political agreement and cooperation will flourish.

6. We have considered the question of the disclosure of detailed information concerning the practical industrial applica-

tion of atomic energy. The military exploitation of atomic energy depends, in large part, upon the same methods and processes as would be required for industrial uses.

We are not convinced that the spreading of the specialized information regarding the practical application of atomic energy, before it is possible to devise effective, reciprocal, and enforceable safeguards acceptable to all nations, would contribute to a constructive solution of the problem of the atomic bomb. On the contrary we think it might have the opposite effect. We are, however, prepared to share, on a reciprocal basis with others of the United Nations, detailed information concerning the practical industrial application of atomic energy just as soon as effective enforceable safeguards against its use for destructive purposes can be devised.

7. In order to attain the most effective means of entirely eliminating the use of atomic energy for destructive purposes and promoting its widest use for industrial and humanitarian purposes, we are of the opinion that at the earliest practicable date a Commission should be set up under the United Nations Organization to prepare recommendations for submission to the Organization.

The Commission should be instructed to proceed with the utmost dispatch and should be authorized to submit recommendations from time to time dealing with separate phases of its work.

In particular the Commission should make specific proposals:

(a) For extending between all nations the exchange of basic scientific information for peaceful ends,

(b) For control of atomic energy to the extent necessary to ensure its use only for peaceful purposes,

(c) For the elimination from national armaments of atomic weapons and of all other major weapons adaptable to mass destruction,

(d) For effective safeguards by way of inspection and other means to protect complying states against the hazards of violations and evasions.

8. The work of the Commission should proceed by separate stages, the successful completion of each one of which will develop the necessary confidence of the world before the next stage is undertaken. Specifically it is considered that the Commission might well devote its attention first to the wide exchange of scientists and scientific information, and as a second stage to the development of full knowledge concerning natural resources of raw materials.

9. Faced with the terrible realities of the application of science to destruction, every nation will realize more urgently than before the overwhelming need to maintain the rule of law among nations and to banish the scourge of war from the earth. This can only be brought about by giving wholehearted support to the United Nations Organization, and by consolidating and extending its authority, thus creating conditions of mutual trust in which all peoples will be free to devote themselves to the arts of peace. It is our firm resolve to work without reservation to achieve these ends.

SOURCE: US Department of State. *Treaties and Other International Acts Series*, 1504

PART TWO

Building the Peace

As a result of the war the entire economy of Europe lay devastated. Industrial production, transportation and the supply of raw materials were negligible. While the difficulties faced by Britain were different from those of the war-ravaged nations of the Continent, they were no less serious. For six years the national economy had been concentrated on the war effort to the exclusion of virtually every other consideration. Lend-Lease—which proved invaluable to the attainment of victory—had served primarily to boost the war effort, rather than to balance the economy. By 1944 British exports had dropped to less than a third of what they had been in 1938; sterling indebtedness had reached £3,355 million in mid-1945 and had risen to £3,700 million by the end of 1946. (In 1939 it had been a mere £476 million.) Moreover, half of Britain's merchant shipping had been lost to enemy action.

After the fall of Japan the predicament faced by Britain suddenly became intensified when, abruptly on 21 August 1945, the United States ended Lend-Lease. Under President Truman's agreement with Congress all supplies already in stock or being delivered would have to be paid for by a thirty-year loan at $2\frac{3}{4}$ per cent.

Three days later Prime Minister Clement Attlee announced that an invitation had been received from the United States 'to enter into immediate conversations to work things out in the manner which will best promote our mutual interests'. Lord Keynes went to Washington to join Lord Halifax, the British Ambassador, to enter the negotiations that led eventually to the financial agreement of 6 December.

Under the terms of the agreement the United States extended a loan of $4,400 million (including $650 million for the postwar residue of Lend-Lease supplies).

Although Keynes told the House of Lords that he would ideally have liked to have received a free grant the agreement did set a relatively generous 2-per-cent interest rate on the loan. Neither interest nor repayment was to begin until 1951 and repayment was to be spread over fifty years. In addition the interest could be waived for a period of years if Britain found this necessary.

Less generously, however, the United States also pressured Britain into agreeing not to increase imperial preferences and, in some cases, even to eliminate these.

Also Britain was required to adhere to the Bretton Woods agreement of July 1944 which set up the International Monetary Fund and the World Bank. This generally desirable move had the undesirable side effect of limiting the British Government's freedom to take steps to maintain the balance of payments.

4 Governments of the US and the UK
FINANCIAL AGREEMENT (6 December 1945)

It is hereby agreed between the Government of the United States of America and the Government of the United Kingdom of Great Britain and Northern Ireland as follows:

1. *Effective date of the Agreement.* The effective date of this Agreement shall be the date on which the Government of the United States notifies the Government of the United Kingdom that the Congress of the United States has made available the funds necessary to extend to the Government of the United Kingdom the line of credit in accordance with the provisions of this Agreement.

2. *Line of credit.* The Government of the United States will extend to the Government of the United Kingdom a line of credit of $3,750,000,000 which may be drawn upon at any time between the effective date of this Agreement and December 31, 1951, inclusive.

3. *Purpose of the line of credit.* The purpose of the line of credit is to facilitate purchases by the United Kingdom of goods and services in the United States, to assist the United Kingdom to meet transitional postwar deficits in its current balance of payments, to help the United Kingdom to maintain adequate reserves of gold and dollars, and to assist the Government of the United Kingdom to assume the obligations of multilateral trade, as defined in this and other agreements.

4. *Amortization and interest.*

(i) The amount of the line of credit drawn by December 31, 1951, shall be repaid in 50 annual installments beginning on December 31, 1951, with interest at the rate of 2 percent per annum. Interest for the year 1951 shall be computed on the amount outstanding on December 31, 1951, and for each year thereafter, interest shall be computed on the amount outstanding on January 1 of each such year.

Forty-nine annual installments of principal repayments and interest shall be equal, calculated at the rate of $31,823,000 for each $1,000,000,000 of the line of credit drawn by December 31, 1951, and the fiftieth annual installment shall be at the rate of $31,840,736.65 for each such $1,000,000,000. Each installment shall consist of the full amount of the interest due and the remainder of the installment shall be the principal to be repaid in that year. Payments required by this section are subject to the provisions of section 5.

(ii) The Government of the United Kingdom may accelerate repayment of the amount drawn under this line of credit.

5. *Waiver of interest payments.* In any year in which the Government of the United Kingdom requests the Government of the United States to waive the amount of the interest due in the installment of that year, the Government of the United States will grant the waiver if:

(*a*) the Government of the United Kingdom finds that a waiver is necessary in view of the present and prospective conditions of international exchange and the level of its gold and foreign exchange reserves *and* (*b*) the International Monetary Fund certifies that the income of the United Kingdom from home-produced exports plus its net income from invisible current transactions in its balance of payments was on the average over the five preceding calendar years less than the average annual amount of United Kingdom imports during 1936–8, fixed at £866 million, as such figure may be adjusted for changes in the price level of these imports. Any amount in excess of £43,750,000 released or paid in any year on account of sterling balances accumulated to the credit of overseas governments, monetary authorities and banks before the effective date of this Agreement shall be regarded as a capital transaction and therefore shall not be included in the above calculation of the net income from invisible current transactions for that year. If waiver is requested for an interest payment prior to that due in 1955, the average income shall be computed for the calendar years from 1950 through the year preceding that in which the request is made.

6. *Relation of this line of credit to other obligations.*

(i) It is understood that any amounts required to discharge obligations of the United Kingdom to third countries outstanding on the effective date of this Agreement will be found from resources other than this line of credit.

(ii) The Government of the United Kingdom will not arrange any long-term loans from governments within the British Commonwealth after December 6, 1945, and before the end of 1951 on terms more favorable to the lender than the terms of this line of credit.

(iii) Waiver of interest will not be requested or allowed under section 5 in any year unless the aggregate of the releases or payments in that year of sterling balances accumulated to the credit of overseas governments, monetary authorities and banks (except in the case of colonial dependencies) before the effective date of this Agreement is reduced proportionately, and unless interest payments due in that year on loans referred to in (ii) above are waived. The proportionate reduction of the releases or payments of sterling balances shall be calculated in relation to the aggregate released and paid in the most recent year in which waiver of interest was not requested.

(iv) The application of the principles set forth in this section shall be the subject of full consultation between the two governments as occasion may arise.

7. *Sterling area exchange agreements.* The Government of the United Kingdom will complete arrangements as early as practicable and in any case not later than one year after the effective date of this Agreement, unless in exceptional cases a later date is agreed upon after consultation, under which immediately after the completion of such arrangements the sterling receipts from current transactions of all sterling area countries (apart from any receipts arising out of military expenditure by the Government of the United Kingdom prior to December 31, 1948, to the extent to which they are treated by agreement with the countries concerned on the same basis as the balances accumulated during the war) will be freely available for current transactions in any currency area without discrimination; with the result that any discrimination arising from the so-called sterling area dollar pool will be entirely removed and that each member of the sterling area will have its current sterling and dollar receipts at its free disposition for current transactions anywhere . . .

SOURCE: US Department of State Bulletin (9 December 1945)

Under any other circumstances, if any other man had been involved, it would have seemed ironic that the first great ringing cry of alarm at the dangers which faced the postwar world from the Soviet bloc should have come, not from the governments in power in Britain or the United States, but from the leader of the opposition in the House of Commons. What gave the sombre warning its force, however, was the fact that it was sounded by Winston Churchill, the architect of victory in war, yet the man whom—inexplicably, in the eyes of many Americans—his countrymen had rejected at the polls in the aftermath of victory.

Churchill's words at Fulton—especially his image of the Iron Curtain

B

that had descended across Europe—are well known, but lose none of their force or eloquence through repetition. What is now often forgotten is that at the time they were delivered many Americans were sharply critical of the British statesman for the stand he took. They suspected that he was seeking to line up the United States with the British in a bloc to counter the Soviet Union (a view that revisionist historians have resurrected recently). The full significance of his remarks was not immediately recognised, nor the fact that he was setting the course of a policy that the Western alliance was to follow for the next fifteen years.

At Fulton, Churchill did not only demonstrate the risks of the precarious balance that had emerged from the war. He also proposed the manner in which the West should respond. He recommended a course of closer military cooperation, the standardisation of weapons and the joint use of forces and bases. He warned that it would be folly to permit unbridled nuclear proliferation. Moreover, he held out a vision of continued, fruitful Anglo-American cooperation that was to be realised in the close cooperative relationship established during the following years.

5 Winston Churchill
SPEECH AT FULTON, MISSOURI (5 March 1946)

. . . The United States stands at this time at the pinnacle of world power. It is a solemn moment for the American democracy. With primacy in power is also joined an awe-inspiring accountability to the future. As you look around you, you must feel not only the sense of duty done but also feel anxiety lest you fall below the level of achievement. Opportunity is here now, clear and shining, for both our countries. To reject it or ignore it or fritter it away will bring upon us all the long reproaches of the aftertime. It is necessary that constancy of mind, persistency of purpose and the grand simplicity of decision shall guide and rule the conduct of the English-speaking peoples in peace as they did in war. We must and I believe we shall prove ourselves equal to this severe requirement.

When American military men approach some serious situation they are wont to write at the head of their directive the words, 'over-all strategic concept.' There is wisdom in this as it leads to clarity of thought. What, then, is the over-all strategic concept which we should inscribe today? It is nothing less than the safety and welfare, the freedom and progress of all the homes and families of all the men and women in all the lands . . .

To give security to these countless homes they must be shielded from the two gaunt marauders—war and tyranny. We all know the frightful disturbance in which the ordinary family is plunged when the curse of war swoops down upon the bread winner and those for whom he works and contrives. The awful ruin of Europe, with all its vanished glories, and of large parts of Asia, glares in our eyes. When the designs of wicked men or the aggressive urge of mighty states dissolve, over large areas, the frame of civilized society, humble folk are confronted with difficulties with which they cannot cope. For them all is distorted, broken or even ground to pulp . . . Our supreme task and duty is to guard the homes of the common people from the horrors and miseries of another war . . .

I now come to the second danger which threatens the cottage home and ordinary people, namely tyranny . . . It is not our duty at this time, when difficulties are so numerous, to interfere forcibly in the internal affairs of countries whom we have not conquered in war, but we must never cease to proclaim in fearless tones the great principles of freedom and the rights of man, which are the joint inheritance of the English-speaking world and which, through Magna Carta, the Bill of Rights, the habeas corpus, trial by jury and the English common law, find their most famous expression in the Declaration of Independence.

All this means that the people of any country have the right and should have the power by constitutional action, by free, unfettered elections, with secret ballot, to choose or change the character or form of government under which they dwell, that freedom of speech and thought should reign, that courts of justice independent of the executive, unbiased by any party, should administer laws which have received the broad assent of large majorities or are consecrated by time and custom. Here are the title deeds of freedom, which should lie in every cottage home. Here is the message of the British and American peoples to mankind. Let us preach what we practice and practice what we preach . . .

Neither the sure prevention of war, nor the continuous rise of world organization will be gained without what I have called the fraternal association of the English-speaking peoples. This means a special relationship between the British Commonwealth and Empire and the United States. This is no time for generalities. I will venture to be precise. Fraternal association requires not only the growing friendship and mutual understanding between our two vast but kindred systems of society but the continuance of the intimate relationships between our military advisers, leading to common study of potential dangers, similarity of weapons and manuals of instruction and interchange of officers and cadets at colleges. It should carry with it the continuance of the present facilities for mutual security by the joint use of all naval and air-force bases in the possession of either country all over the world. This would perhaps double the mobility of the American Navy and Air Force . . .

A shadow has fallen upon the scenes so lately lighted by the Allied victory. Nobody knows what Soviet Russia and its Communist international organization intends to do in the immediate future, or what are the limits, if any, to their expansive and proselytizing tendencies. I have a strong admiration and regard for the valiant Russian people and for my war-time comrade, Marshal Stalin . . . We understand the Russians need to be secure on her western frontiers from all renewal of German aggression. We welcome her to her rightful place among the leading nations of the world. Above all we welcome constant, frequent and growing contacts between the Russian people and our own people on both sides of the Atlantic . . .

From Stettin in the Baltic to Trieste in the Adriatic, an iron curtain has descended across the Continent. Behind that line lie all the capitals of the ancient states of central and eastern Europe. Warsaw, Berlin, Prague, Vienna, Budapest, Belgrade, Bucharest, and Sofia, all these famous cities and the populations around them lie in the Soviet sphere and all are subject in one form or another, not only to Soviet influence but to a very high and increasing measure of control from Moscow . . .

In front of the iron curtain which lies across Europe are other causes for anxiety. In Italy the Communist party is seriously hampered by having to support the Communist trained Marshal Tito's claims to former Italian territory at the head of the Adriatic. Nevertheless the future of Italy hangs in the balance. Again one cannot imagine a regenerated Europe without a strong France. All my public life I have worked for a strong France and I never lost faith in her destiny, even in the darkest hours. I will not lose faith now. However, in a great number of countries, far from the Russian frontiers and throughout the world, Communist fifth columns are established and work in complete unity and absolute obedience to the directions they receive from the Communist center. Except in the British Commonwealth and in this United States, where Communism is in its infancy, the Communist parties or fifth columns constitute a growing challenge and peril to Christian civilization . . .

The outlook is also anxious in the Far East and especially in Manchuria. The agreement which was made at Yalta, to which I was a party, was extremely favorable to Soviet Russia, but it was made at a time when no one could say that the German war might not extend all through the summer and autumn of 1945 and when the Japenese war was expected to last for a further eighteen months from the end of the German war . . .

On the other hand I repulse the idea that a new war is inevitable; still more that it is imminent. It is because I am so sure that our fortunes are in our own hands and that we hold the power to save the future, that I feel the duty to speak out now that I have an occasion to do so. I do not believe that Soviet Russia desires war. What they desire is the fruits of war and the indefinite expansion of their power and doctrines. But what we have to consider here today while time remains, is the permanent prevention of war and the establishment of conditions of freedom and democracy as rapidly as possible in all countries. Our difficulties and dangers will not be removed by closing our eyes to them. They will not be removed by mere waiting to see what happens; nor will they be relieved by a policy of appeasement. What is needed is a settlement and the longer this is delayed the more difficult it will be and the greater our dangers will become. From what I have seen of our Russian friends and allies during the war, I am convinced that there is nothing they admire so much as strength, and there is nothing for which they have less respect than for military weakness. For that reason the old doctrine of a balance of power is unsound. We cannot afford, if we can help it, to work on narrow margins, offering temptations to a trial of strength. If the western democracies stand together in strict adherence to the principles of the United Nations Charter, their influence for furthering these principles will be immense and no one is likely to molest them. If, however, they become divided or falter in their duty, and if these all-important years are allowed to slip away, then indeed catastrophe may overwhelm us all . . .

If the population of the English-speaking commonwealth be added to that of the United States, with all that such co-operation implies in the air, on the sea and in science and industry, there will be no quivering, precarious balance of power to offer its temptation to ambition or adventure. On the contrary, there will be an overwhelming assurance of security . . .

SOURCE: Barton J. Bernstein and Allen J. Matusow (eds). *The Truman Administration: A Documentary History* (New York, 1966)

After the end of the war the Jews who survived the holocaust in Europe became insistent in their demand for an independent national homeland. At the same time Britain's precarious mandate over Palestine became increasingly difficult to administer as communal frictions between Arab and Jew increased. An Anglo-American commission was set up in 1945 to study the political, economic and social conditions in Palestine, the situation of the Jews in Europe, and to make recommendations on possible remedial action. The final report, released in May 1946, made ten recommendations which had been arrived at only after much compromise and discussion. Needless to say, it managed to satisfy neither Arab nor Jew.

One basic difficulty impeding Anglo-American discussions over Palestine came from the active role that Zionist influences played in American politics and in Truman's sensitivity to this pressure. The joint commission was seen by Britain as a means of compelling the United States to assume some positive responsibility in Palestine.

However, on the day the commission's report was released Truman issued a statement which in effect endorsed only those parts which were agreeable to the Zionists and made no mention of American cooperation in implementing the plan. Ernest Bevin, the British Foreign Secretary, worsened the situation by saying tactlessly that American insistence on 100,000 permits being made available to the Jews was because 'they did not want too many of them in New York'.

Finally, after the rejection of a British compromise plan by both the Arabs and the Israelis in February 1947, Britain turned the whole plan over to the youthful United Nations for solution.

6 Anglo-American Committee of Inquiry on Palestine EXCERPTS FROM THE REPORT (20 April 1946)

RECOMMENDATIONS

The European Problem

Recommendation No. 1. We have to report that such information as we received about countries other than Palestine gave no hope of substantial assistance in finding homes for Jews wishing or impelled to leave Europe.

But Palestine alone cannot meet the emigration needs of the Jewish victims of Nazi and Fascist persecution; the whole world shares responsibility for them and indeed for the resettlement of all 'displaced persons'.

We therefore recommend that our Governments together, and in association with other countries, should endeavor immediately to find new homes for all such 'displaced persons', irrespective of creed or nationality, whose ties with their former communities have been irreparably broken.

Though immigration will solve the problems of some victims of persecution, the overwhelming majority, including a considerable number of Jews, will continue to live in Europe. We recommend therefore that our Governments endeavor to secure that immediate effect is given to the provision of the United Nations Charter calling for 'universal respect for, and observance of, human rights and fundamental freedoms for all without distinction as to race, sex, language, or religion'.

Refugee Immigration Into Palestine

Recommendation No. 2. We recommend (a) that 100,000 certificates be authorized immediately for the admission into Palestine of Jews who have been the victims of Nazi and Fascist persecution; (b) that these certificates be awarded as far as possible in 1946 and that actual immigration be pushed forward as rapidly as conditions will permit.

Principles of Government: no Arab, no Jewish State

Recommendation No. 3. In order to dispose, once and for all, of the exclusive claims of Jews and Arabs to Palestine, we regard it as essential that a clear statement of the following principles should be made:

I. That Jew shall not dominate Arab and Arab shall not dominate Jew in Palestine. II. That Palestine shall be neither a Jewish state nor an Arab state. III. That the form of government ultimately to be established, shall, under international guarantees, fully protect and preserve the interests in the Holy Land of Christendom and of the Moslem and Jewish faiths.

Thus Palestine must ultimately become a state which guards

the rights and interests of Moslems, Jews and Christians alike; and accords to the inhabitants, as a whole, the fullest measure of self-government, consistent with the three paramount principles set forth above.

Mandate and United Nations Trusteeship

Recommendation No. 4. We have reached the conclusion that the hostility between Jews and Arabs and, in particular, the determination of each to achieve domination, if necessary by violence, make it almost certain that, now and for some time to come, any attempt to establish either an independent Palestinian state or independent Palestinian states would result in civil strife such as might threaten the peace of the world. We therefore recommend that, until this hostility disappears, the government of Palestine be continued as at present under mandate pending the execution of a trusteeship agreement under the United Nations.

Equality of Standards

Recommendation No. 5. Looking towards a form of ultimate self-government, consistent with the three principles laid down in recommendation No. 3, we recommend that the mandatory or trustee should proclaim the principle that Arab economic, educational and political advancement in Palestine is of equal importance with that of the Jews; and should at once prepare measures designed to bridge the gap which now exists and raise the Arab standard of living to that of the Jews; and so bring the two peoples to a full appreciation of their common interest and common destiny in the land where both belong.

Future Immigration Policy

Recommendation No. 6. We recommend that pending the early reference to the United Nations and the execution of a trusteeship agreement, the mandatory should administer Palestine according to the mandate which declares with regard to immigration that 'The administration of Palestine, while ensuring that the rights and position of other sections of the population are not prejudiced, shall facilitate Jewish immigration under suitable conditions.'

Land Policy

Recommendation No. 7. (a) We recommend that the land transfer regulations of 1940 be rescinded and replaced by regulations based on a policy of freedom in the sale, lease or use of land, irrespective of race, community or creed; and providing adequate protection for the interests of small owners and tenant cultivators. (b) We further recommend that steps be taken to render nugatory and to prohibit provisions in conveyances, leases and agreements relating to land which stipulate that only members of one race, community or creed may be employed on or about or in connection therewith. (c) We recommend that the Government should exercise such close supervision over the Holy Places and localities such as the Sea of Galilee and its vicinity as will protect them from desecration and from uses which offend the conscience of religious people; and that such laws as are required for this purpose be enacted forthwith.

Economic Development

Recommendation No. 8. Various plans for large-scale agricultural and industrial development in Palestine have been presented for our consideration; these projects, if successfully carried into effect, could not only greatly enlarge the capacity of the country to support an increasing population, but also raise the living standards of Jew and Arab alike.

We are not in a position to assess the soundness of these specific plans; but we cannot state too strongly that, however technically feasible they may be, they will fail unless there is peace in Palestine. Moreover their full success requires the willing cooperation of adjacent Arab states, since they are not merely Palestinian projects. We recommend therefore that the examination, discussion and execution of these plans be conducted, from the start and throughout, in full consultation and cooperation not only with the Jewish agency but also with the governments of the neighboring Arab states directly affected.

Education

Recommendation No. 9. We recommend that, in the interests of the conciliation of the two peoples and of general improvement of the Arab standard of living, the educational system of both Jews and Arabs be reformed including the introduction of compulsory education within a reasonable time.

The Need for Peace in Palestine

Recommendation No. 10. We recommend that, if this report is adopted, it should be made clear beyond all doubt to both Jews and Arabs that any attempt from either side, by threats of violence, by terrorism, or by the organization or use of illegal armies to prevent its execution, will be resolutely suppressed.

Furthermore, we express the view that the Jewish agency should at once resume active cooperation with the mandatory in the suppression of terrorism and of illegal immigration, and in the maintenance of that law and order throughout Palestine which is essential for the good of all, including the new immigrants.

Source: US Department of State Bulletin, XIV, 783

The declining influence and rising economic predicament of Britain suddenly became a matter of direct concern to the United States Government on 24 February 1947, when the British chargé d'affaires informed the State Department that Britain could no longer afford to provide aid to Greece and Turkey. Dean Acheson, the aristocratic and strong-willed Under Secretary of State, was in many respects an early exponent of what later came to be called the domino theory. Faced with the impending British withdrawal, he promptly emphasised to the US President that if Greece, then in the throes of a communist insurrection, were lost then Turkey would be untenable. The Soviets could move into the vacuum and seize control of the Dardanelles. The Western stake in the Middle East would be jeopardised and the already shaky economies of Western Europe placed in dire peril.

Following the crisis, Truman was to recall later that the decision he had to make was 'more serious than had ever confronted any president'— a slight if understandable exaggeration.

On 26 February, Acheson recommended a programme of military and financial aid to Greece and Turkey. The following day this was presented to the Congressional leadership. After the Cabinet had been consulted, Truman went before Congress on 12 March with his programme calling for a total of $400 million in aid for the two countries.

The significance of Truman's address went far beyond the immediate predicaments of Greece and Turkey. In it he articulated two principles which were later to emerge as the cornerstones of American policy in the cold war years. The first was that under certain circumstances it was in the American interest to intervene directly anywhere in the world. The second was the concept that the Soviet Union had to be halted before it made any more advances—a conviction which was to be intensified the following year by the collapse of Czechoslovakia.

Initially the President encountered considerable Congressional opposition to his new policy. It was argued that it was imperialistic, too expensive, ignored the United Nations and would lead to war. Some of the opponents of the doctrine later split from the Democrats and emerged in the splinter movement led by Henry Wallace, the former Vice-President.

7 President Truman
THE TRUMAN DOCTRINE (12 March 1947)

The gravity of the situation which confronts the world today necessitates my appearance before a joint session of the Congress. The foreign policy and the national security of this country are involved.

One aspect of the present situation, which I wish to present to you at this time for your consideration and decision, concerns Greece and Turkey.

The United States has received from the Greek Government an urgent appeal for financial and economic assistance. Preliminary reports from the American Economic Mission now in Greece and reports from the American Ambassador in Greece corroborate the statement of the Greek Government that assistance is imperative if Greece is to survive as a free nation.

I do not believe that the American people and the Congress wish to turn a deaf ear to the appeal of the Greek Government . . .

The very existence of the Greek state is today threatened by the terrorist activities of several thousand armed men, led by Communists, who defy the Government's authority at a number of points, particularly along the northern boundaries. A commission appointed by the United Nations Security Council is at present investigating disturbed conditions in Northern Greece and alleged border violations along the frontier between Greece on the one hand and Albania, Bulgaria and Yugoslavia on the other.

Meanwhile, the Greek Government is unable to cope with the situation. The Greek Army is small and poorly equipped. It needs supplies and equipment if it is to restore the authority to the Government throughout Greek territory.

Greece must have assistance if it is to become a self-supporting and self-respecting democracy. The United States must supply this assistance. We have already extended to Greece certain types of relief and economic aid but these are inadequate. There is no other country to which democratic Greece can turn. No other nation is willing and able to provide the necessary support for a democratic Greek Government.

The British Government, which has been helping Greece, can give no further financial or economic aid after March 31. Great Britain finds itself under the necessity of reducing or liquidating its commitments in several parts of the world, including Greece.

We have considered how the United Nations might assist in this crisis. But the situation is an urgent one requiring imme-

diate action, and the United Nations and its related organizations are not in a position to extend help of the kind that is
required . . .

Greece's neighbor, Turkey, also deserves our attention. The
future of Turkey as an independent and economically sound
state is clearly no less important to the freedom-loving peoples
of the world than the future of Greece. The circumstances in
which Turkey finds itself today are considerably different from
those of Greece. Turkey has been spared the disasters that have
beset Greece. And during the war, the United States and Great
Britain furnished Turkey with material aid.

Nevertheless, Turkey now needs our support.

Since the war Turkey has sought financial assistance from
Great Britain and the United States for the purpose of effecting
that modernization necessary for the maintenance of its national
integrity.

That integrity is essential to the preservation of order in the
Middle East.

The British Government has informed us that, owing to its
own difficulties, it can no longer extend financial or economic
aid to Turkey. As in the case of Greece, if Turkey is to have the
assistance it needs, the United States must supply it. We are the
only country able to provide that help.

I am fully aware of the broad implications involved if the
United States extends assistance to Greece and Turkey, and I
shall discuss these implications with you at this time.

One of the primary objectives of the foreign policy of the
United States is the creation of conditions in which we and
other nations will be able to work out a way of life free from
coercion. This was a fundamental issue in the war with Germany and Japan. Our victory was won over countries which
sought to impose their will, and their way of life, upon other
nations . . .

The peoples of a number of countries of the world have recently had totalitarian regimes forced upon them against their
will. The Government of the United States has made frequent

protests against coercion and intimidation, in violation of the Yalta Agreement, in Poland, Rumania, and Bulgaria. I must also state that in a number of other countries there have been similar developments.

At the present moment in world history nearly every nation must choose between alternative ways of life. The choice is too often not a free one.

One way of life is based upon the will of the majority, and is distinguished by free institutions, representative government, free elections, guarantees of individual liberty, freedom of speech and religion, and freedom from political oppression.

The second way of life is based upon the will of a minority forcibly imposed upon the majority. It relies upon terror and oppression, a controlled press and radio, fixed elections, and the suppression of personal freedoms.

I believe that it must be the policy of the United States to support free peoples who are resisting attempted subjugation by armed minorities or by outside pressures.

I believe that we must assist free peoples to work out their own destinies in their own way.

I believe that our help should be primarily through economic and financial aid, which is essential to economic stability and orderly political processes.

The world is not static and the status quo is not sacred. But we cannot allow changes in the status quo in violation of the Charter of the United Nations by such methods as coercion, or by such subterfuges as political infiltration. In helping free and independent nations to maintain their freedom, the United States will be giving effect to the principles of the Charter of the United Nations . . .

SOURCE: White House Documents (12 March 1947)

After the aid programme to Greece and Turkey had been launched it was time to turn to the perilous situation in Europe. During a visit to the Continent, General George Marshall, the US Secretary of State, had been shaken at what he had found. Britain, especially, had been hard hit by the worst winter of the century, which had accentuated the country's already desperate economic state. The launching of the Truman doctrine had prepared the ground for a similar large scale programme in the far more vital areas of Western Europe. On 8 May 1947, Acheson used the unusual forum of the Delta Council Meeting in Cleveland, Mississippi, to deliver a speech which paved the way for Marshall's famous address at Harvard University the following month. In his speech Acheson gave a comprehensive outline of the deteriorating situation that the Marshall proposals were designed to tackle. To ensure that it received the widest audience he took the precaution of notifying in advance a select handful of British correspondents about the significance of his remarks. Subtly, Acheson emphasised to his predominantly agricultural and business audience that American aid was in the national interest, a theme that would be sounded repeatedly whenever the subject of foreign aid was raised. He noted that American exports to Europe far exceeded imports, leaving the foreign countries with the problem of paying for the goods and services they received. Europe needed far more than what it was getting, but could not pay for what it was obtaining.

Europe must import more. This, he argued, was a matter of common sense, not charity. It was the duty of the United States to help Europe, because by so doing, it was serving its own best interests.

Acheson later remarked: 'Bevin had thrown me the ball and I had to run with it. I now decided to throw it in the air.'

8 Dean Acheson
SPEECH AT CLEVELAND, MISSISSIPPI (8 May 1947)

When Secretary of State Marshall returned from the recent meeting of the Council of Foreign Ministers in Moscow he did not talk to us about ideologies or armies. He talked about food and fuel and their relation to industrial production, and the relation of industrial production to the organisation of Europe, and the relation of the organisation of Europe to the peace of the world.

The devastation of war has brought us back to elementals, to the point where we see clearly how short is the distance from food and fuel either to peace or to anarchy.

Here are some of the basic facts of life with which we are primarily concerned today is the conduct of foreign relations:

The first is that most of the countries of Europe and Asia are today in a state of physical destruction or economic dislocation, or both. Planned scientific destruction of the enemy's resources carried out by both sides during the war has left factories destroyed, fields impoverished and without fertiliser or machinery to get them back in shape, transportation systems wrecked, populations scattered and on the borderline of starvation, and long-established business and trading connections disrupted.

Another grim fact of international life is that two of the greatest workshops of Europe and Asia—Germany and Japan —upon whose production Europe and Asia were to an important degree dependent before the war, have hardly been able even to begin the process of reconstruction because of the lack of a peace settlement. As we have seen, recent efforts at Moscow to make progress towards a settlement for Germany and Austria have ended with little accomplishment. Meanwhile, political instability in some degree retards revival in nearly every country of Europe and Asia.

A third factor is that unforeseen disasters—what the lawyers call 'acts of God'—have occurred to the crops of Europe. For two successive years unusually severe droughts have cut down food production. And during the past winter storms and floods and excessive cold unprecedented in recent years have swept northern Europe and England with enormous damage to agricultural and fuel production. These disasters have slowed down the already slow pace of reconstruction, have impeded recovery of exports, and have obliged many countries to draw down irreplaceable reserves of gold and foreign exchange which had been earmarked for the importation of reconstruction materials, for the purchase of food and fuel for subsistence.

The accumulation of these grim developments has produced a disparity between production in the United States and production in the rest of the world that is staggering in its proportions. The United States has been spared physical destruction during the war. Moreover, we have been favored with unusually bountiful agricultural crops in recent years. Production in this country is today running at the annual rate of two hundred and ten billion dollars.

Responding to this highly abnormal relationship between production in the United States and the production in the rest of the world, the United States Government has already authorised and is carrying out an extensive program of relief and reconstruction. We have contributed nearly three billion dollars to foreign relief. We have taken the lead in the organisation of the International Bank for Reconstruction and Development and the International Monetary Fund, and have subscribed to these two institutions to the extent of almost six billion dollars. We have increased the capacity of the ExportImport Bank to make loans abroad by almost three billion dollars. We have made a direct loan of three and three quarter billion dollars to Great Britain. We are proposing this year to contribute a half billion dollars for relief and reconstruction in the Philippines, and a billion dollars to relief in occupied areas. The President's recommendations for aid to Greece and Turkey to the extent of four hundred million dollars and for postUNRRA relief to the extent of three hundred and fifty million dollars are still under consideration by Congress. And there are a few other smaller items.

These measures of relief and reconstruction have been only in part suggested by humanitarianism. Your Congress has authorised and your Government is carrying out a policy of relief and reconstruction today chiefly as a matter of national self-interest. For it is generally agreed that until the various countries of the world get on their feet and become self-supporting there can be no political or economic stability in the world and no lasting peace or prosperity for any of us. Without outside aid, the process of recovery in many countries would take so long as to give rise to hopelessness and despair. In these conditions freedom and democracy and the independence of nations could not long survive, for hopeless and hungry people often resort to desperate measures. The war will not be over until the people of the world can again feed and clothe themselves and face the future with some degree of confidence.

The contribution of the United States towards world livelihood and reconstruction is best measured today not in terms of money but in terms of the commodities which we ship abroad. It is commodities—food, clothing, coal, steel, machinery—that the world needs, and it is commodities that we must concentrate our attention upon . . .

In return for the commodities and services which we expect to furnish the world this year, we estimate that we will receive commodities and services from abroad to the value of about eight billion dollars. This is just about half as much as we are exporting. This volume of imports is equal to about two weeks' work of all the factories, farms, mines, and laborers of the United States, and consists largely of things which are not produced in this country in sufficient quantity. We wish that the imports were larger, but the war-devastated world is just not able to supply more.

The difference between the value of the goods and services which foreign countries must buy from the United States this year and the value of the goods and services they are able to supply to us this year will therefore amount to the huge sum of about eight billion dollars.

How are foreigners going to get the U.S. dollars necessary to cover this huge difference? And how are they going to get the U.S. dollars to cover a likely difference of nearly the same amount next year? These are some of the most important questions in international relations today . . .

The facts of international life . . . mean that the United States is going to have to undertake further emergency financing of foreign purchases if foreign countries are to continue to buy in 1948 and 1949 the commodities which they need to sustain life and at the same time rebuild their economies. Requests for further United States aid may reach us through the International Bank, or through the Export-Import Bank, or they may be of a type which existing national and international institutions are not equipped to handle and therefore may be made directly through diplomatic channels. But we know now that further financing, beyond existing authorisations, is going to be needed. No other country is able to bridge the gap in commodities or dollars . . .

Since world demand exceeds our ability to supply, we are goint to have to concentrate our emergency assistance in areas where it will be most effective in building world political and economic stability, in promoting human freedom and democratic institutions, in fostering liberal trading policies, and in strengthening the authority of the United Nations.

This is merely common sense and sound practice. It is in keeping with the policy announced by President Truman in his special message to Congress on March 12 on aid to Greece and Turkey. Free peoples who are seeking to preserve their independence and democratic institutions and human freedoms against totalitarian pressures, either internal or external, will receive top priority for American reconstruction aid. This is no more than frank recognition, as President Truman said, 'that totalitarian regimes imposed on free peoples, by direct or indirect aggression, undermine the foundations of international peace and hence the security of the United States' . . .

Not only do human beings and nations exist in narrow economic margins, but also human dignity, human freedom, and democratic institutions.

It is one of the principal aims of our foreign policy today to use our economic and financial resources to widen these margins. It is necessary if we are to preserve our own freedoms and our own democratic institutions. It is necessary for our national security. And it is our duty and our privilege as human beings.

Source: US Department of State Bulletin, XVI, 991

Although it was Dean Acheson who first originated the idea of a pro-
gramme of reconstruction assistance for Europe, this became linked
irretrievably with the name of General Marshall, the US Secretary of
State, who outlined it in his famous address at Harvard University.

In his speech Marshall repeated many of the same themes that
Acheson had first articulated at Cleveland, Mississippi, but used his
more influential forum to appeal to Europe to cooperate by stating its
needs. Then, he indicated, the United States would be ready to extend aid.

He stressed that there had been a 'dislocation of the entire fabric of the
European economy'—a dislocation that was even more severe than that
wrought by war. He emphasised that rehabilitation would require a far
longer period of time and effort than had been anticipated. Industry was
not producing enough goods to exchange for food; farmers could not buy
what they needed and had no incentive to produce more; governments
were forced to use their dwindling reserves of foreign currency and credit
to buy food abroad. It was logical for the United States to help in
'breaking the vicious cycle'. American policy, Marshall stressed, was not
directed at any government or doctrine, but against 'hunger, poverty,
desperation and chaos'. However, he warned 'any government which
manoeuvres to block the recovery of other nations cannot expect help from
us'.

Participation in the plan was open to the Soviet Union and the other
East European countries. However, the requirement that participating
nations must open their national economic records for inspection proved
too much for the Soviet Union, which rejected the plan—as the United
States undoubtedly expected it would. The Soviet rejection also meant
that all other states in the Soviet bloc had to follow suit.

9A George C. Marshall
THE MARSHALL PLAN (5 June 1947)

I need not tell you gentlemen that the world situation is very
serious. That must be apparent to all intelligent people. I think
one difficulty is that the problem is one of such enormous complexity that the very mass of facts presented to the public by
press and radio make it exceedingly difficult for the man in the

street to reach a clear appraisement of the situation. Furthermore, the people of this country are distant from the troubled areas of the earth and it is hard for them to comprehend the plight and consequent reactions of the long-suffering peoples, and the effect of those reactions on their governments in connection with our efforts to promote peace in the world.

In considering the requirements for the rehabilitation of Europe the physical loss of life, the visible destruction of cities, factories, mines, and railroads was correctly estimated, but it has become obvious during recent months that this visible destruction was probably less serious than the dislocation of the entire fabric of European economy. For the past 10 years conditions have been highly abnormal. The feverish preparation for war and the more feverish maintenance of the war effort engulfed all aspects of national economies. Machinery has fallen into disrepair or is entirely obsolete. Under the arbitrary and destructive Nazi rule, virtually every possible enterprise was geared into the German war machine. Long-standing commercial ties, private institutions, banks, insurance companies and shipping companies disappeared through loss of capital, absorption through nationalization or by simple destruction. In many countries, confidence in the local currency has been severely shaken. The breakdown of the business structure of Europe during the war was complete. Recovery has been seriously retarded by the fact that 2 years after the close of hostilities a peace settlement with Germany and Austria has not been agreed upon. But even given a more prompt solution of these difficult problems, the rehabilitation of the economic structure of Europe quite evidently will require a much longer time and greater effort than had been foreseen.

There is a phase of this matter which is both interesting and serious. The farmer has always produced the foodstuffs to exchange with the city dweller for the other necessities of life. This division of labor is the basis of modern civilization. At the present time it is threatened with breakdown. The town and city industries are not producing adequate goods to exchange with the food-producing farmer. Raw materials and fuel are in short supply. Machinery is lacking or worn out. The farmer or the peasant cannot find the goods for sale which he desires to purchase. So the sale of his farm produce for money which he cannot use seems to him an unprofitable transaction. He, therefore, has withdrawn many fields from crop cultivation and is using them for grazing. He feeds more grain to stock and finds for himself and his family an ample supply of food, however short he may be on clothing and the other ordinary gadgets of civilization. Meanwhile people in the cities are short of food and fuel. So the governments are forced to use their foreign money and credits to procure these necessities abroad. This process exhausts funds which are urgently needed for reconstruction. Thus a very serious situation is rapidly developing which bodes no good for the world. The modern system of the division of labor upon which the exchange of products is based is in danger of breaking down.

The truth of the matter is that Europe's requirements for the next 3 or 4 years of foreign food and other essential products— principally from America—are so much greater than her present ability to pay that she must have substantial additional help, or face economic, social, and political deterioration of a very grave character.

The remedy lies in breaking the vicious circle and restoring the confidence of the European people in the economic future of their own countries and of Europe as a whole. The manufacturer and the farmer throughout wide areas must be able and willing to exchange their products for currencies the continuing value of which is not open to question.

Aside from the demoralizing effect on the world at large and the possibilities of disturbances arising as a result of the desperation of the people concerned, the consequences to the economy of the United States should be apparent to all. It is logical that the United States should do whatever it is able to do to assist in the return of normal economic health in the world, without which there can be no political stability and no assured peace. Our policy is directed not against any country or doctrine but against hunger, poverty, desperation, and chaos. Its purpose should be the revival of a working economy in the world so as to permit the emergence of political and social conditions in which free institutions can exist. Such assistance, I am convinced, must not be on a piecemeal basis as various crises develop. Any assistance that this Government may render in the future should provide a cure rather than a mere palliative. Any government that is willing to assist in the task of recovery will find full cooperation, I am sure, on the part of the United States Government. Any government which maneuvers to block the recovery of other countries cannot expect help from us. Furthermore, governments, political parties, or groups which seek to perpetuate human misery in order to profit therefrom politically or otherwise will encounter the opposition of the United States.

It is already evident that, before the United States Government can proceed much further in its efforts to alleviate the situation and help start the European world on its way to recovery, there must be some agreement among the countries of Europe as to the requirements of the situation and the part those countries themselves will take in order to give proper effect to whatever action might be undertaken by this Government. It would be neither fitting nor efficacious for this Government to undertake to draw up unilaterally a program designed to place Europe on its feet economically. This is the business of the Europeans. The initiative, I think, must come from Europe. The role of this country should consist of friendly aid in the drafting of a European program and of later support of such a program so far as it may be practical for us to do so. The program should be a joint one, agreed to by a number, if not all European nations.

An essential part of any successful action on the part of the United States is an understanding on the part of the people of America of the character of the problem and the remedies to be applied. Political passion and prejudice should have no part.

With foresight, and a willingness on the part of our people to face up to the vast responsibility which history has clearly placed upon our country, the difficulties I have outlined can and will be overcome.

SOURCE: US Department of State Bulletin, XVI, 1159

9B Ernest Bevin
SPEECH TO THE FOREIGN PRESS ASSOCIATION
(13 June 1947)

. . . Notwithstanding that we are the centre of a great Empire and Commonwealth we recognize that we are more than ever linked with the destinies of Europe. We are . . . a European nation and must act as such.

We have spent in two wars the accumulations from hundreds of years of effort in defending not so much our territory but our soul and the liberty of the world. But if anybody in the world has got it in his head that Britain is down and out, please get it out. We have genius, science, and productive capacity, and, while we have paid the price, I venture to prophesy that in a few years' time we shall be back where we have been hitherto.

We welcome the inspiring lead given to us and the peoples of Europe by Mr. Marshall, the American Secretary of State. His speech at Harvard will rank, I think, as one of the greatest speeches made in world history. It seemed to me to focus a need, and to have behind it the conception of a great cooperation between Europe and the wonderful and powerful western hemisphere. I can only say to other nations that when the United States throws a bridge to link east and west it would be disastrous for ideological or other reasons to frustrate the United States in that great endeavour.

On this occasion—just as they did when they proposed the Four-Power Treaty in Europe—it again seems that this great new and wonderful country, with all its great and potential wealth, is acting in the most unselfish manner in an endeavour to use her capacity to save Europe from another ruin and to rehabilitate Europe as urgently as possible. We in this country are exploring urgently and actively how best to respond to that lead, and must in this work consult France.

SOURCE: *The Times* (14 June 1947)

PART THREE

Soviet Challenge and Western Response

As part of their general desire to foster European recovery, the Western Powers determined that the three western zones of Germany should be brought into greater economic unity. As a step in this development General Lucius Clay, the chief of the American zone of occupation, in March 1948 initiated discussions of a currency reform in the Anglo-American zones. The Russians, foreseeing that West Germany was about to become merged in what they saw as an anti-Soviet grouping, responded with a partial blockade of western traffic into Berlin.

In June, General Clay boldly declared he would introduce the new currency into West Berlin. At the same time the allies made it known they would go forward with the formation of a West German government. The Soviets responded in some fury. Marshal Stalin argued that as the West had abandoned the idea of German unification, there was no longer any point in maintaining Berlin as a future capital. The allies, he said, should retire to their own zones. On 23 June he ordered a total blockade on all ground traffic into Berlin from the West. At the end of July the allies responded with a counter-blockage, stopping rail passage through their zones of traffic to and from the Soviet zone. The cordon around Berlin, which lasted until 12 May 1949, was overcome by an unprecedented use of air transport to fly a steady stream of supplies into the beleaguered city, with the allies ferrying in as much as 13,000 tons of material a day.

59

From the Soviet point of view, the blockade was a failure, since the Russians were unable to prevent the unification of West Germany. On the allied side the blockade had the effect of strengthening Anglo-American resolution and intensifying Western suspicions of Soviet intentions.

10 Governments of the US and the UK
NOTE ON THE BERLIN BLOCKADE
(6 July 1948)

The United States Government wishes to call to the attention of the Soviet Government the extremely serious international situation which has been brought about by the actions of the Soviet Government in imposing restrictive measures on transport which amount now to a blockade against the sectors in Berlin occupied by the United States, United Kingdom and France. The United States Government regards these measures of blockade as a clear violation of existing agreements concerning the administration of Berlin by the four occupying Powers.

The rights of the United States as a joint occupying Power in Berlin derive from the total defeat and unconditional surrender of Germany. The international agreements undertaken in connexion therewith by the Governments of the United States, United Kingdom, France and the Soviet Union defined the zones in Germany and the sectors in Berlin which are occupied by these powers. They established the quadripartite control of Berlin on a basis of friendly cooperation which the Government of the United States earnestly desires to continue to pursue.

These agreements implied the right of free access to Berlin. This right has long been confirmed by usage. It was directly specified in a message sent by President Truman to Premier Stalin on 14th June, 1945, which agreed to the withdrawal of United States forces to the zonal boundaries, provided satisfactory arrangements could be entered into between the military commanders, which would give access by rail, road and air to United States forces in Berlin. Premier Stalin replied on 16th June, suggesting a change in date but no other alteration in the plan proposed by the President. Premier Stalin then gave assurances that all necessary measures would be taken in accordance with the plan. Correspondence in a similar sense took place between Premier Stalin and Mr. Churchill. In accordance with this understanding, the United States, whose armies had penetrated deep into Saxony and Thuringia parts of the Soviet zone, withdrew its forces to its own area of occupation in Germany and took up its position in its own sector in Berlin. Thereupon the agreements in regard to the occupation of Germany and Berlin went into effect. The United States would not have so withdrawn its troops from a large area now occupied by the Soviet Union had there been any doubt whatsoever about the observance of its agreed right of free access to its sector of Berlin. The right of the United States to its position in Berlin thus stems from precisely the same source as the right of the Soviet Union. It is impossible to assert the latter and deny the former.

It clearly results from these undertakings that Berlin is not a part of the Soviet zone, but is an international zone of occupation. Commitments entered into in good faith by the zone commanders, and subsequently confirmed by the Allied Control Authority, as well as practices sanctioned by usage, guarantee the United States together with other Powers, free access to Berlin for the purpose of fulfilling its responsibilities as an occupying Power. The facts are plain. Their meaning is clear. Any other interpretation would offend all the rules of comity and reason.

In order that there should be no misunderstanding whatsoever on this point, the United States Government categorically asserts that it is in occupation of its sector in Berlin with free access thereto as a matter of established right deriving from the defeat and surrender of Germany and confirmed by formal agreements among the principal Allies. It further declares that it will not be induced by threats, pressure or other actions to abandon these rights. It is hoped that the Soviet Government entertains no doubts whatsoever on this point.

This Government now shares with the Governments of France and the United Kingdom the responsibility initially undertaken at Soviet request on 7th July, 1945, for the physical well-being of 2,400,000 persons in the western sectors of Berlin. Restrictions recently imposed by the Soviet authorities in Berlin have operated to prevent this Government and the Governments of the United Kingdom and of France from fulfilling that responsibility in an adequate manner.

The responsibility which this Government bears for the physical wellbeing and the safety of the German population in its sector of Berlin is outstandingly humanitarian in character. This population includes hundreds of thousands of women and children, whose health and safety are dependent on the continued use of adequate facilities for moving food, medical supplies and other items indispensable to the maintenance of human life in the western sectors of Berlin. The most elemental of those human rights which both our Governments are solemnly pledged to protect are thus placed in jeopardy by these restrictions. It is intolerable that any one of the occupying authorities should attempt to impose a blockade upon the people of Berlin.

The United States Government is therefore obliged to insist that in accordance with existing agreements the arrangements for the movement of freight and passenger traffic between the Western zones and Berlin be fully restored. There can be no question of delay in the restoration of these essential services since the needs of the civilian population in the Berlin area are imperative.

Holding these urgent views regarding its rights and obligations in the United States sector of Berlin, yet eager always to resolve controversies in the spirit of fair consideration for the view points of all concerned, the Government of the United States declares that duress should not be invoked as a method of attempting to dispose of any disagreements which may exist between the Soviet Government and the Government of the United States in respect of any aspect of the Berlin situation.

Such disagreements if any should be settled by negotiation or by way of the other peaceful methods provided for in Article 33 of the Charter in keeping with our mutual pledges as co-partners in the United Nations. For these reasons the Government of the United States is ready as a first step to participate in negotiations in Berlin among the four Allied Occupying Authorities for the settlement of any question in dispute arising out of the administration of the City of Berlin. It is, however, a prerequisite that the lines of communication and the movement of persons and goods between the United Kingdom, the United States and the French sectors in Berlin and the Western zones shall have been fully restored.

SOURCE: UK Command papers 7534, p 47; Annex IIA, *Germany 1947–1949*

The genesis of the North Atlantic Treaty lay in the Treaty of Brussels, under which the Western European nations attempted to cooperate in the military field. In his inaugural address of 20 January 1949, President Truman had proposed that the United States should provide military aid and equipment for nations to cooperate in maintaining peace and security.

The NATO Treaty came as an outcome of the belief—prompted by years of what appeared to have been continuous Soviet pressure and duplicity—that strength was a necessary condition of international stability. The United States commitment to the defence of Europe came to be viewed as a means of maintaining the morale of the exposed European nations.

The most notable absentees from the Treaty—signed on 4 April 1949 —were Spain, which was excluded because of the deeply rooted ideological opposition to the Franco regime; Eire, which refused to join so long as Ireland remained divided; and neutral Sweden.

Truman asked the US Senate to ratify the Treaty and called on both houses of Congress to approve a military aid programme costing $1,450 *million in the first year. Final approval of the programme was assured by Truman's announcement on 23 September that the Soviet Union had conducted its first nuclear test during the summer. The Mutual Defence Assistance Act was passed three days later.*

11A Dean Acheson
SPEECH FOR THE NORTH ATLANTIC TREATY
(18 March 1949)

The paramount purposes of the pact are peace and security. If peace and security can be achieved in the North Atlantic area, we shall have gone a long way to assure peace and security in other areas as well.

The achievement of peace and security means more than that in the final outcome we shall have prevented war and brought about the settlement of international disputes by peaceful means. There must be conviction of people everywhere that war will be prevented and that disputes will be settled peacefully. In the most practical terms, true international peace and security require a firm belief by the peoples of the world that they will not be subjected to unprovoked attack, to coercion and intimidation, to interference in their own affairs. Peace and security require confidence in the future, based on the assurance that the peoples of the world will be permitted to improve their conditions of life, free from fear that the fruits of their labor may be taken from them by alien hands . . .

It is important to keep in mind that the really successful national and international institutions are those that recognize and express underlying realities. The North Atlantic community of nations is such a reality. It is based on the affinity and natural identity of interests of the North Atlantic powers.

The North Atlantic treaty which will formally unite them is the product of at least 350 years of history and perhaps more. There developed on our Atlantic Coast a community, which has spread across the continent, connected with Western Europe by common institutions and moral and ethical beliefs.

Similarities of this kind are not superficial, but fundamental. They are the strongest kind of ties, because they are based on moral conviction, an acceptance of the same values in life.

The very basis of Western civilization, which we share with the other nations bordering on the North Atlantic, and which all of us share with many other nations, is the ingrained spirit of restraint and tolerance. This is the opposite of the Communist belief that coercion by force is a proper method of hastening the inevitable. Western civilization has lived by mutual restraint and tolerance. This civilization permits and stimulates free inquiry and bold experimentation. It creates the environment of freedom, from which flows the greatest amount of ingenuity, enterprise, and accomplishment . . .

Now successful resistance to aggression in the modern world requires modern arms and trained military forces. As a result of the recent war, the European countries joining in the pact are generally deficient in both requirements. The treaty does not bind the United States to any arms program. But we all know that the United States is now the only democratic nation with the resources and productive capacity to help the free nations of Europe to recover their military strength.

Therefore, we expect to ask the Congress to supply our European partners some of the weapons and equipment they need to be able to resist aggression. We also expect to recommend military supplies for other free nations which will co-operate with us in safeguarding peace and security.

In the compact world of today the security of the United States cannot be defined in terms of boundaries and frontiers. A serious threat to international peace and security anywhere in the world is of direct concern to this country. Therefore it is our policy to help free peoples to maintain their integrity and independence, not only in Western Europe, not only in the Americas, but wherever the aid we are able to provide can be effective . . .

Allegations that aggressive designs lie behind this country's signature of the Atlantic pact can rest only on a malicious misrepresentation or a fantastic misunderstanding of the nature and aims of American society . . .

The United States is waging peace by throwing its full strength and energy into the struggle, and we shall continue to do so.

We sincerely hope that we can avoid strife, but we cannot avoid striving for what is right. We devoutly hope we can have genuine peace, but we cannot be complacent about the present uneasy and troubled peace.

A secure and stable peace is not a goal we can reach all at once and for all time. It is a dynamic state, produced by effort and faith, with courage and justice. The struggle is continuous and hard. The prize is never irrevocably ours.

To have this genuine peace we must constantly work for it. But we must do even more. We must make it clear that armed attack will be met by collective defense, prompt and effective.

That is the meaning of the North Atlantic pact.

SOURCE: *New York Times* (19 March 1949)

11B NATO
TEXT OF THE NORTH ATLANTIC TREATY
(4 April 1949)

The Parties to this Treaty reaffirm their faith in the purposes and principles of the Charter of the United Nations and their desire to live in peace with all peoples and all governments.

They are determined to safeguard the freedom, common heritage and civilisation of their peoples, founded on the principles of democracy, individual liberty and the rule of law.

They seek to promote stability and well-being in the North Atlantic area.

They are resolved to unite their efforts for collective defense and for the preservation of peace and security.

They therefore agree to this North Atlantic Treaty:

Article 1

The Parties undertake, as set forth in the Charter of the United Nations, to settle any international disputes in which they may be involved by peaceful means in such a manner that international peace and security, and justice, are not endangered, and to refrain in their international relations from the threat or use of force in any manner inconsistent with the purposes of the United Nations.

Article 2

The Parties will contribute toward the further development of peaceful and friendly international relations by strengthening their free institutions, by bringing about a better understanding of the principles upon which these institutions are founded, and by promoting conditions of stability and well-being. They will seek to eliminate conflict in their international economic policies and will encourage economic collaboration between any or all of them.

Article 3

In order more effectively to achieve the objectives of this Treaty, the Parties, separately and jointly, by means of continuous and effective self-help and mutual aid, will maintain and develop their individual and collective capacity to resist armed attack.

Article 4

The Parties will consult together whenever, in the opinion of any of them, the territorial integrity, political independence or security of any of the Parties is threatened.

Article 5

The Parties agree that an armed attack against one or more of them in Europe or North America shall be considered an attack against them all; and consequently they agree that, if such an armed attack occurs, each of them, in exercise of the right of individual or collective self-defense recognised by Article 51 of the Charter of the United Nations, will assist the Party or Parties so attacked by taking forthwith, individually and in concert with the other Parties, such action as it deems necessary, including the use of armed force, to restore and maintain the security of the North Atlantic area.

Any such armed attack and all measures taken as a result thereof shall immediately be reported to the Security Council. Such measures shall be terminated when the Security Council has taken the measures necessary to restore and maintain international peace and security.

Article 6

For the purpose of Article 5, an armed attack on one or more of the Parties is deemed to include an armed attack—

(i) on the territory of any of the Parties in Europe or North America, on the Algerian Departments of France, on the territory of Turkey or the islands under the jurisdiction of any of the Parties in the North Atlantic area north of the Tropic of Cancer;

(ii) on the forces, vessels or aircraft of any of the Parties, when in or over these territories or any other area in Europe in which occupation forces of any of the Parties were stationed on the date when the Treaty entered into force or the Mediterranean Sea or the North Atlantic area north of the Tropic of Cancer.

Article 7

The Treaty does not affect, and shall not be interpreted as affecting, in any way the rights and obligations under the Charter of the Parties which are members of the United Nations, or the primary responsibility of the Security Council for the maintenance of international peace and security.

Article 8

Each Party declares that none of the international engagements now in force between it and any other of the Parties or any third state is in conflict with the provisions of this Treaty, and undertakes not to enter into any international engagements in conflict with this Treaty.

Article 9

The Parties hereby establish a council, on which each of them shall be represented, to consider matters concerning the implementation of this Treaty. The council shall be so organised as to be able to meet promptly at any time. The council shall set up such subsidiary bodies as may be necessary; in particular it shall establish immediately a defense committee which shall recommend measures for the implementation of Articles 3 and 5.

Article 10

The Parties may, by unanimous agreement, invite any other European state in a position to further the principles of this Treaty and to contribute to the security of the North Atlantic area to accede to this Treaty. Any state so invited may become a party to the Treaty by depositing its instrument of accession with the Government of the United States of America. The Government of the United States of America will inform each of the Parties of the deposit of each such instrument of accession.

Article 11

This Treaty shall be ratified and its provisions carried out by the Parties in accordance with their respective constitutional processes. The instruments of ratification shall be deposited as soon as possible with the Government of the United States of America, which will notify all the other signatories of each deposit. The Treaty shall enter into force between the states which have ratified it as soon as the ratification of the majority of the signatories, including the ratifications of Belgium, Canada, France, Luxembourg, the Netherlands, the United Kingdom and the United States, have been deposited and shall come into effect with respect to other states on the date of deposit of their ratifications.

Article 12

After the treaty has been in force for ten years, or at any time thereafter, the Parties shall, if any of them so requests, consult together for the purpose of reviewing the Treaty, having regard for the factors then affecting peace and security in the North Atlantic area, including the development of universal as well as regional arrangements under the Charter of the United Nations for the maintenance of international peace and security.

Article 13

After the Treaty has been in force for twenty years, any Party may cease to be a party one year after its notice of denunciation has been given to the Government of the United States of America, which will inform the Governments of the other Parties of the deposit of each notice of denunciation . . .

SOURCE: US Department of State. *Treaties and Other International Acts Series*, 1964

The Truman administration's Mutual Defence Assistance Programme (MDAP) was submitted to Congress immediately after the North Atlantic Treaty had been ratified on 25 July 1949.

In his accompanying message Truman based his request on the need to keep the peace and the fear that some members of the United Nations were prepared to use force or threaten force. He stressed that the United States had assumed world leadership and this implied an obligation to plan ahead, as in the earlier decision to extend aid to Greece and Turkey.

The President asked for $1,450 million to finance supplies which would be delivered during the next two years, including $50 million which had already been requested to continue aid to Greece and Turkey.

Congress approved a bill providing $1,314 million, to be allocated at the President's discretion, on 26 September 1949—just three days after the President had disclosed that the Soviet Union had conducted its first nuclear test during the summer.

The drafts of the proposed agreements were published in November, but problems developed in the one relating to Britain. As originally drafted the programme would have hampered British exports to the Commonwealth. This was resolved through a number of separate annexes to the agreement.

12 Governments of the UK and the US
MUTUAL DEFENCE ASSISTANCE AGREEMENT
(27 January 1950)

The Governments of the United Kingdom of Great Britain and Northern Ireland and the United States of America;

Being parties to the North Atlantic Treaty signed at Washington on 4th April 1949;

Considering their reciprocal pledges under Article 3 of the North Atlantic Treaty separately and jointly with the other parties, by means of continuous and effective self-help and mutual aid, to maintain and develop their individual and collective capacity to resist armed attack;

Desiring to foster international peace and security, within the framework of the Charter of the United Nations through measures which will further the ability of nations dedicated to the purposes and principles of the Charter to participate effectively in arrangements for individual and collective self-defence in support of those purposes and principles;

Reaffirming their determination to give their full co-operation to the efforts to provide the United Nations with armed forces as contemplated by the Charter and to obtain agreement on universal regulation and reduction of armaments under adequate guarantee against violation;

Recognising that the increased confidence of free peoples in their own ability to resist aggression will advance economic recovery;

Taking into consideration the support that has been brought to these principles by the Government of the United Kingdom in affording military assistance to other parties of the North

Atlantic Treaty and by the Government of the United States of America in enacting the Mutual Defence Assistance Act of 1949 which provides for the furnishing of military assistance to nations which have joined with it in collective security arrangements;

Desiring to set forth the conditions which will govern the furnishing of military assistance by one contracting Government to the other under this Agreement;

Have agreed as follows:—

Article I

1. Each contracting Government, consistently with the principle that economic recovery is essential to international peace and security and must be given clear priority, and in accordance with its obligations under Article 3 of the North Atlantic Treaty, will make available to the other such equipment, materials, services, or other military assistance as the contracting Government furnishing such assistance may authorise, in accordance with detailed arrangements from time to time to be made between them. The Government of the United Kingdom in fulfilment of its obligations under Article 3 of the North Atlantic Treaty will furnish or continue to furnish to other parties to the North Atlantic Treaty such equipment, materials, services, or other military assistance as it may authorise. The furnishing of assistance by the Government of the United States of America under this Agreement will be under the provisions, and subject to all the terms, conditions, and termination provisions of the Mutual Defence Assistance Act of 1949, acts amendatory and supplementary thereto and appropriation acts thereunder.

2. Such assistance shall be so designed as to promote the integrated defence of the North Atlantic area and to facilitate the development of, or be in accordance with, defence plans under Article 9 of the North Atlantic Treaty approved by each contracting Government.

Article II

1. Each contracting Government undertakes to make effective use of assistance received pursuant to Article I of this Agreement—

  (*a*) for the purpose of promoting an integrated defence of the North Atlantic area, and for facilitating the development of defence plans under Article 9 of the North Atlantic Treaty; and

  (*b*) in accordance with defence plans formulated by the North Atlantic Treaty Organisation, recommended by the North Atlantic Treaty Council and Defence Committee, and agreed to by the two contracting Governments.

2. Neither contracting Government, without the prior consent of the other, will devote assistance furnished to it by the other contracting Government to purposes other than those for which it was furnished.

Article III

In the common security interest of both contracting Governments, each contracting Government undertakes not to transfer to any person not an officer or agent of such contracting Government, or to any other nation, title to or possession of any equipment, materials, or services, furnished on a grant basis, without the prior consent of the contracting Government furnishing such equipment, materials, or services . . .

SOURCE: US Department of State Bulletin (13 February 1950), 247

If any one individual may be said to have kept the spirit of the Atlantic alliance alive during the years after the war it was Winston Churchill. Born of a British father and an American mother, he was always regarded by the Americans as something of a private possession of theirs. It was Churchill who during the war typified to most Americans the British spirit of resistance, as he still typified it. His electoral defeat in 1945

*was incomprehensible on the other side of the Atlantic. In opposition,
through the determined manner in which he spoke out on behalf of the
alliance, he continued to earn respect. Back in office, the aging Churchill
was a welcome spokesman for the Anglo-American cause. A speech he
delivered to the American society in London on Independence Day 1950
is typical of Churchill's respect for his dual heritage and the firm
manner in which he continued to oppose what he saw as the Soviet
threat.*

13 Winston Churchill
SPEECH TO THE AMERICAN SOCIETY
IN LONDON (4 July 1950)

. . . It was Bismarck who said in the closing years of his life that
the most potent factor in human society at the end of the nine-
teenth century was the fact that the British and American
peoples spoke the same language. He might well have added,
what was already then apparent, that we had in common a very
wide measure of purpose and ideals arising from our institutions, our literature and our common law. Since then, on the
anvil of war, we have become so welded together that what
might have remained for generations an interesting historical
coincidence has become the living and vital force which pre-
serves Christian civilization and the rights and freedom of mankind. Nearly two months have passed since the Ambassador
talked over with me the invitation with which you have
honoured me. Mr Lew Douglas is an intimate war comrade of
mine, and one of the best friends from across the Atlantic which
our country had in the struggle; and that is saying a lot. He is
esteemed throughout this island and we all have felt the utmost
sympathy for him in his accident, and admiration for the
courage with which he has surmounted so much physical pain.
No one I am sure can do more to prevent misunderstandings—
diplomatic or otherwise—between our two countries than His
Excellency the American Ambassador.

When I accepted your invitation I could not foresee that

when the date arrived we should once again be brothers in arms, engaged in fighting for exactly the same cause that we thought we had carried to victory five years ago. The British and Americans do not war with races or governments as such. Tyranny, external or internal, is our foe whatever trappings or disguises it wears, whatever language it speaks, or perverts. We must forever be on our guard, and always vigilant against it— in all this we march together. Not only, if need be, under the fire of the enemy but also in those realms of thought which are consecrated to the rights and the dignity of man, and which are so amazingly laid down in the Declaration of Independence, which has become a common creed on both sides of the Atlantic Ocean.

The inheritance of the English-speaking world, vast and majestic though it is in territory and resources, derives its glory as a moral unity from thought and vision widely spread in the minds of our people and cherished by all of those who under-stand our destiny. As you may have heard (I don't want to give away any secrets) we had a General Election here a few months ago by which a Parliament was returned very evenly balanced but still more sharply divided; but divided not by small matters but by issues which cut deep into our national life. We have not developed to any extent over here the bipartisan conduct of external policy by both great parties like that which has in these later years so greatly helped the United States. Nevertheless, once the deep gong of comradeship between kindred nations strikes, resounds and reverberates, and when our obligations to the United Nations are staring us in the face, we shall allow no domestic party quarrels—grievous though they may be—to mar the unity of our national or international action. You can count on Britain, and not only Britain. Four years ago, when President Truman, whom we salute tonight, took me to Westminster College at Fulton in Missouri I ventured to offer the American people my counsel, and I said, 'Let no man underrate the abid-ing power of the British Empire and Commonwealth. Do not suppose that we shall not come through these dark years of privation as we came through the glorious years of agony, or that half a century from now will not see 70,000,000 or 80,000,000 Britons spread throughout the world and united in defence of our traditions, our way of life, and the world causes which you and we espouse.' In the increasing unity of the Anglo-American thought and action resides the main foundation of the freedom and progress of all the men in all the lands. Let us not weary, let us not lose confidence in our mission, let us not fail in our duty in times of stress, let us not flinch if danger comes.

We must ask ourselves whether danger—I mean the danger of a third world war, has come nearer because of what has happened in the last week, and is happening now. I do not think, myself, that the danger has grown greater. But then, I thought it very serious before. It all depends where you start thinking in these matters. I must say that we—Britons and Americans—and the many States and nations associated with us have had hard luck. The Russian Communists have built up an empire far beyond the dreams of the Tsars out of a war in which they might have been conquered or driven beyond the Ural mountains in spite of the bravery with which the Russian Army fought for its native soil. They would have been conquered or driven out but for the immense diversionary aid of Britain and the United States on land and sea and, above all, in the air. And also the vital supplies which had cost so much self-denial, and peril—and the Ambassador knows a lot about all that because the shipping on which everything depended was throughout influenced in the most effective manner by his personal care and courage. Not only do the Soviets hold at the present time all the famous capitals of Europe east of the line— which I call 'the Iron Curtain' drawn from Stettin to Trieste, not only are they endeavouring with great cruelties to compel these many States and countries to adopt the Communist system and become incorporated in the Soviet mass, but they have gained also vast populations in Asia, including practically the whole of China. And they are pressing forward in insatiable, imperialist ambition wherever any weakness on the part of the free world gives them an opportunity.

Thus, I say we have had hard luck, just when we thought we had finished with Hitler and Mussolini, with Nazism and Fascism, we have Stalin and Communism lumping up against us representing the former Hitler tyranny in barbaric form and Asiatic guise. We had hoped that the task of this hard-pressed generation was done. Your poet Walt Whitman said: 'Now understand me well it is provided in the essence of things that from any fruition of success, no matter what, shall come forth something to make a greater struggle necessary.' We pray this may not be so. These hard decrees may be the lot of the human race in its unending struggle for existence, but the question which we have to consider tonight, and in regard to which the Ambassador laid before you in a cogently related argument many essential facts, is whether our dangers have been increased by the Communist act of aggression in Korea. I agree with the British Government speakers that they have not been increased. How does this new menace differ in principle from the Berlin blockade, two years ago, which together we faced with composure and overcame by the Allied airlift, mainly carried by American planes but in which we bore an important share? It differs in one major fact. We are told that the Kremlin oligarchy now know how to make the atomic bomb. That is the one new fact. To that extent there is a change to our disadvantage. It certainly seems to me that there is a better hope of a general settlement with Soviet Russia following on the defeat of aggression in Korea on a localized scale, than that we should drift on while large quantities of these devastating weapons are accumulated. Indeed I feel that there is nothing more likely to bring on a third world war than drift.

It is always difficult for free democracies, governed in the main by public opinion from day to day, to cope with the designs of dictator States and totalitarian systems. But hitherto we have held our own, or we should not be here tonight. We have only to be morally united and fearless, to give mankind the best hope of avoiding another supreme catastrophe. But I must say one thing before I sit down. It is of vital consequence to these hopes of world peace that what the Communists have begun in Korea should not end in their triumph. If that were to happen a third world war, under conditions even more deadly than now exist, would certainly be forced upon us, or hurled upon us before long. It is fortunate that the path of duty, and of safety, is so plainly marked out before our eyes, and so widely recognized by both our nations and governments, and by the large majority, the overwhelming majority of the member States comprised in the United Nations Organization.

We owe it not only to ourselves, but to our faith in an institution, if not a world government at least a world protection from aggressive war, not to fail in our duty now. Thus we shall find the best hopes of peace and surest proof of honour. The League of Nations failed not because of its noble conceptions, but because these were abandoned by its members. We must not ask to be taught this hard lesson twice. Looking around this obscure, tumultuous scene, with all its uncertainties as it presents itself to us tonight, I am sure we shall not be guilty of such incurable folly; we shall go forward; we shall do our duty; we shall save the world from a third world war. And should it come in spite of all our efforts, we shall not be trampled down into serfdom and ruin.

Source: Winston S. Churchill. *In the Balance* (New York 1952)

PART FOUR

Strains on the Alliance

A jaundiced and highly cantankerous view of the value of America's alliance with Western Europe was expressed in late 1950 by Herbert Hoover, whose opinion as that of the only living ex-president carried a certain weight. In a broadcast speech he said that, apart from Britain, the countries of Western Europe were unwilling to even make preparations to resist communist aggression and that no money or American troops would be sent to Europe until a unified European army was formed. Similar views were expressed by Senator Robert Taft and by Joseph Kennedy, the father of the future president, who argued that Iceland was more important to the defence of the United States than Berlin.

The views of such diehard isolationists failed to sway Truman, as they have failed to influence subsequent presidents. On 19 December 1950, after declaring a state of emergency and establishing an office of defence mobilisation, he dispatched additional troops to Europe.

14 Herbert Hoover
EXTRACT FROM A BROADCAST SPEECH
(19 October 1950)

. . . The immediate problem which now confronts us is: How can we reorganize our instrumentalities for peace so as to give the world renewed hope? How can we secure peace—even an uneasy peace?

Before I make some suggestions, we must coldly appraise the world situation in which we find ourselves.

1. Our great hope is the United Nations. For five years, with the one exception of the Korean action when the Russians were away on a blackmail strike, they have paralyzed that organization.

2. Nothing will stop Red military aggression except an effective organized phalanx of the non-Communist world which will freeze the ambitions of the Kremlin.

3. We are told by many military authorities that Stalin could put 175 mobilized combat divisions on the European front within ninety days. We are told that they have 30,000 tanks, thousands of planes and the atom bomb.

We are told they have large reserve forces. We are told that the Iron Curtain States have large armies poised for action. We are told they have huge forces in North Asia equipped by Russia.

In contrast we are told that the European nations now in the North Atlantic Alliance do not have available to Europe more than thirty active combat divisions with some air and naval power, with which to meet this horde from behind the Iron Curtain. We are told that South Asia has but little military strength to oppose the Communists.

4. The industrial potential of the United States can be overpowering in the long run. But Stalin, now having also the industrial power of the Iron Curtain States, can arbitrarily concentrate it on preparedness.

Western Europe with a larger population than the United States has as large or greater industrial power than that of Stalin. It is being little occupied in preparedness. It could be quickly mobilized and could constitute a doubly overwhelming balance of industrial power.

5. We must realize, and the world must realize, that 160,000,000 Americans cannot alone maintain the safety of the world against 800,000,000 Communists on the fronts of both Europe and Asia.

Nor can we, out of our resources and manpower, contribute more than a minority part in such a phalanx of force.

6. We are told by the civilian and military leaders of our Government that we stand in the greatest of perils. We have inaugurated an immense military program.

The consequences of this program to our economic life are already evident. Under it taxes will take a greater portion of our national income than that taken by most non-Communist countries in Europe.

Already we are in the midst of a disastrous wave of inflation from its pressures. We must defer many needed improvements.

We can stand this for possibly two or three years pending a genuine rally by the non-Communist world to their full part in defense. But we must in time have relief from a large part of that burden.

We cannot carry the load for long without fulfilling Stalin's hopes of bleeding us economically to impotence.

7. There are three sources from which real military defense must come:

First. The European nations in the North American Alliance;

Second. The other non-Communist nations who are members of the United Nations, such as, Canada, Latin America, the Middle East, South Africa, Australia, New Zealand and some of the smaller South Asian countries.

Third. And there is the United States.

We will successfully clean up the Korean aggression under General MacArthur's brilliant generalship and teach a lesson.

However, our greatest danger point to all Western Civilization is Western Europe. It is obvious, with the threats in Asia, that the United States can supply only a minor part of this huge European deficiency even with our present program.

The time has therefore come to speak frankly what is in the mind of many Americans today. And I speak not only as one who has witnessed two world wars, but with substantial military advice.

We know that the European nations now in the North

Atlantic Pact (with American aid) have reached a greater industrial productivity than they had before either the First or Second World War.

They have larger populations and more manpower than in those wars. In both those two wars, these peoples put in the field in ninety days over 140 equipped and trained combat divisions in addition to naval and air forces.

When the fabulous expenditures of various loans, together with the Marshall Plan and the North Atlantic Pact were laid before the American people, certain results were promised.

It was emphasized that besides economic and social objectives these gigantic sums would build the European nations into a united military defense against aggression upon Western Civilization. It was represented as the American first line of defense.

We consented to these sacrifices primarily on this promise. It has been costly. Outside of Lend-Lease during the war, we have spent since the war ended in gifts, and loans (which are also bound to be gifts) almost 20 billions in Europe on this faith.

We have not begrudged these huge sacrifices. But the result has been deeply disappointing to a growing body of Americans.

Competent observers are daily raising the serious question as to whether these nations, outside of Britain, have the will to fight, or even the will to preparedness. The actions and statements of their own leaders give little evidence of any real determination.

In confirmation, I need only to quote Winston Churchill, who stated, in a public address, a few weeks ago:

> Imposing conferences have been held between military chiefs and experts, and a pretentious façade has been displayed by the governments responsible for our safety.
>
> In fact, however, apart from the establishment of the American bomber base in England, nothing has been done to give any effective protection to our peoples from being subjugated or destroyed by the Russian Communist armies with their masses of armor and aircraft.

I and others have given what warnings we could, but, as in the past, they fell on unheeding ears or were used to sustain the false accusation of war-mongering.

Mr. Churchill seemed to think Europe had only two years in which to arm.

Our American officials in the recent conference of Foreign Ministers again urged the necessity of a unified European defense army embracing German components. That proposal has again been defeated or delayed.

All this situation has come as a great shock to thinking Americans. These failures raise serious questions.

Are we being misled as to the seriousness of this situation? Have these nations such convincing evidence of the Kremlin's good intentions that they are not interested in defense?

Has Karl Marx paralyzed the will of nations for independence? Do they expect the United States and Britain to carry the whole load in case of attack?

The time has come when the American people should speak out in much stronger tones than the diplomatic phrases of conference halls.

We should be willing to aid but, if Western Europe wants defense from the Communist tide, they must do most of it themselves—and do it fast.

Someone proposed that we at once increase our forces in Europe to ten combat divisions. That would be only a slaughter of American boys unless many times that number were standing by their sides.

We should say, and at once, that we shall provide no more money until a definitely unified and sufficient European army is in sight. And further that ten American divisions will not be landed until then.

Nor is such an army in Europe even with American forces alone sufficient to dull Kremlin ambitions in both Europe and Asia . . .

SOURCE: *New York Times* (20 October 1950)

The Chinese intervention in Korea brought home to the United States the effective limitation of its power in the postwar world. The Truman administration had to face either going to war with China, and possibly with the Soviet Union, or returning to the ceasefire line and status quo as it existed before the North Korean invasion. The tension inherent in the situation became readily apparent when President Truman, at a news conference on 29 November 1950, in an unguarded moment declared that if the United Nations authorised military action against China, General Douglas MacArthur might be empowered to use the atomic bomb. He added that there had always been consideration of using the bomb. The President's casual statement created a storm in the House of Commons and Prime Minister Attlee went almost immediately to Washington. He took a set of questions with him and bluntly expressed his concern that the United States might be on the point of pulling out of Korea, a move that might lead on the rebound to a full scale war with China. At the same time he urged the United States to negotiate with China. In a communiqué issued following Attlee's meeting with the President, the two men agreed to expand rapidly their military capabilities and arms production. During his visit, the British Prime Minister expressed his views clearly and in detail in a speech to the National Press Club.

15 Clement Attlee
SPEECH AT THE NATIONAL PRESS CLUB, WASHINGTON (6 December 1950)

Let me turn to the position as it is today. Our two countries are two of the leading countries in the United Nations. We are engaged in a great adventure, the adventure of peace. Believing that if we are to base peace on such foundations we must resist aggression, we are, together with others, seeking by our action in Korea to assert the rule of law.

We are loyal members of the United Nations. The United States is bearing the major part of the burden of asserting the rule of law. Our forces are fighting alongside yours. You may be certain that, in fair or foul weather, where the Stars and

Stripes fly in Korea, the British flag will fly beside them. We stand by our duty. We stand by our friends.

The times are critical. It is idle to deny that the forces of the United Nations have suffered a serious setback. This is not the time for criticism. We must seek to find how best to help those who are bearing this burden.

Let me say here that the achievement of General MacArthur and his troops will go down in history as most notable. With slender forces he defended South Korea obstinately, and then, passing to the offensive, in a brilliantly conceived campaign, routed the North Korean armies.

The fact that, faced with overwhelming odds, the United Nations forces are now in difficulties, should not obscure what was skilful and resolute leadership. None the less, we have to recognize that, owing to the intervention of the Chinese, the military situation has gravely deteriorated in the last few days.

It is our task here to review the world situation in the light of these events and consider carefully our further course of action. Let me say here that we must always beware of taking short views dictated by our emotions. We must always recall that military objectives are means to an end, not ends in themselves. The purpose of military operations by the United Nations in the Far East is to halt aggression, to see the rule of law respected and to establish lasting conditions of peace. We must always bear in mind that the peoples of the Far East have to live as neighbors—and we want them as good neighbors. Our long-term object, therefore, is to get rid of the causes of war.

That does not mean that we have any intention of indulging in what is called appeasement—a word of ill omen. I am told that there are people who believe that that is what I have come here to do. That is not true. We all know from our own bitter experience that appeasement does not pay.

We in Britain are deeply concerned with all that goes on in Asia, for we have a long and intimate association with its peoples. India, Pakistan and Ceylon have in the last few years become free and equal partners in the British Commonwealth of Nations. The Burmese, another people with whom we have old ties of friendship, have elected to be independent. There are the peoples such as those of Malaya, who are in process of working toward self-government.

We have, too, a very close relation with the peoples of the Middle East.

You see, therefore, that at many points the United Kingdom is in close touch with that great land mass of Asia and all the fringes of that great land. We are vitally concerned with what goes on there.

So we naturally bring into our discussions in Washington the viewpoints we derive from our special position.

I am giving you some of the thoughts which form the background of the policy of the British Government toward China. I know our policy has not always been understood here and sometimes is criticized. We are asked how we can recognize and have diplomatic relations with the Government of China, when its policies are in contradiction to the United Nations objectives in Korea and when its nationals are engaged in conflict with our own forces.

My answer to these criticisms is quite straightforward and realistic. The Chinese People's Government has control of all the mainland territory that we know as China. It commands the obedience of 400,000,000 Chinese who inhabit that territory. These are stubborn facts and it is no good shutting our eyes to them. Are we to refuse to recognize these facts, however unpleasant they may be? Are we to cut ourselves off from all contact with one-sixth of the inhabitants of the world, from all chance of making our views known to their rulers? Our recognition of the Chinese People's Government was the recognition of an obvious fact; and our attempt to establish full diplomatic relations with them sprang from the motives to which I have referred.

Now, you will have seen that we recently published the Colombo plan for cooperative economic development in Southeast Asia. The second title of the plan is, I think, significant; it

is 'New Horizons in the East'. That title expresses the hope
which we and our fellow-members of the Commonwealth have
put into this plan. That plan grew out of a meeting of the
foreign ministers of the Commonwealth at Colombo.

Because we are persuaded that military and political policies
are not enough, there must be an economic and social policy.
Our aim is to try to get rid of these terrible extremes of poverty
that you find in the East that form places at which all kinds of
dangerous movements may breed . . .

SOURCE: *New York Times* (7 December 1950)

THE ATLANTIC ADMIRAL

*One of the minor irritations which bedevilled Anglo-American relations
—and which had some significance in that it reflected the sharp shift in
the balance of power between the allies since the war—was the row over
the appointment of a supreme allied commander for the Atlantic. The
Royal Navy had traditionally regarded the Atlantic Ocean as its special
preserve and in Britain the Conservative opposition was quick to react
with outrage and injured pride to the appointment of an American to the
supreme command. The Attlee government, after some deliberation, chose
to accept the inevitable, and announced its decision on 21 February 1951.
In a later statement, on the 26th, Attlee explained that the American
supreme commander would have a British deputy and the command
would be divided into an eastern and a western area, commanded respectively by a British and an American admiral.*

*The agreement was criticised by the opposition on the grounds that
there was no need for a single commander and that it was desirable to
give him power to transfer forces from the eastern to the western area of
the ocean. However, when the Conservatives returned to power they made
no attempt to reverse the agreement.*

16 Clement Attlee
STATEMENT ON THE ORGANISATION OF THE
NORTH ATLANTIC COMMANDS (26 February 1951)

I wish to make a short statement on the question of the appointment of a Supreme Commander Atlantic. As I promised when the matter was raised in the House on 22nd February, I have again looked into this matter of the command organisation of the North Atlantic ocean. The House will appreciate that this matter forms only one part of the general plans which are taking shape within the North Atlantic Treaty Organisation under the direction of the Standing Group, which comprises representatives of the United States, United Kingdom and France.

One of the most important features of these plans in relation to the North Atlantic ocean is an agreement on the system of command which will obtain in war. Preliminary arrangements must, however, necessarily be made in peace-time in order to ensure quick and easy transition to war if the need arises.

The area which will be under the Supreme Commander is the North Atlantic ocean, excluding the Mediterranean and British European coastal waters. This ocean will include an eastern and a western area. The eastern area, which for us will be the most vital and crucial, will be under the command of a British admiral, in association with the Coastal Command of the Royal Air Force. This British admiral will be the Commander-in-Chief, Home Fleet—an appointment at present held by Admiral Sir Philip Vian. In his capacity of Commander-in-Chief of the Eastern Atlantic, he would, in time of war, exercise command not only over British Forces, but also over Forces of the United States Navy and those of other North Atlantic Treaty Organisation Powers. Conversely, the American admiral commanding the Western Atlantic would, likewise, control British and other North Atlantic Treaty Organisation Forces.

As the House will no doubt realise, the whole problem embracing both command and areas in the North Atlantic ocean has for some time past been fully discussed in all its details, not only by the British and American Chiefs of Staff, but also by the representatives of other Powers interested in the Atlantic, namely, France, Canada, Norway, Denmark, Belgium, Holland, Portugal, and Iceland. In the light of the experience of the last war it has been agreed on both sides of the Atlantic that it is of the utmost importance that an overall Supreme Commander for the North Atlantic ocean should be appointed in order that the naval and Air Forces specifically assigned to him, not only from this country and from the United States, but from the other North Atlantic Treaty Organisation Powers, should be used to the best advantage throughout the whole of these waters.

The outstanding lesson of the Battle of the Atlantic in the late war was that the Atlantic is one battlefield in which the mobile threat represented by the submarine must be matched by an equally flexible system of defence. Too often during the last war, we had to wait until serious losses had been incurred, or great opportunities missed while discussion went on in Washington and London about the re-disposition of naval or Air Forces. Thus all our experience of that time proved that there is a need for a single command in the Atlantic which can allocate and re-allocate Forces to meet the shifting threat as it develops. One of the principal duties of the Supreme Commander will be to move Forces to the area where the danger is greatest and to make representations, when the need arises, for the particular requirements of the Atlantic in a global war ...

SOURCE: House of Commons Debates, 5th series, vol 484, 1751–4

THE EUROPEAN ARMY

One of the earlier movements towards European unity, the collapse of which left a legacy of mistrust for the future, was the ill-starred attempt to form a European army. The British Government, mindful of the long and respected tradition of the British army, refused to allow it to become merged in any multi-national force. This action laid the ground for suspicions that would later prejudice Britain's initial attempts to become associated with the Common Market. The whole concept of the European army failed after the foreign ministers of the six European nations were unable to reach an agreement on the financing and political control of the proposed army.

17 Winston Churchill
SPEECH IN THE HOUSE OF COMMONS
(6 December 1951)

Coming now to more controversial topics, I do not feel there
ought to be any great difference between us about the European
Army. We are, I believe, most of us agreed that there should be
a European Army and that Germany must take an honourable
place in it. When I proposed this in Strasbourg 18 months ago
I said—perhaps I may be permitted to quote myself when I
find it convenient—

> I am very glad that the Germans amid their own problems
> have come here to share our perils and augment our strength.
> They ought to have been here a year ago. A year has been
> wasted, but still it is not too late. There is no revival of Europe,
> no safety or freedom for any of us except in standing together
> united and unflinching. I ask this Assembly to assure our
> German friends that if they throw in their lot with us we shall
> hold their safety and freedom as sacred as our own.

This assurance has now been formally given by the Allied
Governments. I went on:

> There must be created, and in the shortest possible time, a
> real defensive front in Europe. Great Britain and the United
> Nations must send large forces to the Continent. France must
> again revive her famous Army. We welcome our Italian com-
> rades. All—Greece, Turkey, Holland, Belgium, Luxemburg,
> the Scandinavian States—must bear their share and do their
> best.

We seem to have made good progress since then. General
Eisenhower is in supreme command on the Continent. All the
Powers mentioned have contributed, or are contributing, or are
about to contribute, contingents and many of their contingents
are growing. The front is not covered yet. The potential aggressor has a vast superiority of numbers. Nevertheless, the gather-

ing of our deterrents has been continued. As things have developed, my own ideas have always been as follows. There is the NATO Army. Inside the NATO Army there is the European Army, and inside the European Army there is the German Army. The European Army should be formed by all the European parties to NATO dedicating from their own national armies their quota of divisions to the Army or Armies now under General Eisenhower's command.

At Strasbourg in 1950 the Germans did not press for a national army. On the contrary, they declared themselves ready to join a European Army without having a national army. Dr. Adenauer has renewed to us this assurance, and that is still the German position and their preference—no national army. This is a very great and helpful fact which we must all take into consideration. The size and strength of any German army, whether contingent or otherwise, and its manufacture of weapons, would in any case have to be agreed between the Allied Powers concerned. There, in short, is the policy which I have always advocated and which I am very glad to find is steadily going forward.

Difficulties have, however, arisen about the texture of the European Army. Should it be an amalgam of the European nations divested of all national characteristics and traditions, or should it be composed of elements essentially national but woven together by alliance, common organisation and unified command? On this point the discussions have at times assumed an almost metaphysical character, and the logic of continental minds has produced a scheme for what is called the European Defence Community. That is, at least, an enlightened if not an inspiring title The European Defence Force, which is to be a vital element in the defence of Western Europe, will be closely and effectively associated with the British Forces which constitute another element in the same defence system through their common allegiance to NATO.

The European Defence Community has not yet taken its final shape. The Paris Conference has been sitting for nine months, and it is now on the point of producing its Report. I am sorry the late Government did not send a delegation to this Conference instead of only an observer. The technical discussions have proceeded smoothly and in great detail, and at last the far-reaching political issues which have been raised and which surround the military questions have been reached. We do not know how these will be settled, and we have had no voice or share in the long argument. As soon as the Conference reaches its final conclusions we shall consider the way to establish the most effective form of association with the resultant organisations. In this way a European Army, containing a German contribution of agreed size and strength, will stand alongside the British and United States Armies in a common defensive front. That after all, is what really matters to the life or death of the free world.

As far as Britain is concerned, we do not propose to merge in the European Army but we are already joined to it. Our troops are on the spot, and we shall do our utmost to make a worthy and effective contribution to the deterrents against aggression and to the causes of freedom and democracy which we seek to serve. These matters will, of course, require to be further discussed as the weeks pass by, and we shall probably know much more about what is the decision taken on the Continent than we can attempt to anticipate and imagine at this moment.

Source: House of Commons Debates, 5th series, vol 494, 2594-6

THE PERSIAN OIL DISPUTE

Both Britain and the United States regarded Iran as an important element in the barriers against Soviet expansion to the south, fears of which had been stimulated immediately after the war by the abortive Soviet attempt to set up autonomous Azerbaijani and Kurdish republics and obtain oil concessions in northern Iran. The American policy of building up Iran's military strength was badly disrupted by the Anglo-Iranian oil dispute. At the same time the dispute awakened in Britain latent suspicions over United States motives in the Near East and fears that the United States was secretly seeking to obtain ripe new concessions for the big American oil companies. At the time it was nationalised by the Iranian Government the Anglo-Iranian Oil Company furnished about 6 per cent of the world's oil supplies, or a quarter of the entire oil imports of Britain.

The Iranian Government approved the plan for the immediate takeover of the company's assets and operations on 1 May 1951, soon after the mercurial Mohammed Mossadegh became Prime Minister.

In Washington representatives of various American oil companies held an emergency meeting at the State Department. The department in its official statement of 18 May promised that no American company would step into the place of the Anglo-Iranian Oil Company if it was evicted.

The statement was a salvation for the British. At the same time it brought down on the Americans the outrage and anger that the Iranians had hitherto reserved for the British.

Despite constant American attempts at mediation, the crisis dragged on through the summer and for the next two years, until, on 19 August 1953, Mossadegh was ousted in a royalist coup that had been actively promoted by the United States Central Intelligence Agency.

18 US Department of State
STATEMENT ON THE ANGLO-PERSIAN OIL DISPUTE (18 May 1951)

The United States is deeply concerned by the dispute between the Iranian and British Governments over Iranian oil. We are firm friends of both Iran and Great Britain and are sincerely interested in the welfare of each country. The United States wants an amicable settlement to this dispute, which is serious not only to the parties directly concerned but also to the whole free world. We have followed the matter closely and have told both countries where we stand. The views which we have expressed have related to the broad aspects of the problem, as it has not been appropriate for us to advise with respect to specific terms of arrangements which might be worked out.

Since the United States attitude has been the subject of some speculation, it is deemed advisable to describe the position which we have taken in our talks with representatives of Iran and Great Britain.

We have stressed to the Governments of both countries the need to solve the dispute in a friendly way through negotiation and have urged them to avoid intimidation and threats of unilateral action.

In our talks with the British Government, we have expressed the opinion that arrangements should be worked out with the Iranians which give recognition to Iran's expressed desire for greater control over and benefits from the development of its petroleum resources. While the United States has not approved or disapproved the terms of any particular British proposal, it is pleased to note a sincere desire on the part of the British to negotiate with the Iranians on all outstanding issues.

We fully recognize the sovereign rights of Iran and sympathize with Iran's desire that increased benefits accrue to that country from the development of its petroleum. In talks with the Iranian Government, we have pointed out the serious effects of any unilateral cancellation of clear contractual relationships which the United States strongly opposes. We have stressed the importance of the Iranians achieving their legitimate objectives through friendly negotiation with the other party, consistent with their international responsibilities. This would have the advantage of maintaining confidence in the future commercial investments in Iran and, indeed, in the validity of contractual arrangements all over the world.

Iran has been urged, before it takes final action, to analyze carefully the practical aspects of this problem. In this connection, we have raised the question of whether or not the elimination of the established British oil company from Iran would in fact secure for Iran the greatest possible benefits. We have pointed out that the efficient production and refining of

Iranian oil requires not only technical knowledge and capital but transport and marketing facilities such as those provided by the company. We have also pointed out that any uncertainty as to future availability of Iranian supplies would cause concern on the part of customers which might lead to shifts in their source of supply with a consequent decreased revenue to Iran.

Those United States oil companies which would be best able to conduct operations such as the large-scale and complex industry in Iran have indicated to this Government that they would not in the face of unilateral action by Iran against the British company be willing to undertake operations in that country. Moreover, petroleum technicians of the number and competence required to replace those presently in Iran are not, due to extreme shortages of manpower in this specialized field, available in this country or in other countries.

The United States believes that Iran and Great Britain have such a strong mutuality of interests that they must and will find some way, through friendly negotiation, of reestablishing a relationship which will permit each party to play its full role in the achievement of their common objectives. Through such negotiation it is felt that Iran's basic desires and interests can best be realized, the legitimate British interests preserved, and the essential flow of Iranian oil into the markets of the free world maintained.

The United States has repeatedly expressed its great interest in the continued independence and territorial integrity of Iran and has given and will continue to give concrete evidence of this interest.

SOURCE: US Department of State Bulletin (28 May 1951), 851

THE MIDDLE EAST COMMAND

Allied policy towards the Middle East was marked by a seemingly endless series of attempts to link the Arab states in a single command as a counter to Soviet expansion. One of the more determined of these efforts was the declaration of 10 November 1951 in which the United States,

*Britain, and France, joined by Turkey, set up a Middle East Command
to secure the defence of the Arab world. The declaration led to a pre-
dictable denunciation from the Soviet Union. In their discussions with
the Arabs the four powers emphasised that they were not seeking to
create a body which would intervene in internal disputes in the area, but
the command never had much impact in controlling the conflicting and
turbulent forces loose in the Arab world.*

19 Governments of the US, the UK, France and Turkey
DECLARATION ON A MIDDLE EAST COMMAND
(10 November 1951)

In proceeding with their announced intention to establish the
Middle East Command, the Governments of the United States,
United Kingdom, France and Turkey state that they are
guided by the following principles:

1. The United Nations is a world response to the principle
that peace is indivisible and that the security of all states is
jeopardized by breaches of the peace anywhere; at the same
time it is incumbent upon the states of any area to be willing
and able to undertake the initial defense of their area.

2. The defense of the Middle East is vital to the free world
and its defense against outside aggression can be secured only
by the co-operation of all interested states.

3. The Middle East Command is intended to be the center
of co-operative efforts for the defense of the area, as a whole;
the achievement of peace and security in the area through the
Middle East Command will bring with it social and economic
advancement.

4. A function of the Middle East Command will be to assist
and support the states willing to join in the defense of the
Middle East and to develop the capacity of each to play its
proper role in the defense of the area as a whole against outside
aggression. It will not interfere in problems and disputes arising
within the area. The establishment of the Middle East Command in no way affects existing arrangements relating to

such matters, notably the armistice agreements and the United States–United Kingdom–French Tripartite Declaration of May 1950.

5. The task of the Middle East Command at the outset will be primarily one of planning and providing the Middle East States on their request with assistance in the form of advice and training. Requests for arms and equipment made by states in the area willing to join in its defense of sponsoring states in a position to assist in this connection will be filled by them to the extent possible following the co-ordination of such requests through the Middle East Command.

6. The Supreme Allied Commander Middle East will command forces placed at his disposal and will develop plans for the operations of all forces within the area (or to be introduced into the area) in time of war or international emergency. However, the placing of forces under the command of the Supreme Allied Commander Middle East in peacetime is not a prerequisite for joining in the common effort for the defense of the Middle East. Movement of those troops placed under the command of the Supreme Allied Commander Middle East to or within the territories of states joining in the defense of the Middle East will be made only with the agreement of the state or states concerned and in full accord with their national independence and sovereignty . . .

SOURCE: US Department of State Bulletin (19 November 1951), 817

PART FIVE

Conciliation at the Summit

The death of Marshal Stalin on 5 March 1953 was immediately seen as removing the major obstacle towards improved relations between East and West. But the dominant mood was still one of uncertainty over the future course of events when, with characteristic impetuosity, Sir Winston Churchill presented to the House of Commons his proposal for a summit conference.

Sir Winston began by noting that the government's immediate aim was a truce in Korea. He then discussed Indo-China and Egypt before turning to Europe.

Finally, moving on to the subject of relations with the Soviet Union, the Prime Minister noted that there had recently been a number of encouraging gestures from Moscow and added that it was a mistake to assume that nothing could be settled until everything was settled. The Soviets had the right to expect guarantees against a repeat of the 1940 invasion and assurances that Poland would remain friendly. For these and other reasons a conference at the highest level should be held without delay.

Sir Winston's bold speech had an immediate impact. France and India expressed their approval. In the United States, however, reactions were considerably more cautious. Some critics accused the Prime Minister of resurrecting the spectre of appeasement—an allegation that was to bedevil every attempt to ease East-West relations for nearly twenty years.

Sir Winston's ill-advised reference to Locarno also aroused concern in West Germany.

For its part the US State Department issued a non-commital statement, observing that any conference should be preceded by some concrete expression of Soviet sincerity—in Korea, for example.

The immediate outcome of the speech was a plan to hold a three-power meeting in Bermuda at the end of May, although this was postponed because of, first, one of the recurrent French political crises, and then Sir Winston's illness. Instead the British, French, and United States' foreign ministers met in Washington.

None the less, by his important speech Sir Winston had set the seed of what was to become a recurrent obsession of his successor prime ministers —the belief that a meeting at the summit could automatically resolve many of the outstanding problems affecting international relations. In addition, such conferences would assure Britain's place among the big powers.

20 Winston Churchill
SPEECH PROPOSING A MEETING AT THE SUMMIT (11 May 1953)

... The scene today, its scale and its factors, is widely different, and yet I have a feeling that the master thought which animated Locarno might well play its part between Germany and Russia in the minds of those whose prime ambition it is to consolidate the peace of Europe as the key to the peace of mankind. Russia has a right to feel assured that as far as human arrangements can run the terrible events of the Hitler invasion will never be repeated, and that Poland will remain a friendly Power and a buffer, though not, I trust, a puppet State.

I venture to read to the House again some words which I wrote exactly eight years ago, 29th April, 1945, in a telegram I sent to Mr. Stalin:

'There is not much comfort', I said, 'in looking into a future where you and the countries you dominate, plus the Communist Parties in many other States, are all drawn up on one

side, and those who rally to the English-speaking nations and
their associates or Dominions are on the other. It is quite obvious
that their quarrel would tear the world to pieces, and that all of
us leading men on either side who had anything to do with that
would be shamed before history. Even embarking on a long
period of suspicions, of abuse and counter-abuse, and of oppos-
ing policies would be a disaster hampering the great developments of world prosperity for the masses which are attainable
only by our trinity. I hope there is no word or phrase in this
outpouring of my heart to you which unwittingly gives offence.
If so, let me know. But do not, I beg you, my friend Stalin,
underrate the divergences which are opening about matters
which you may think are small to us but which are symbolic of
the way the English-speaking democracies look at life.'

I feel exactly the same about it today.

I must make it plain that, in spite of all the uncertainties and
confusion in which world affairs are plunged, I believe that a
conference on the highest level should take place between the
leading Powers without long delay. This conference should not
be overhung by a ponderous or rigid agenda, or led into mazes
and jungles of technical details, zealously contested by hordes
of experts and officials drawn up in vast, cumbrous array. The
conference should be confined to the smallest number of Powers
and persons possible. It should meet with a measure of informality and a still greater measure of privacy and seclusion.
It might well be that no hard-faced agreements would be
reached, but there might be a general feeling among those
gathered together that they might do something better than
tear the human race, including themselves, into bits.

For instance, they might be attracted, as President Eisenhower has shown himself to be, and as 'Pravda' does not challenge, by the idea of letting the weary, toiling masses of mankind
enter upon the best spell of good fortune, fair play, well-being,
leisure and harmless happiness that has ever been within their
reach or even within their dreams.

I only say that this might happen, and I do not see why anyone should be frightened at having a try for it. If there is not at

the summit of the nations the will to win the greatest prize and the greatest honour ever offered to mankind, doom-laden responsibility will fall upon those who now possess the power to decide. At the worst the participants in the meeting would have established more intimate contacts. At the best we might have a generation of peace.

I have now finished my survey of the world scene as I see it and as I feel about it today. I express my thanks to the House for the great consideration with which I have been treated. I hope I have contributed a few thoughts which may make for peace and help a gentler breeze to blow upon this weary earth. But there is one thing I have to say before I end, and without it all the hopes I have ventured to indulge would be utterly vain. Whatever differences of opinion may be between friends and allies about particular problems or the general scale of values and sense of proportion which we should adopt, there is one fact which stands out overwhelmingly in its simplicity and force. If it is made good every hope is pardonable. If it is not made good all hopes fall together.

This would be the most fatal moment for the free nations to relax their comradeship and preparations. To fail to maintain our defence effort up to the limit of our strength would be to paralyse every beneficial tendency towards peace both in Europe and in Asia. For us to become divided among ourselves because of divergences of opinion or local interests, or to slacken our combined efforts would be to end for ever such new hope as may have broken upon mankind and lead instead to their general ruin and enslavement. Unity, vigilance and fidelity are the only foundations upon which hope can live.

SOURCE: House of Commons Debates, vol 515, col 883–898

THE BERMUDA CONFERENCE

With widespread disarray in the Western camp over policy towards both Europe and the Middle East, the Bermuda Conference, which had been postponed in May, was finally held in December.

*In the communiqué the three powers declared their conviction that a
united Europe was essential for achieving greater prosperity and stability
in Europe, and also that a European defence community was a necessary
part of the alliance.*

*However, no definite Anglo-American commitments to European
defence, which many in France had hoped for, were forthcoming.*

*At a subsequent meeting of the NATO Council in Paris, Bidault
tried to obtain the safeguards he sought through NATO, even going so
far as to hint that France might have to resort to certain unspecified
accommodations with the Soviet Union. The dominant Anglo-American
alliance treated his threats with the contempt they deserved.*

21 President Eisenhower, Sir Winston Churchill and M Joseph Laniel
COMMUNIQUE ISSUED AFTER THE MEETING
(8 December 1953)

Our meeting symbolised and confirmed the unity of purpose of
our three countries. We found ourselves in accord on our
analysis of the problems confronting us and have agreed on
various measures essential for their solution.

Confident that our united strength is the best guarantee of
peace and security we are resolved to maintain our joint efforts
to perfect it. If the danger of aggression now appears less imminent we attribute this to the mounting strength of the free
world and the firmness of its policies.

We shall remain resolute in maintaining our solidarity and
vigilant against efforts to divide us.

With their material and moral resources we are confident
that the free peoples can provide both for their security and for
their well-being. We dedicate ourselves to work together toward
these ends.

The North Atlantic Treaty is and will remain the foundation
of our common policy.

We discussed means of developing the defensive capacity of
our alliance. Lord Ismay, the secretary-general of the North

Atlantic Treaty Organisation, was present at the conversations on this subject.

In the continuing development of a United Europe, including Germany, we see the best means of achieving greater prosperity, security and stability for its free peoples. We reaffirmed that the European Defence Community is needed to assure the defensive capacity of the Atlantic Community, of which it will be an integral part within this framework.

It will ensure intimate and durable co-operation between the United Kingdom and United States forces, and the forces of the European Defence Community on the continent of Europe.

The French Minister for Foreign Affairs explained the problems facing his Government in regard to the European Defence Community.

We cannot accept as justified or permanent the present division of Europe. Our hope is that in due course peaceful means will be found to enable the countries of Eastern Europe again to play their part as free nations in a free Europe.

Our three Governments will lose no opportunity for easing the tensions that beset the world and for reassuring all nations that they have no cause to fear that the strength of the West will be invoked in any cause of wrongful violence.

On the contrary, it is the fundamental principle of the United Nations Organisation, which we serve, that the guarantees against aggression shall be universal in their application.

We are confident that if we remain strong, united and steadfast it will become possible gradually to solve the stubborn problems which have so long been unsettled.

In this spirit we have examined the latest Note from the Soviet Government. We approved the text of our replies which should lead to an early meeting of the four Foreign Ministers.

Our hope is that this meeting will make progress towards the reunification of Germany in freedom and the conclusion of an Austrian State Treaty, and thus toward the solution of other major international problems.

We reviewed the situation in the Far East. The immediate

object of our policy continues to be the convening of the political conference provided for in the Korean armistice agreement.

This will provide the means for reaching a peaceful settlement of the Korean question and for making progress in restoring more normal conditions in the Far East and South-East Asia.

In Indo-China we salute the valiant forces of France and of the three associated states of Indo-China fighting within the French Union to protect the independence of Cambodia, Laos and Viet-Nam.

We recognise the vital importance of their contribution to the defence of the free world. We will continue to work together to restore peace and stability in this area.

Our meetings have re-enforced our solidarity, strengthened our resolve and fortified our hopes. Confident in our common purposes and united in our views we shall persevere in our policies whose sole aim is to foster and assure peace.

SOURCE: *The Daily Telegraph* (9 December 1953)

SOUTH-EAST ASIA TREATY ORGANISATION
The fall of Dien Bien Phu and the end of the first Indo-China war, coupled with the refusal of President Eisenhower to intervene on the side of the French, created a dilemma for John Foster Dulles, the American Secretary of State. Swiftly he tried to restore some influence for American foreign policy in South-East Asia by setting up an Asian counterpart of NATO. Under the terms of the agreement establishing the South-East Asia Treaty Organisation (SEATO), the allies agreed to consult if any signatory felt threatened. They would act together against an aggressor if they could unanimously agree on the nature of the action they would take. Protection for South Vietnam, Laos and Cambodia was covered under a separate protocol. SEATO never developed into an effective counterpart of the Atlantic alliance—too many countries were not members and it was too much a white man's club. It may indirectly have contributed to communist feelings of encirclement and certainly failed to stop the Indo-China war breaking out again.

22 SEATO
SOUTH-EAST ASIA COLLECTIVE DEFENCE TREATY, MANILA (8 September 1954)

The Parties to this Treaty,

Recognising the sovereign equality of all the Parties,

Reiterating their faith in the purposes and principles set forth in the Charter of the United Nations and their desire to live in peace with all peoples and all governments,

Reaffirming that, in accordance with the Charter of the United Nations, they uphold the principle of equal rights and self-determination of peoples, and declaring that they will earnestly strive by every peaceful means to promote self-government and to secure the independence of all countries whose peoples desire it and are able to undertake its responsibilities,

Desiring to strengthen the fabric of peace and freedom and to uphold the principles of democracy, individual liberty and the rule of law, and to promote the economic well-being and development of all peoples in the Treaty area,

Intending to declare publicly and formally their sense of unity, so that any potential aggressor will appreciate that the Parties stand together in the area, and

Desiring further to co-ordinate their efforts for collective defence for the preservation of peace and security,

Therefore agree as follows:

Article One

The Parties undertake, as set forth in the Charter of the United Nations, to settle any international disputes in which they may be involved by peaceful means in such a manner that international peace and security and justice are not endangered, and to refrain in their international relations from the threat or use of force in any manner inconsistent with the purposes of the United Nations.

Article Two
In order more effectively to achieve the objectives of this Treaty, the Parties, separately and jointly, by means of continuous and effective self-help and mutual aid will maintain and develop their individual and collective capacity to resist armed attack and to prevent and counter subversive activities directed from without against their territorial integrity and political stability.

Article Three
The Parties undertake to strengthen their free institutions, and to co-operate with one another in the further development of economic measures, including technical assistance, designed both to promote economic progress and social well-being and to further the individual and collective efforts of Governments toward these ends.

Article Four
1. Each Party recognises that aggression by means of armed attack in the treaty area against any of the Parties or against any State or territory which the Parties by unanimous agreement may hereafter designate, would endanger its own peace and safety, and agrees that it will in that event act to meet the common danger in accordance with its constitutional processes.

Measures taken under this paragraph shall be immediately reported to the Security Council of the United Nations.

2. If, in the opinion of any of the Parties, the inviolability or the integrity of the territory or the sovereignty or political independence of any Party in the treaty area or of any other State or territory to which the provision of paragraph 1 of this Article from time to time apply is threatened in any way other than by armed attack or is affected or threatened by any fact or situation which might endanger the peace of the area, the Parties shall consult immediately in order to agree on the measures which should be taken for the common defence.

3. It is understood that no action on the territory of any State designated by unanimous agreement under paragraph 1 of this Article or on any territory so designated shall be taken except at the invitation or with the consent of the Government concerned ...

SOURCE: US Department of State, *Treaties and Other International Acts*, 3170

THE GENEVA CONFERENCE

The idea of a summit conference, which Sir Winston Churchill had stimulated with such brilliance in 1953, finally germinated at Geneva two years later. The conference was given added impetus by rising concern over nuclear armaments and the continued escalation of military expenditures. In March 1955, Sir Winston again expressed his belief in the summit concept. The conclusion of the Austrian State Treaty also appeared to be evidence of a new, more conciliatory approach on the part of the Soviets. Finally, on 10 May, the Western powers suggested a meeting of heads of government, followed by a second meeting in which the issues raised in the first would be explored in detail. In a swift and promising reaction, the Soviet Union accepted the idea of a conference on 26 May.

The divergences between the two sides rapidly began to emerge, though, at the first session of the conference on 18 July. The Western delegates all stressed that German unity was the primary issue. The Soviet delegate, Marshal Bulganin, retorted that 'security' was the central concern, stressing the need for a system of collective security and measures to end the arms race, ban atomic weapons, and limit atomic energy to peaceful uses.

It was no surprise that the practical results of the conference were disappointing and there was little evidence of any change of position on either side. But the conference did show that it was still possible to meet on friendly terms and without excessive recrimination. To this limited extent it might be accounted a muted success.

23A United States, Britain and France
NOTE TO THE SOVIET UNION (10 May 1955)

The Governments of France, the United Kingdom, and the United States believe that the time has now come for a new effort to resolve the great problems which confront us. We, therefore, invite the Soviet Government to join with us in an effort to remove sources of conflict between us.

We recognize that the solution of these problems will take time and patience. They will not be solved at a single meeting nor in a hasty manner. Indeed, any effort to do so could set back real progress toward their settlement. Accordingly, we think it would be helpful to try a new procedure for dealing with these problems.

In view of their complexity and importance, our suggestion is that these problems be approached in two stages. We think it would be fruitful to begin with a meeting of the Heads of Government, accompanied by their Foreign Ministers, for an exchange of views. In the limited time for which the Heads of Government could meet, they would not undertake to agree upon substantive answers to the major difficulties facing the world. Such a meeting could, however, provide a new impetus by establishing the basis for the detailed work which will be required.

For this purpose the Heads of Government could devote themselves to formulating the issues to be worked on and to agreeing on methods to be followed in exploring solutions. We further propose that the Foreign Ministers, to assist the Heads of Government in their task, should come together shortly in advance of the meeting of the Heads of Government and at the same place.

This first stage would lay the foundation for the second stage in which the problems would be examined in detail by such methods, organs, and participants as it appears will be most fruitful according to the nature of the issues. This work should be started as soon as practicable after the meeting of the Heads of Government.

This procedure would facilitate the essential preparation and orderly negotiation most likely to bring about agreements by progressive stages. The important thing is to begin the process promptly and to pursue it with patience and determination.

We hope that this proposal will commend itself to the Soviet Union as a useful basis for progress toward better relations between us. If the Soviet Union agrees that an early meeting of the Heads of Government to explore such a program would be useful, we suggest that our Foreign Ministers settle through diplomatic channels or otherwise upon a time and place for such a meeting. The forthcoming meeting of the Foreign Ministers at Vienna for the signing of the Austrian State Treaty might provide an opportunity for preliminary discussion of this proposal.

SOURCE: US Department of State Publication 6046, *The Geneva Conference of Heads of Government July 18–23, 1955*, 6–7

23B United States, France, United Kingdom and the USSR
DIRECTIVE TO THE FOREIGN MINISTERS
(23 July 1955)

The Heads of Government of France, the United Kingdom, the U.S.S.R. and the U.S.A., guided by the desire to contribute to the relaxation of international tension and to the consolidation of confidence between states, instruct their Foreign Ministers to continue the consideration of the following questions with regard to which an exchange of views has taken place, at the Geneva Conference, and to propose effective means for their solution, taking account of the close link between the reunification of Germany and the problems of European security, and the fact that the successful settlement of each of these problems would serve the interests of consolidating peace.

1. European Security and Germany. For the purpose of establishing European security with due regard to the legitimate interests of all nations and their inherent right to individual and collective self-defence, the Ministers are instructed to consider various proposals to this end, including the following: A security pact for Europe or for a part of Europe, including provisions for the assumption by member nations of an obligation not to resort to force and to deny assistance to an aggressor; limitation, control, and inspection in regard to armed forces and armaments; establishment between East and West of a zone in which the disposition of armed forces will be subject to mutual agreement; and also to consider other possible proposals pertaining to the solution of this problem.

The Heads of Government, recognizing their common responsibility for the settlement of the German question and the reunification of Germany, have agreed that the settlement of the German question and the reunification of Germany by means of free elections shall be carried out in conformity with the national interests of the German people and the interests of European security. The Foreign Ministers will make whatever arrangements they may consider desirable for the participation of, or for consultation with, other interested parties.

2. Disarmament

The Four Heads of Government,

Desirous of removing the threat of war and lessening the burden of armaments,

Convinced of the necessity, for secure peace and for the welfare of mankind, of achieving a system for the control and reduction of all armaments and armed forces under effective safeguards,

Recognizing that achievements in this field would release vast material resources to be devoted to the peaceful economic development of nations, for raising their well-being, as well as for assistance to underdeveloped countries,

Agree:

(1) for these purposes to work together to develop an acceptable system for disarmament through the Sub-Committee of the United Nations Disarmament Commission;

(2) to instruct their representatives in the Sub-Committee in the discharge of their mandate from the United Nations to take account in their work of the views and proposals advanced by the Heads of Government at this Conference;

(3) to propose that the next meeting of the Sub-Committee be held on August 29, 1955, at New York;

(4) to instruct the Foreign Ministers to take note of the proceedings in the Disarmament Commission, to take account of the views and proposals advanced by the Heads of Government at this Conference and to consider whether the four Governments can take any further useful initiative in the field of disarmament.

3. Development of Contacts between East and West

The Foreign Ministers should by means of experts study measures, including those possible in organs and agencies of the United Nations, which could (a) bring about a progressive elimination of barriers which interfere with free communications and peaceful trade between people and (b) bring about such freer contacts and exchanges as are to the mutual advantage of the countries and peoples concerned.

4. The Foreign Ministers of the Four Powers will meet at Geneva during October to initiate their consideration of these questions and to determine the organisation of their work.

SOURCE: US Department of State Publication 6046, *The Geneva Conference of Heads of Government July 18–23, 1955*, 67–8

PART SIX

The Suez Crisis

The Egyptian nationalisation of the Suez Canal Company, on 20 July 1956, came as Nasser's swift reaction to the Anglo-American withdrawal of their offer to help finance the Aswan Dam. It led with inexorable pace to the collapse of the shaky Western attempt to work with Egypt in building an anti-Soviet buffer in the Middle East, and then, three months later, to the greatest division in the Anglo-American alliance in this century.

More than any other event, the Suez crisis marks the true divide in the postwar history of the special relationship. The relationship survived, it is true, but it would never again recover its former intensity. Suez revealed to the British the extent to which their military power and influence had declined since 1945. In collaboration with France and Israel, Britain tried to launch a comparatively limited operation against a small country. It failed ignominiously through its inability to collect sufficient forces quickly enough to act before the world community's alarm was aroused. It would never again be rash enough to attempt such a venture.

The brusque and insensitive manner in which the United States turned against Britain brought out all the latent anti-Americanism that was to be found in large sections of both political parties at Westminster. Those who had argued persistently that it was unwise to place too much reliance on the special relationship felt that their suspicions had been vindicated.

The United States, which had helped to precipitate the crisis by with-drawing its financial support for the Aswan Dam had, it was argued, failed to help its most loyal ally when it was trapped in the consequences of its actions.

The situation was intensified by the scarcely veiled contempt Sir Anthony Eden, the Prime Minister, had for John Foster Dulles, the US Secretary of State, whom he suspected, with some justice, of exercising an overbearing influence on President Eisenhower's judgement.

In an attempt to avoid the breach that was later to occur, Eden sent a letter to Eisenhower on 6 September emphasising the common concerns of their two nations in the Middle East and the need to cooperate in bringing pressure on the Egyptian Government. The American response was cool. The United States was reluctant, in view of its firmly anti-communist policy, to appear to 'gang up' with the colonialist powers against Egypt. Dulles saw the conflict less as one involving national interests—there were few that affected the United States, in any case—than a business dispute involving a monopolistic public utility of international value.

24 Sir Anthony Eden
LETTER TO PRESIDENT EISENHOWER
(6 September 1956)

Thank you for your message and writing thus frankly.

There is no doubt as to where we are agreed and have been agreed from the very beginning, namely that we should do everything we can to get a peaceful settlement. It is in this spirit that we favoured calling the twenty-two power conference and that we have worked in the closest co-operation with you about this business since. There has never been any question of our suddenly or without further provocation resorting to arms, while these processes were at work. In any event, as your own wide knowledge would confirm, we could not have done this without extensive preparation lasting several weeks.

This question of precautions has troubled me considerably and still does. I have not forgotten the riots and murders in Cairo in 1952, for I was in charge here at the time when Winston was on the high seas on his way back from the United States.

We are both agreed that we must give the Suez committee every chance to fulfil their mission. This is our firm resolve. If the committee and subsequent negotiations succeed in getting Nasser's agreement to the London proposals of the eighteen powers, there will be no call for force. But if the committee fails, we must have some immediate alternative which will show that Nasser is not going to get his way. In this connection we are attracted by Foster's suggestion, if I understand it rightly, for the running of the canal by the users in virtue of their rights under the 1888 Convention. We heard about this from our Embassy in Washington yesterday. I think that we could go along with this, provided that the intention was made clear by both of us immediately the Menzies mission finishes its work. But unless we can proceed with this, or something very like it, what should the next step be?

You suggest that this is where we diverge. If that is so I think that the divergence springs from a difference in our assessment of Nasser's plans and intentions. May I set out our view of the position.

In the nineteen-thirties Hitler established his position by a series of carefully planned movements. These began with the occupation of the Rhineland and were followed by successive acts of aggression against Austria, Czechoslovakia, Poland, and the West. His actions were tolerated and excused by the majority of the population of Western Europe. It was argued either that Hitler had committed no act of aggression against anyone, or that he was entitled to do what he liked in his own territory, or that it was impossible to prove that he had any ulterior designs, or that the Covenant of the League of Nations did not entitle us to use force and that it would be wiser to wait until he did commit an act of aggression.

In more recent years Russia has attempted similar tactics. The blockade of Berlin was to have been the opening move in a campaign designed at least to deprive the Western powers of their whole position in Germany. On this occasion we fortunately reacted at once with the result that the Russian design was never unfolded. But I am sure that you would agree that it would be wrong to infer from this circumstance that no Russian design existed.

Similarly the seizure of the Suez Canal is, we are convinced, the opening gambit in a planned campaign designed by Nasser to expel all Western influence and interests from Arab countries. He believes that if he can get away with this, and if he can successfully defy eighteen nations, his prestige in Arabia will be so great that he will be able to mount revolutions of young officers in Saudi Arabia, Jordan, Syria and Iraq. (We know that he is already preparing a revolution in Iraq, which is the most stable and progressive.) These new Governments will in effect be Egyptian satellites if not Russian ones. They will have to place their united oil resources under the control of a united Arabia led by Egypt and under Russian influence. When that moment comes Nasser can deny oil to Western Europe and we here shall all be at his mercy.

There are some who doubt whether Saudi Arabia, Iraq and Kuwait will be prepared even for a time to sacrifice their oil revenues for the sake of Nasser's ambitions. But if we place ourselves in their position I think the dangers are clear. If Nasser says to them, 'I have nationalized the Suez Canal. I have successfully defied eighteen powerful nations including the United States, I have defied the whole of the United Nations in the matter of the Israel blockade, I have expropriated all Western property. Trust me and withhold oil from Western Europe. Within six months or a year, the Continent of Europe will be on its knees before you.' Will the Arabs not be prepared to follow this lead? Can we rely on them to be more sensible than were the Germans? Even if the Arabs eventually fall apart again as they did after the early Caliphs, the damage will have been done meanwhile.

In short we are convinced that if Nasser is allowed to defy the eighteen nations it will be a matter of months before revolution breaks out in the oil-bearing countries and the West is wholly deprived of Middle Eastern oil. In this belief we are fortified by the advice of friendly leaders in the Middle East.

The Iraqis are the most insistent in their warnings; both Nuri and the Crown Prince have spoken to us several times of the consequences of Nasser succeeding in his grab. They would be swept away.

[I then gave the President an account of three other warnings which we had received, each from a different Middle Eastern country: as the authors of these warnings are still alive, I do not propose to make their names public.]

The difference which separates us today [my message continued] appears to be a difference of assessment of Nasser's plans and intentions and of the consequences in the Middle East of military action against him.

You may feel that even if we are right it would be better to wait until Nasser has unmistakably unveiled his intentions. But this was the argument which prevailed in 1936 and which we both rejected in 1948. Admittedly there are risks in the use of force against Egypt now. It is, however, clear that military intervention designed to reverse Nasser's revolutions in the whole continent would be a much more costly and difficult undertaking. I am very troubled, as it is, that if we do not reach a conclusion either way about the canal very soon one or other of these eastern lands may be toppled at any moment by Nasser's revolutionary movements.

I agree with you that prolonged military operations as well as the denial of Middle East oil would place an immense strain on the economy of Western Europe. I can assure you that we are conscious of the burdens and perils attending military intervention. But if our assessment is correct, and if the only alternative is to allow Nasser's plans quietly to develop until this country and all Western Europe are held to ransom by Egypt acting at Russia's behest it seems to us that our duty is plain. We have many times led Europe in the fight for freedom. It would be an ignoble end to our long history if we accepted to perish by degrees.

SOURCE: Sir Anthony Eden. *The Eden Memoirs: Full Circle* (1960), 464–7

After the beginning of tripartite discussions on the Suez Canal in late July 1956, the United States' aim was to try and keep the parties talking and avoid hasty action. Prior to the first London Conference, the British had hoped that at the last moment the Americans would join them in taking action. After all, Eden reasoned, Dulles himself had spoken of the need to make 'Nasser disgorge'. Later, though, Dulles reverted to form and denied his intention of meeting 'violence with violence'. He stressed that the United States had never given any commitments on the course it would follow if the conference should fail. Then, in a further statement, the United States gave notice that its object was the 'safeguarding of the legitimate interests of Egypt'. The warning could hardly have been more specific.

The London Conference, the mission of the Australian Prime Minister, Sir Robert Menzies, and Anglo-French suspicions that the United States was engaged in clandestine negotiations with the Egyptians had only brought a deterioration of the situation when Dulles produced his plan for a Suez Canal Users' Association. The reaction from Britain and France was cool. Eden queried why Dulles should have gone back to the points produced by the London Conference in August. Dulles doubtless hoped that economic pressure would bring Egypt to terms, but this was not to be. Egypt suffered little and was in any case able to recruit enough pilots abroad to keep traffic flowing through the canal.

25 John Foster Dulles
PROPOSAL FOR A SUEZ CANAL USERS'
ASSOCIATION (13 September 1956)

The United States, as has been made clear, seeks a just and peaceful solution of the Suez question. Within this context, we gave whole-hearted cooperation to the London Conference of twenty-two nations. There, eighteen countries, including the United States, representing over 90 percent of the ownership of vessels passing through the Canal, joined in an expression of views designed to furnish, we thought, a proper and reasonable basis for working out the question of the operation of the Canal in accordance with the 1888 Convention. These views were presented and explained to the Government of Egypt by a Five Nation Committee under the Chairmanship of the Right Honorable Robert Menzies, the Prime Minister of Australia. The Government of Egypt was unwilling to agree to negotiate on the basis which the overwhelming majority of the users suggested. In these circumstances, it had to be considered what further steps could be taken towards a just, yet peaceful, settlement.

Prime Minister Eden in his speech yesterday set forth the concept of an association of users of the Suez Canal. Prior to his making that speech, the United States had informed him that if the United Kingdom alone or in association with others should propose a users' association to be organized by the 18 sponsors of the London proposals, or such of them as were so disposed, and perhaps others, the United States would participate in such a users' association. We assume that such an organization would act as agent for the users and would exercise on their behalf the rights which are theirs under the 1888 Convention and seek such cooperation with Egypt as would achieve the results designed to be guaranteed by that Convention.

The eighteen nations, meeting in London, joined in a common approach to the problem, feeling that it was to their best interest to concert their efforts.

Certain things are, I think, clear:

1. The user nations have rights under the 1888 Treaty;
2. These rights cannot legally be nullified by unilateral Egyptian action;
3. It is normal for users to seek to work in association when rights which they possess jointly are in jeopardy.

So we think it is wise that voluntary cooperation among the users of the Canal should continue. We do not believe that their rights can be adequately safeguarded if each nation, much less if each ship, fends for itself. We believe that, under present circumstances, practical cooperation with Egypt can be effectively achieved only if the users are organized so that they can deal jointly with Egypt and Egypt deal with them jointly.

We are thus prepared to participate in a users' organization on the basis which I indicated. It is our thought that the users' association would, among other things, provide qualified pilots for the users' ships; would initially receive the dues from the ships of members of the association passing through the Canal, which sums would be used to defray the expenses of the organization and to pay appropriate compensation to Egypt for its contribution to the maintenance of the Canal and the facilities of transit; and so far as practical arrange for the pattern of traffic of the member vessels through the Canal.

It is our hope that perhaps practical on-the-spot arrangements for cooperation can be achieved without prejudice to the rights of anyone. This may provide a provisional *de facto* working arrangement until formal agreements can be reached.

Of course, we recognize that what is now suggested provides no permanent solution. We shall be unremitting in our efforts to seek by peaceful means a just solution giving due recognition to the rights of all concerned, including Egypt.

It is in this spirit that the United States and, we hope, other Suez Canal users, will seek association with each other . . .

SOURCE: US Department of State Publications 6392, 335

Dulles had already succeeded in enraging the British by saying earlier in an interview that the United States would not 'try to shoot its way through the Canal', and would send its ships around the Cape instead if necessary. Moreover, he added that Britain and France could not count on American support if they resorted to war. Not surprisingly Eden saw this as amounting to the Americans torpedoing their own plan as soon as they had launched it.

On 2 October, Dulles worsened the situation at a press conference by sharply drawing a distinction between American policy and that of

Britain and France. Furthermore, he then called attention to the different role to be played by the United States and by the 'so-called colonial powers'.

26 John Foster Dulles
PRESS CONFERENCE ON SUEZ CANAL USERS' ASSOCIATION (2 October 1956)

. . . As far as the formula for the users association is concerned, there is no detectable change, at least not detectable to me, between what it now is and what was planned, at least as far as the United States is concerned, and as we made known to the British and the French before the project was publicly launched in any way. There was drawn up a draft of the charter, so to speak, the articles of the users association, and what is coming into being today is almost exactly what was planned at that time. There is talk about the 'teeth' being pulled out of it. There were never 'teeth' in it, if that means the use of force.

Now there has been some difference in our approach to this problem of the Suez Canal. This is not an area where we are bound together by treaty. Certain areas we are by treaty bound to protect, such as the North Atlantic Treaty area, and there we stand together and I hope and believe always will stand absolutely together.

There are also other problems where our approach is not always identical. For example, there is in Asia and Africa the so-called problem of colonialism. Now there the United States plays a somewhat independent role. You have this very great problem of the shift from colonialism to independence which is in process and which will be going on, perhaps, for another 50 years, and there I believe the role of the United States is to try to see that that process moves forward in a constructive evolutionary way and does not either come to a halt or take a violent revolutionary turn which would be destructive of very much good. I suspect that the United States will find that its role, not only today but in the coming years, will be to try to aid that process, without identifying itself 100 percent either with the so-called colonial powers or with the powers which are primarily and uniquely concerned with the problem of getting their independence as rapidly as possible. I think we have a special role to play and that perhaps makes it impractical for us, as I say, in every respect to identify our policies with those of other countries on whichever side of that problem they find their interest.

SOURCE: US Department of State Bulletin (15 October 1956), 577

Neither the two London conferences nor the subsequent resort to the United Nations succeeded in resolving the dispute over the Suez Canal, or in bridging the widening gap between the United States and the Anglo-French alliance. Although negotiations continued throughout October, these appeared to have been concerned more with form than with a real attempt to reach agreement. In any case, events in the Middle East rapidly took command, culminating in the Israeli assault on Egypt.

As soon as the Anglo-French ultimatum to Egypt had expired on 31 October 1956, and armed attacks were launched, the American response was strong and shocking to the Anglo-French leadership. Despite all the prior evidence, it appeared the two allies still considered that in the final resort the United States would hold back from condemning their course of action.

Eisenhower went on radio and television on the evening of 31 October to hail what he prematurely called the 'new day' in Eastern Europe, where it briefly appeared the Hungarian revolt had achieved its objectives, and to condemn the joint action against Egypt. He pledged there would be no United States involvement in the hostilities and condemned the military actions as 'scarcely to be reconciled with the principles and purposes of the United Nations'.

27 President Eisenhower
BROADCAST ADDRESS ON DEVELOPMENTS IN EASTERN EUROPE AND THE MIDDLE EAST
(31 October 1956)

Tonight I report to you as your President.

We all realize that the full and free debate of a political campaign today surrounds us. But the events and issues I wish to place before you this evening have no connection whatsoever with matters of partisanship. They are concerns of every American—his present and his future.

I wish, therefore, to give you a report of essential facts so that you—whether belonging to either one of our two great parties, or to neither—may give thoughtful and informed consideration to this swiftly changing world scene.

The changes of which I speak have come in two areas of the world—Eastern Europe and the Middle East.

In Eastern Europe there seems to appear the dawn of a new day. It has not been short or easy in coming.

After World War II, the Soviet Union used military force to impose on the nations of Eastern Europe governments of Soviet choice—servants of Moscow.

It has been consistent United States policy, without regard to political party, to seek to end this situation and to fulfil the wartime pledge of the United Nations that these countries, overrun by wartime armies, would once again know sovereignty and self-government.

We could not, of course, carry out this policy by resort to force. Such force would have been contrary both to the best interests of the Eastern European peoples and to the abiding principles of the United Nations. But we did help to keep alive the hope of these peoples for freedom.

Beyond this, they needed from us no education in the worth of national independence and personal liberty, for, at the time of the American Revolution, it was many of them who came to our land to aid our cause. Recently the pressure of the will of these peoples for national independence has become more and more insistent.

A few days ago, the people of Poland with their proud and deathless devotion to freedom moved to secure a peaceful transition to a new government. And this government, it seems, will strive genuinely to serve the Polish people.

And all the world has been watching dramatic events in Hungary where this brave people, as so often in the past, have offered their very lives for independence from foreign masters. Today, it appears, a new Hungary is rising from this struggle, a Hungary which we hope from our hearts will know full and free nationhood . . .

I now turn to that other part of the world where, at this moment, the situation is somber. It is not a situation that calls for extravagant fear or hysteria. It invites our most serious concern.

I speak, of course, of the Middle East. This ancient crossroads of the world was, as we all know, an area long subject to colonial rule. This rule ended after World War II, when all countries there won full independence. Out of the Palestinian mandated territory was born the new State of Israel.

These historic changes could not, however, instantly banish animosities born of the ages. Israel and her Arab neighbors soon found themselves at war with one another. And the Arab nations showed continuing anger toward their former colonial rulers, notably Great Britain and France.

The United States through all the years since the close of World War II has labored tirelessly to bring peace and stability to this area.

We have considered it a basic matter of United States policy to support the new State of Israel and at the same time to strengthen our bonds both with Israel and with the Arab countries. But unfortunately, through all these years, passion in the area threatened to prevail over peaceful purpose and, in one form or another, there has been almost continuous fighting.

This situation recently was aggravated needlessly by an

Egyptian policy including rearmament with Communist weapons. We, for our part, felt this to be a misguided policy on the part of the Government of Egypt. The State of Israel, for its part, felt increasing anxiety for its safety. And Great Britain and France feared more and more that Egyptian policies threatened what they regard as their 'lifeline' of the Suez Canal.

These matters came to a crisis on July 26th of this year, when the Egyptian Government seized the Universal Suez Canal Company. For 90 years, ever since the inauguration of the canal, that company had operated the canal, largely under British and French technical supervision.

There were some among our allies who urged an immediate reaction to this event by use of force. We insistently urged otherwise, and our wish prevailed—through a long succession of conferences and negotiations for weeks and months, with participation by the United Nations. And there, only a short while ago, on the basis of agreed principles, it seemed that an acceptable accord was within our reach. But the direct relations of Egypt with both Israel and France kept worsening to a point at which first Israel, then France and Great Britain also, determined that, in their judgment, there could be no protection of their vital interests without resort to force.

Upon this decision, events followed swiftly. On Sunday the Israeli Government ordered total mobilization. On Monday, their armed forces penetrated deeply into Egypt and to the vicinity of the Suez Canal, nearly 100 miles away. And on Tuesday, the British and French Governments delivered a 12-hour ultimatum to Israel and Egypt—now followed up by armed attack against Egypt.

The United States was not consulted in any way about any phase of these actions. Nor were we informed of them in advance.

As it is the manifest right of any of these nations to take such decisions and actions, it is likewise our right—if our judgment so dictates—to disagree. We believe these actions to have been taken in error. For we do not accept the use of force as a wise or proper instrument for the settlement of international disputes.

To say this in this particular instance is in no way to minimize our friendship with these nations nor our determination to retain and to strengthen the bonds among us. And we are fully aware of the grave anxieties of Israel, of Britain, and of France. We know that they have been subjected to grave and repeated provocations.

The present fact, nonetheless, seems clear: The actions taken can scarcely be reconciled with the principles and purposes of the United Nations to which we have all subscribed. And, beyond this, we are forced to doubt even if resort to war will for long serve the permanent interests of the attacking nations.

Now we must look to the future.

In the circumstances I have described, there will be no United States involvement in these present hostilities. I therefore have no plan to call the Congress in special session. Of course, we shall continue to keep in contact with congressional leaders of both parties. At the same time it is—and it will remain—the dedicated purpose of your Government to do all in its power to localize the fighting and to end the conflict.

We took our first measure in this action yesterday. We went to the United Nations Security Council with a request that the forces of Israel return to their own land and that hostilities in the area be brought to a close. This proposal was not adopted, because it was vetoed by Great Britain and France.

The processes of the United Nations, however, are not exhausted. It is our hope and intent that this matter will be brought before the United Nations General Assembly. There, with no veto operating, the opinion of the world can be brought to bear in our quest for a just end to that tormenting problem. In the past the United Nations has proved able to find a way to end bloodshed. We believe it can and will do so again.

My fellow citizens, as I review the march of world events in recent years, I am ever more deeply convinced that the processes of the United Nations need further to be developed and strengthened. I speak particularly of increasing its ability to secure justice under international law.

In all the recent troubles in the Middle East, there have indeed been injustices suffered by all nations involved. But I do not believe that another instrument of justice—war—is the remedy for these wrongs.

There can be no peace without law. And there can be no law if we were to invoke one code of international conduct for those who oppose us and another for our friends.

The society of nations has been slow in developing means to apply this truth. But the passionate longing for peace on the part of all peoples of the earth compels us to speed our search for new and more effective instruments of justice. The peace we seek and need means much more than mere absence of war. It means the acceptance of law, and the fostering of justice, in all the world. To our principles guiding us in this quest we must stand fast. In so doing we can honor the hopes of all men for a world in which peace will truly and justly reign.

SOURCE: US Department of State Bulletin (12 November 1956), 743

The editorial opinions of the respected Times *of London had for so long been associated in the public mind—inaccurately—with those of the British government, that it came as a surprise when* The Times *clearly differed with the government over the Suez intervention. In measured terms it stated its deep reservations over the outcome of the joint Anglo-French action and its likely consequences for the Anglo-American alliance. The firm opposition of* The Times *was an eloquent measure of the deep divisions in Britain over the wisdom of the military attack on Egypt.*

28 'The Times'
LEADING ARTICLE ON SUEZ, 'A LACK OF CANDOUR' (2 November 1956)

. . . But as to whether, or at least at what point, President Eisenhower and Mr Dulles were aware of our intentions was left vague. The impression is that they were not in the picture until these intentions had become an irrevocable decision. Now there is much that can be said about the United States' conduct not only in recent weeks but over many years. The world might well not be in the mess it is today if President Roosevelt had been less suspicious of British intentions and had acted differently towards the Russians. There had been more than one occasion during the Suez Crisis when Mr Dulles had caused his British colleagues justifiable bewilderment. It was thoroughly unfair that for a time the American press presented a picture to the world of an America anxious to take the Suez dispute to the United Nations and held back only by the reluctance of Britain when in fact it was Mr Dulles himself, and up to very recently indeed, who was restraining the British Government's desire to go there.

But when all this has been said it is still no excuse if the Prime Minister failed to keep the President in the picture. Sir Anthony Eden said in the House that the moment the British and French governments had reached conclusions he 'authorised the dispatch of a full message to the United States explaining our action'. But there is here a dilemma. If the decisions were come to on the spur of the moment, without previous consideration, calculation, or argument, then a most grave step was taken with surprising levity; if, on the other hand, they were only the final crystallisation of a process of deliberation then there was time to keep the American informed.

It is necessary to stress the word 'informed'. Mr Gaitskell went too far when he implied that Britain needed America's agreement. There will always be the greatest anxiety on both sides of the Atlantic that the English-speaking peoples should whenever possible march in step. But Britain is not a satellite. On the other hand, we and the United States are allies, and the closeness of our association and understanding should be such that it can withstand honest disagreement if that is inevitable. What it cannot withstand is a lack of candour. Again there are different levels of communication. Throughout history, these have always comprised those that were official and unofficial.

Sir Winston Churchill added that of the 'Former Naval Person' and the President. It has hitherto been thought that Sir Anthony Eden had carried this on. If that is so, and President Eisenhower was even unofficially aware of what was in the Prime Minister's mind, then most of the present indignation and surprise of the American administration is unjustified. If, on the other hand, in spite of all the close links of the past, the President did not know what was in the minds of the British and French governments, then the error was grave indeed. 'I hold it perfectly justifiable to deceive the enemy', Sir Winston Churchill said in 1942, 'even if at the same time your own people are for a while misled. There is one thing, however, which you must never do, and that is to mislead your ally.' This is no side issue. It is one of the most vital in the present crisis. On Britain's and America's ability to trust each other, even in disagreement, the peace of the world depends.

SOURCE: *The Times* (2 November 1956)

A failure of British policy in the Suez intervention was that it confused the United States acceptance of Britain's special interest in the Middle East with acceptance of the British attempt to force an 'international' governing body on the Canal. Also the British assertion, voiced with most conviction by Eden, that Nasser should be destroyed to keep the Soviet Union out of the Middle East had little impact on the United States, where the dangers of a vacuum were strongly perceived. In fact, had it not been for the simultaneous Hungarian uprising, there might even have been an unprecedented degree of Soviet-American cooperation in halting the Anglo-French action.

The deterioration of Anglo-American relations alarmed all friends of the United States in Britain, not least Churchill and Macmillan. Churchill, in a final intervention in world affairs, sent a letter to Eisenhower in an attempt to restore relations between the two allies. On 12 December 1956, when Dulles and George Humphrey, the US Treasury Secretary, were in London, Macmillan had a long talk with the latter and then made an instructive note on American attitudes.

29 Harold Macmillan
THE CONSEQUENCES OF SUEZ

. . . An unfortunate aspect of the Suez episode was the breach in Anglo-American friendship. There was an equal sense of disillusionment on both sides. It seemed as if the long tradition of close co-operation which had been brought to such a high degree of confidence and respect was now seriously, if not fatally damaged. In an attempt to restore the President's balance of view, Churchill sent a personal letter to him. I did not know of this until much later; it was a striking—and the last—intervention of the old statesman in world affairs. In the absence of Eden, the letter was passed through the United States Embassy, for Churchill did not want either the Foreign Office or the Secretariat at Number 10 to know of his action. He sent, however, a copy to the Queen. It is so deeply moving that I cannot refrain from quoting it in full.

There is not much left for me to do in this world and I have neither the wish nor the strength to involve myself in the present political stress and turmoil. But I do believe, with unfaltering conviction, that the theme of the Anglo-American alliance is more important today than at any time since the war. You and I had some part in raising it to the plane on which it has stood. Whatever the arguments adduced here and in the United States for or against Anthony's action in Egypt, it will now be an act of folly, on which our whole civilisation may founder, to let events in the Middle East come between us.

There seems to be growing misunderstanding and frustration on both sides of the Atlantic. If they be allowed to develop, the skies will darken and it is the Soviet Union that will ride the storm. We should leave it to the historians to argue the rights and wrongs of all that has happened during the past years. What we must face is that at present these events have left a situation in the Middle East in which spite, envy and malice prevail on the one hand and our friends are beset by bewilderment and uncertainty for the future. The Soviet Union is attempting to move into this dangerous vacuum, for you must have no doubt that a

E

triumph for Nasser would be an even greater triumph for them.

The very survival of all that we believe in may depend on our setting our minds to forestalling them. If we do not take immediate action in harmony, it is no exaggeration to say that we must expect to see the Middle East and the North African coastline under Soviet control and Western Europe placed at the mercy of the Russians. If at this juncture we fail in our responsibility to act positively and fearlessly we shall no longer be worthy of the leadership with which we are entrusted.

I write this letter because I know where your heart lies. You are now the only one who can so influence events both in UNO and the free world as to ensure that the great essentials are not lost in bickerings and pettiness among the nations. Yours is indeed a heavy responsibility and there is no greater believer in your capacity to bear it or well-wisher in your task than your old friend

Winston S. Churchill

The President sent a long letter in reply, clearly of his own composition and in his own hand. I feel certain that Churchill's appeal was of material assistance when we had to begin in the following year the difficult task of re-establishing the old relations, without loss of dignity or retraction of our own positions, but with full sincerity and, happily, with full success.

On the more immediate issues the American Government was now ready to assist us. It was, of course, a little wounding to feel that we were to be given a 'reward' for our submission to American pressure. Nevertheless, I was not foolish enough to refuse, even though the conditions were somewhat distasteful. We received generous help to meet our urgent needs. In addition I was able to begin a negotiation with Humphrey which led to a revision of the American loan in our favour. The old and somewhat obscure waiver clauses were replaced by provisions giving the British Government the right to defer up to seven annual instalments in all, both of principal and interest, until the year 2000.

On 12 December both Foster Dulles and Humphrey were in London. I had an interesting talk with Humphrey, of which I made a note at the time, on the general position; especially as regards the difficulties facing British and American companies in the Middle East.

I said that I felt that now was the time to get on with a long-term policy and try to get a fundamental settlement of all the problems. I expressed the view that this was the Achilles heel of the free world, and that the Russians would be much more likely to try and bring Western Europe down by bringing disorder into the Middle East than by trying a frontal attack on Europe itself. Mr. Humphrey agreed with this view. He then began to develop this following theme: The whole principle of American life was free competition—cartels, trusts and so forth were contrary to their philosophy. This was all right at home, but when they found themselves trading abroad it meant that their companies were at a great disadvantage. This was particularly the case now in the Middle East. Ten years ago the companies were the big shots and the sheikhs were very naïve. Now the sheikhs were the big shots and bullied the companies, who were terrified of them. The companies could not get together because of the Sherman Anti-Trust Law. If one oil man spoke to another, he was liable to be sent to gaol. The Government of the United States did not know what to do. He expressed the view that some new philosophy must be developed which, while preserving free competition and private enterprise in general, would put these arrangements made in foreign countries under some governmental guarantee of authority. I then mentioned the Abadan settlement and the strength which I thought the consortium had given. He agreed. He also thought that what we had done in Iraq had helped because the people saw some result of all its wealth. The position in Saudi Arabia and the other sheikhdoms was much weaker. I replied that I thought that we ought to get down to studying this together and try to get a rapid settlement of the oil and of the political problems of the Middle East. He liked the idea of an Anglo-American study group in Washington, where this could be studied both from the point of view of the oil companies, and so forth, and from the point of view of a longer term political settlement . . .

SOURCE: Harold Macmillan. *Riding the Storm* (1971), 175–8

THE BERMUDA MEETING

The new Conservative Government under Harold Macmillan, which was formed on 10 January 1957, after the sudden resignation of Eden, made the improvement of relations with the United States the first order of its business. At the end of January, Duncan Sandys, then Minister of Defence, was sent to Washington where, though little of importance was achieved, he was able to perform the valuable function of breaking the ice. In March the Prime Minister flew to Bermuda for talks with President Eisenhower. Through these meetings some of the fabric of cooperation that had been ruptured by the Suez venture was restored. Anxiety over the future of the Middle East and events in Central Europe acted as the stimulus to bring the two sides together; although the United States was still nervous about becoming too closely associated with British and French policies.

At Bermuda the two leaders agreed that 'certain guided missiles' (intermediate range ballistic missiles) should be made available to Britain by the American forces. But no agreement was reached on the Middle East. The talks had a further untoward and unwelcome significance in that they were regarded with considerable suspicion by France. The French resented the fact the United States was unwilling to hold a tripartite meeting and felt they were being relegated to a subordinate position in the alliance. In this manner were the seeds of future conflict nurtured.

30 President Eisenhower and Harold Macmillan
COMMUNIQUE ON THE TALKS (24 March 1957)

The President of the United States and the Prime Minister of the United Kingdom, assisted by the United States Secretary of State and the British Foreign Secretary and other advisers, have exchanged views during the past three days on many subjects of mutual concern. They have conducted their discussions with the freedom and frankness permitted to old friends. In a world of growing interdependence they recognize their responsibility to seek to coordinate their foreign policies in the interests of peace with justice.

Among the subjects discussed in detail were common problems concerning the Middle East, Far East, NATO, European Cooperation, the reunification of Germany, and Defense.

The President and the Prime Minister are well satisfied with the results of this Conference, at which a number of decisions have been taken. They intend to continue the exchange of views so well begun.

The agreements and conclusions reached on the main subjects discussed at the Conference are annexed.

ANNEX I

1. Recognition of the value of collective security pacts within the framework of the United Nations, and the special importance of NATO for both countries as the cornerstone of their policy in the West.

2. Reaffirmation of common interest in the development of European unity within the Atlantic Community.

3. Agreement on the importance of closer association of the United Kingdom with Europe.

4. Agreement on the benefits likely to accrue for European and world trade from the plans for the common market and the Free Trade Area, provided they do not lead to a high tariff bloc; and on the desirability that all countries should pursue liberal trade policies.

5. Willingness of the United States, under authority of the recent Middle East joint resolution, to participate actively in the work of the Military Committee of the Baghdad Pact.

6. Reaffirmation of intention to support the right of the German people to early reunification in peace and freedom.

7. Sympathy for the people of Hungary; condemnation of repressive Soviet policies towards the peoples of Eastern Europe, and of Soviet defiance of relevant United Nations resolutions.

8. Agreement on the need for the speedy implementation of recent resolutions of the United Nations General Assembly dealing with the Gaza Strip and the Gulf of Aqaba.

9. Agreement on the importance of compliance both in letter and in spirit with the Security Council Resolution of October 13 concerning the Suez Canal, and on support for the efforts of the Secretary-General to bring about a settlement in accordance with its provisions.

10. Joint declaration on policy regarding nuclear tests (See Annex II).

11. Agreement in principle that, in the interest of mutual defense and mutual economy, certain guided missiles will be made available by the United States for use by British forces . . .

SOURCE: US Department of State Bulletin (8 April 1957), 561

PART SEVEN

Disarmament

After several years of inconclusive negotiations over disarmament, the Soviet Union on 10 May 1955 had startled the West by producing a plan which adopted many of the elements of an Anglo-French proposal that had been drifting around for about a year. The Soviets dropped their demand for a flat one-third cut in conventional forces, accepting instead the force levels proposed by the allies, and abandoned their insistence on beginning the process of disarmament with the elimination of nuclear weapons. At this point the United States suddenly developed second thoughts about the merits of the Anglo-French proposals, observing, correctly, that the Soviet response had failed to be specific on methods of control.

In March 1956, Britain and France produced a revised version of their plan, omitting specific provisions for the elimination of nuclear weapons, while—as a concession to Soviet views—providing for significant reductions in conventional armaments in the first stage.

By July 1956, the Russians had come to accept the Western suggestions on force levels, but added their own new demands for an unconditional ban on the use of nuclear weapons, the limitation of other nations, armed forces, and an immediate ban on nuclear tests.

All disarmament discussions were interrupted by the Hungarian revolt and the Suez crisis, but were revived with some seriousness thereafter. Eisenhower, Macmillan and the Soviet leaders had all frequently declared their support for disarmament, but the major stumbling blocks were still the American fear of surprise attack—with its Pearl Harbour

*connotations—and the Soviet refusal to accept methods of national
control and verification.*

*Also, the NATO allies were at a sharp disadvantage—their strategy
called for a military strength which, unlike that of Russia, had not yet
been met. This meant that the allies were generally somewhat more
hesitant than the Soviets to embrace various schemes for partial or complete disarmament, to the propoganda advantage of Moscow. Approaches
by the West on disarmament were hampered during the 1950s and much
of the 1960s by the Western desire to secure simultaneous political
settlements, including the reunification of Germany.*

*In August 1957, Dulles intervened personally in the negotiations with
a series of proposals to cope with the problem of surprise attack, which
were embodied in the allied working paper of that month.*

*His first alternative was for an area of inspection comprising the
whole of Canada, the United States, and the Soviet Union. If the
Soviets objected to this, as seemed inevitable, they were offered a zone
covering the whole territory of the three nations north of the Arctic
Circle, plus parts of Greenland and Norway.*

*The Soviets were also, under a third option, offered two alternative
zones in Europe. The new initiative proposed that a working group of
experts should be set up to examine the technical problems of the various
inspection areas.*

*The Soviets refused to go beyond their own proposals, however,
arguing that the plan excluded America's forward bases in Africa, the
Near East and the Far East. In November the Russians, after more
fruitless wrangling, brought matters to a head by walking out of the
Disarmament Commission.*

31 Governments of Canada, France, the UK and the US
JOINT STATEMENT ON TEMPORARY SUSPENSION
OF NUCLEAR EXPLOSIONS (2 July 1957)

1. The delegations of Canada, France, the United Kingdom
and the United States welcome the acceptance by the delegation of the Union of Soviet Socialist Republics of the requirement of inspection posts with appropriate scientific instruments,

equipment, and facilities, to be set up for the purposes of control and detection of nuclear testing. This is an essential requirement which the four delegations of the Western Powers had long proposed and upon which they had insisted. They note that the Soviet Union proposes that these inspection posts should be located within the territories of the USSR, the United States, the United Kingdom and Pacific Ocean areas.

2. Soviet acceptance of this principle now brings within the realm of possibility a temporary suspension of nuclear testing as part of an agreement for a first step in disarmament. This temporary cessation would be subject, of course, to precise agreement on its duration and timing, on the installation and location (with, of course, the consent of the countries concerned) of the necessary controls, including inspection posts, and on its relationship to other provisions of a first-stage agreement. These provisions would include the first steps to halt the growth of armaments and to reverse the trend by initial reductions in armed forces and designated armaments, with the necessary initial measures of inspection, and the cessation of production of fissionable materials for weapons purposes under conditions to be agreed.

3. The delegations of Canada, France, the United Kingdom and the United States propose that a group of experts under the direction of the five delegations meet on (date) to proceed with the design of the inspection system to verify the suspension of nuclear test explosions and that the Chairmen of the five delegations proceed with the consideration of the necessary relationship of this provision for the temporary suspension of nuclear testing to the other provisions of the first-stage disarmament agreement.

SOURCE: United Nations Documents D/112 (1 August 1957), Annex II

The increasing French sense of isolation was stimulated when Mac-

millan visited Washington in October 1957, the first visit to the White House of a Western statesman since the launching of Sputnik. At the time, Le Monde referred to the 'resurrection of an Anglo-Saxon directorate', which was seeking to dominate the Western alliance. The 'declaration of common purpose'—itself a suspicious term—which was issued following the meeting spoke in general terms about the need for more widespread sharing of classified information in nuclear matters, but the French were properly doubtful that much of this information was likely to be extended to them. French alarm was further stimulated in November when Britain and the United States declared they had decided to ship small arms to Tunisia. Paris was certain that some of these arms might find their way to Algeria and there was an immediate outcry from the French.

32 President Eisenhower and Harold Macmillan
DECLARATION OF COMMON PURPOSE
(25 October 1957)

We have met together as trusted friends of many years who have come to head the Governments of our respective countries. These two countries have close and historic ties, just as each has intimate and unbreakable ties with other free countries.

Recognising that only in the establishment of a just peace can the deepest aspirations of free peoples be realised, the guiding purpose of our deliberations has been the determination of how best to utilise the moral, intellectual and material strength of our two nations in the performance of our full share of those tasks that will more surely and promptly bring about conditions in which peace can prosper. One of these tasks is to provide adequate security for the free world.

The free nations possess vast assets, both material and moral. These in the aggregate are far greater than those of the Communist world. We do not ignore the fact that the Soviet rulers can achieve formidable material accomplishments by concentrating upon selected developments and scientific applications, and by yoking their people to this effort. Despotisms have often been able to produce spectacular monuments. But the price has been heavy.

For all peoples yearn for intellectual and economic freedom, the more so if from their bondage they see others manifest the glory of freedom. Even despots are forced to permit freedom to grow by an evolutionary process, or in time there will be violent revolution. This principle is inexorable in its operation.

Already it has begun to be noticeable even within the Soviet orbit. If the free nations are steadfast, and if they utilise their resources in harmonious co-operation, the totalitarian menace that now confronts them will in good time recede.

In order, however, that freedom may be secure and show its good fruits, it is necessary first that the collective military strength of the free nations should be adequate to meet the threat against them. At the same time, the aggregate of the free world's military expenditure must be kept within limits compatible with individual freedom. Otherwise we risk losing the very liberties which we seek to defend.

These ideas have been the central theme of our conversations which, in part, were participated in by M. Spaak, the Secretary-General of NATO.

In application of these ideas, and as an example which we believe can and should spread among the nations of the free world, we reached the following understanding:

1. The arrangements which the nations of the free world have made for collective defence and mutual help are based on the recognition that the concept of national self-sufficiency is now out of date. The countries of the free world are inter-dependent, and only in genuine partnership, by combining their resources and sharing tasks in many fields, can progress and safety be found. For our part, we have agreed that our two countries will henceforth act in accordance with this principle.

2. Our representatives to the North Atlantic Council will urge an enlarged Atlantic effort in scientific research and development in support of greater collective security and

the expansion of current activities of the task force working in this field under the Council's decision of last December.

3. The President of the United States will request the Congress to amend the Atomic Energy Act* as may be necessary and desirable to permit of close and fruitful collaboration of scientists and engineers of Great Britain, the United States, and other friendly countries.

4. The disarmament proposals made by the western representatives on the disarmament sub-committee in London and approved by all members of NATO are a sound and fair basis for an agreement which would reduce the threat of war and the burden of armaments. The indefinite accumulation of nuclear weapons and the indiscriminate spreading of the capacity to produce them should be prevented. Effective and reliable inspection must be an integral part of initial steps in the control and reduction of armaments.

5. In the absence of such disarmament as we are seeking, international security now depends not merely upon local defensive shields but upon reinforcing them with the deterrent and retaliatory power of nuclear weapons. So long as the threat of international Communism persists, the free nations must be prepared to provide for their own security. Because the free world measures are purely defensive and for security against outside threat, the period for which they must be maintained cannot be foreseen.

It is not within the capacity of each nation acting alone to make itself fully secure. Only collective measures will

---

* 'The close war-time co-operation of the United States with Canada and the United Kingdom on research and development of sources of nuclear energy largely ceased in 1946, on the passing of the US Atomic Energy Act (the MacMahon Act). This Act set up a US Atomic Energy Commission, empowered to take over all US resources related to atomic energy. It laid down severe restrictions on the dissemination of classified information on the subject, and, in effect, clamped down on the continued exchange of information between scientists of the three countries. Freer exchange of information was permitted by a new US Atomic Energy Act in 1954 but this excluded information relating to the design or fabrication of atomic weapons.' *Commonwealth Survey*, 29 October 1957, p 943.

suffice. These should preferably be found by implementing the provisions of the United Nations Charter for forces at the disposal of the Security Council.

But if the Soviet Union persists in nullifying these provisions by veto, there must otherwise be developed a greater sense of community security. The framework for this exists in collective defence arrangements now participated in by nearly 50 free nations, as authorised by the Charter. All members of this community, and other free nations which so desire, should possess more knowledge of the total capabilities of security that are in being and in prospect.

There should also be provided greater opportunity to assure that this power will in fact be available in case of need for their common security, and that it will not be misused by any nation for purposes other than individual and collective self-defence, as authorised by the Charter of the United Nations.

For our part we regard our possession of nuclear weapons power as a trust for the defence of the free world.

6. Our two countries plan to discuss these ideas with all of their security partners. So far as the North Atlantic Alliance is concerned, the December meeting may, perhaps, be given a special character in this respect. This has been discussed with the secretary-general of NATO, M. Spaak.

7. In addition to the North Atlantic Treaty, the South-East Asia Collective Defence Treaty, the Bagdad Pact and other security arrangements constitute a strong bulwark against aggression in the various treaty areas.

There are also vitally important relationships of a somewhat different character. There is the Commonwealth; and in the western hemisphere, the Organisation of American States. There are individual mutual defence agreements and arrangements to which the United States is a party.

8. We recognise that our collective security efforts must be supported and reinforced by co-operative economic action. The present offers a challenging opportunity for improvement of trading conditions and the expansion of trade throughout the free world. It is encouraging that plans are developing for a European free trade area in association with the European common market. We recognise that especially in the less developed countries there should be a steady and significant increase in standards of living and economic development.

9. We took note of specific factors in the ideological struggle in which we are engaged. In particular, we were in full agreement that:

Soviet threats directed against Turkey give solemn significance to the obligation, under Article 5 of the North Atlantic Treaty, to consider an armed attack against any member of the alliance as an attack against all;

The reunification of Germany by free elections is essential. At the Geneva conference of 1955, Mr. Khrushchev and Mr. Bulganin agreed to this with us and our French allies. Continued repudiation of that agreement and continued suppression of freedom in eastern Europe undermine international confidence and perpetuate an injustice, a folly, and a danger.

The President and the Prime Minister believe that the understandings they have reached will be increasingly effective as they become more widespread between the free nations. By co-ordinating the strength of all free peoples, safety can be assured, the danger of Communist despotism will in due course be dissipated, and a just and lasting peace will be achieved.

SOURCE: *Commonwealth Survey* (29 October 1957), 943–4

The year 1958 neared its end on a note of some optimism, with hopes that an easing of the threat of nuclear conflict might finally be in sight.

On 22 August the United States had addressed a note to the Soviet Union undertaking to enter negotiations for a suspension of nuclear weapons tests and for setting up an international control system. Eisenhower issued a simultaneous declaration that, if the American offer to negotiate were accepted, the United States would stop testing for a year from the date on which negotiations began. The proposals were accepted by the Soviet Union and, after a brief delay, by Britain.

A tests conference opened at Geneva on 31 October 1958. Although some progress was made in the next eighteen months, the conference failed to fulfil the major expectations it had aroused at the beginning. None the less the suspension of tests continued to be observed by all countries except France.

At Easter 1959, Selwyn Lloyd, the Secretary of State for Foreign Affairs, gave the House of Commons a full report on the progress made by the Anglo-American side in the negotiations.

33 Selwyn Lloyd
STATEMENT IN THE HOUSE OF COMMONS
(27 April 1959)

I will begin by saying something about the conference on nuclear tests, at Geneva. As the House knows, new Notes from Mr. Khrushchev to President Eisenhower and my right hon. Friend the Prime Minister have just been sent. Translations of these did not reach me until Saturday night and there has, therefore, been little time for study and none for discussion with the United States Government, but I shall refer to those Notes in the course of what I have to say.

The position of this conference on nuclear tests at the time of the Easter Recess was that, of the five major areas of disagreement, three had been satisfactorily resolved. When the conference started, the Soviet delegation wanted an agreement to ban all tests separately from and before an agreement as to the details of an effective control system. After considerable discussion, it was agreed that the details of the control system should be negotiated during the conference and should be embodied within the treaty and its annexes. That was the first major hurdle, but it was successfully overcome.

The second matter was the relationship of the agreement on the discontinuance of tests with real disarmament. At the beginning of the conference, the United States and United Kingdom Governments offered to suspend tests for a year and to prolong the suspension provided that an effective control system was being set up satisfactorily and provided, also, that progress was being made towards real disarmament. The Soviet Government, however, preferred that the whole of these negotiations should be confined to the problem of tests, and they objected to that second proviso which I have just mentioned about progress towards measures of real disarmament. The United States and United Kingdom Governments decided to waive that proviso. We made this concession to the Soviet views, although we still want this agreement to provide an impetus towards real disarmament.

That was the second matter. The third matter was the duration of the agreement. We had some difficulty in persuading the Soviet representatives of the point that a treaty cannot continue to be binding on a country when it is not observed by the co-signatories. After some discussion, however, agreement has been reached on a draft article on the duration of the treaty. That matter, too, has therefore been disposed of.

The two final issues have been on the staffing and the facilities of the control posts and inspection teams and the circumstances in which the latter should operate. We regard both these as vital elements in the agreement. We are not again going to accept the kind of arrangement which at present exists in Korea, where the work of the control organ has been hamstrung throughout because there has had to be unanimity between the four members of the organ. The Swiss and the Swedish observers have been unable to take any action except by agreement with the Polish and the Czech representatives. Consequently, throughout the whole of that agreement there has never been effective inspection.

I believe that the first of the two matters, staffing and facilities, are negotiable. The Russians maintain that the control posts should be operated by nationals of the territory on which they are situated, with a few observers from the other side to see that there was no monkey business with the instruments. They have advanced from that opening position, first, by admitting the possibility of an increase in the number of these observers, and, secondly, by agreeing that these observers should actually take part in the technical work of the post.

The Russians still insist that a very limited number of persons from what is called 'the other side' should accompany the inspection team. In other words, they still seem to hanker after self-inspection, which, of course, we cannot accept. Nevertheless, I believe that in due course we shall reach agreement upon the composition both of the control posts and of the inspection teams and upon their facilities. I had a full discussion on these matters with Mr. Gromyko when we were in the Soviet Union, and I am hopeful about agreement upon that matter.

The fifth and most important area of difference relates to the veto. The veto is of special importance in relation to underground tests, because, to detect whether or not there has been an underground test it is vital to have an on-site inspection. Rather different considerations apply to tests in the atmosphere. The Soviet position up to now has been that there must be unanimity that there is something to be investigated—in other words, that an event has taken place which could have been a nuclear explosion. Secondly, they claim that there must also be unanimity before an inspection group can be dispatched to the site of the suspected incident. On both those points we feel that we cannot accept a veto.

One idea for breaking this disagreement is a British idea which was discussed in Moscow and in Washington by the Prime Minister with Mr. Khrushchev and President Eisenhower, and which is mentioned in Mr. Khrushchev's Note. It is that each side should have the right of a limited number of inspections each year which could not be challenged by the other side. There would be free choice to select for inspection a limited number from the suspicious cases disclosed by instruments at the control posts. On a golfing analogy, each side should have a certain number of bisques, X in number [Hon. Member: 'What is that?']. A bisque is a stroke which can be taken at any time by the opponent of the person by whom it is given. I am glad to add to the right hon. Gentleman's knowledge . . .

Source: House of Commons Debates, vol 604, 898–901

PART EIGHT

Cooperation in Defence

The US Atomic Energy Act (the MacMahon Act) of 1946 had formally forbidden the exchange of nuclear information—a step which infuriated the British, who considered, with reason, that since they had been intimately involved in the early development of the atomic bomb they should continue to benefit from the fruits of their association.

In 1954 the act was amended to permit a limited degree of nuclear cooperation between the United States and other NATO countries.

It was not until 1958 that the provisions of the act were substantially eased to the benefit of Britain.

At the end of 1957, three weeks after the launch of Sputnik by the Soviet Union, Eisenhower promised Macmillan he would seek to amend the MacMahon Act to permit a close partnership between the United States and Britain in nuclear development to be restored.

The amendments, as they passed the US Congress, were clearly designed to benefit Britain, and only Britain. They authorised the transfer of information, nuclear materials and non-nuclear parts of atomic weapons to any nation that had made 'substantial progress' in the development of an atomic weapons capability. Clearly Britain was the only country which met this definition. The amendments had the effect of further excluding France and stimulating the French to take the expensive decision to build their own independent nuclear deterrent. Such Europeanists in the US State Department as George Ball were later to criticise the nuclear amendments as perpetuating the special relationship to the eventual disadvantage of Britain when applying for membership in the Common Market.

34 Governments of the UK and the US
ATOMIC ENERGY AGREEMENT, WASHINGTON
(3 July 1958)

The Government of the United Kingdom of Great Britain and Northern Ireland on its own behalf and on behalf of the United Kingdom Atomic Energy Authority and the Government of the United States of America.

> Considering that their mutual security and defense require that they be prepared to meet the contingencies of atomic warfare;

> Considering that both countries have made substantial progress in the development of atomic weapons;

> Considering that they are participating together in international arrangements pursuant to which they are making substantial and material contributions to their mutual defense and security;

> Recognizing that their common defense and security will be advanced by the exchange of information concerning atomic energy and by the transfer of equipment and materials for use therein;

> Believing that such exchange and transfer can be undertaken without risk to the defense and security of either country; and

> Taking into consideration the United States Atomic Energy Act of 1954, as amended, which was enacted with these purposes in mind,

Have agreed as follows:

Article I
General Provision

While the United States and the United Kingdom are participating in an international arrangement for their mutual defense and security and making substantial and material contributions thereto, each Party will communicate to and exchange with the other Party information, and transfer materials and equipment to the other Party, in accordance with the provisions of this Agreement provided that the communicating or transferring Party determines that such cooperation will promote and will not constitute an unreasonable risk to its defense and security.

Article II
Exchange of Information

A. Each Party will communicate to or exchange with the other Party such classified information as is jointly determined to be necessary to:

1. the development of defense plans;
2. the training of personnel in the employment of and defense against atomic weapons and other military applications of atomic energy;
3. the evaluation of the capabilities of potential enemies in the employment of atomic weapons and other military applications of atomic energy;
4. the development of delivery systems compatible with the atomic weapons which they carry; and
5. research, development and design of military reactors to the extent and by such means as may be agreed.

B. In addition to the cooperation provided for in paragraph A of this Article each Party will exchange with the other Party other classified information concerning atomic weapons when, after consultation with the other Party, the communicating Party determines that the communication of such information is necessary to improve the recipient's atomic weapon design, development and fabrication capability.

Article III
Transfer of Submarine, Nuclear Propulsion Plant and Materials

A. The Government of the United States will authorize, subject to terms and conditions acceptable to the Government of the United States, a person to transfer by sale to the Government of the United Kingdom or its agent one complete submarine nuclear propulsion plant with such spare parts therefor as may be agreed by the Parties and to communicate to the Government of the United Kingdom or its agent (or to both) such classified information as relates to safety features and such classified information as is necessary for the design, manufacture and operation of such propulsion plant. A person or persons will also be authorized, for a period of ten years following the date of entry into force of this Agreement and subject to terms and conditions acceptable to the Government of the United States, to transfer replacement cores or fuel elements for such plant.

B. The Government of the United States will transfer by sale agreed amounts of U-235 contained in uranium enriched in the isotope U-235 as needed for use in the submarine nuclear propulsion plant transferred pursuant to paragraph A of this Article, during the ten years following the date of entry into force of this Agreement on such terms and conditions as may be agreed. If the Government of the United Kingdom so requests, the Government of the United States will during such period reprocess any material sold under the present paragraph in facilities of the Government of the United States, on terms and conditions to be agreed, or authorize such reprocessing in private facilities in the United States. Enriched uranium recovered in reprocessing such materials by either Party may be purchased by the Government of the United States under terms and conditions to be agreed. Special nuclear material recovered in reprocessing such materials and not purchased by the Government of the United States may be returned to or retained by the Government of the United Kingdom and any U-235 not purchased by the Government of the United States will be credited to the amounts of U-235 to be transferred by the Government of the United States under this Agreement.

C. The Government of the United States shall be compensated for enriched uranium sold by it pursuant to this Article at the United States Atomic Energy Commission's published charges applicable to the domestic distribution of such material in effect at the time of the sale. Any purchase of enriched uranium by the Government of the United States pursuant to this Article shall be at the applicable price of the United States Atomic Energy Commission for the purchase of enriched uranium in effect at the time of purchase of such enriched uranium.

D. The Parties will exchange classified information on methods of reprocessing fuel elements of the type utilized in the propulsion plant to be transferred under this Article, including classified information on the design, construction and operation of facilities for the reprocessing of such fuel elements.

E. The Government of the United Kingdom shall indemnify and hold harmless the Government of the United States against any and all liabilities whatsoever (including third-party liability) for any damage or injury occurring after the propulsion plant or parts thereof, including spare parts, replacement cores or fuel elements are taken outside the United States, for any cause arising out of or connected with the design, manufacture, assembly, transfer or utilization of the propulsion plant, spare parts, replacement cores or fuel elements transferred pursuant to paragraph A of this Article . . .

SOURCE: UK Command Papers 537

A remarkable display of renewed Anglo-American cooperation came with the joint landings in Lebanon and Jordan in July 1958. The intervention followed swiftly on the Iraq revolution and the murder of the pro-western Prime Minister Nuri es-Said on 14 July. The day after the coup Eisenhower announced that in response to an urgent plea from President Chamoun of Lebanon, American forces would be stationed in that country to protect American lives and encourage the Lebanese Government.

On 17 July, the British Government sent troops to Amman in response to an appeal from King Hussein the previous evening, saying that there was a Syrian plot against his kingdom.

Although confused in both motive and execution, the allied intervention did have the result of stabilising the situation to a remarkable degree. British troops were finally withdrawn from Jordan by 2 November 1958.

35 Harold Macmillan
STATEMENT IN THE HOUSE OF COMMONS
(17 July 1958)

Within a matter of minutes after the end of the debate yesterday, I was given a telegram from Her Majesty's Representative in Jordan. This contained the first news that we had had that King Hussein and the Prime Minister of Jordan had made a request for the immediate despatch of British forces to Jordan.

In making this request, the King and the Prime Minister said that Jordan was faced with an imminent attempt by the United Arab Republic to create internal disorder and to overthrow the present régime, on the pattern of recent events in Iraq ... They went on to say that Jordan's territorial integrity was threatened by the movement of Syrian forces towards her northern frontier and by the infiltration of arms across it. They had information that a *coup* organised by the United Arab Republic would be attempted today.

I asked the Cabinet to meet late last night to consider this request.

From our own sources we had received up to date intelligence which clearly showed that the apprehensions of the Jordan Government were well founded, and that an attempt was indeed being organised for today.

The Government accordingly decided to accede to the request, and British forces are, in fact, being sent by air to Jordan from Cyprus.

The purpose of this military assistance is to stabilise the situation in Jordan by helping the Jordanian Government to resist aggression and threats to the integrity and independence of their country.

Our troops will be under the orders of the local British commander who will act with the agreement of the King and Government of Jordan.

The Jordan Government have made a similar request for help to the United States Government, who are considering it urgently in the light of their other commitments in the area. Her Majesty's Government's decision was taken after full consultation with the United States Government, and our action has the full support and approval of the United States Government.

The decision of Her Majesty's Government is being reported to the United Nations, and we are making it clear to the United Nations that if arrangements can be made by the Security Council to protect the lawful Government of Jordan from the external threat, and so maintain international peace and security, the action which we have taken will be brought to an end.

We have informed the other Commonwealth countries, and also the North Atlantic Treaty Organisation Council, of the action we have taken and the reasons which have led to the Government's decision.

SOURCE: House of Commons Debates, vol 591, coll 1438–9

THE POLARIS BASE AGREEMENT

In defence matters the special relationship which so disturbed the French continued in full force. In February 1960 Britain and the United States reached an agreement to set up a ballistic missile early warning station at Fylingdales in Yorkshire. The station was primarily designed to assist the United States, but it also gave Britain a very brief notice of any surprise attack. For the British Government it was seen as improving the credibility of the deterrent by providing about fifteen minutes in which to permit the V-bomber force to take off.

The reliance on the V-bomber force led to a further understanding which was to become a major source of friction in the next two years. When Macmillan visited Washington in March 1960, he discussed with Eisenhower the possibility of obtaining the then-planned Skybolt missiles

to extend the life of the V-bomber force beyond the mid-1960s. On 13
April, Harold Watkinson, Britain's Minister of Defence, announced
that the proposed British 'Blue Streak' land-based missile was being
abandoned and the purchase of Skybolt was being considered. In June the
understanding was confirmed and a detailed agreement was signed in
September.

Already, though, the weapon that was to make Skybolt obsolete even
before it made its first flight was about to come into service. In November,
Macmillan announced that the Government was making available base
facilities at Holy Loch in Scotland to the American Polaris fleet. The
agreement, he maintained against strongly voiced Labour opposition,
would strengthen the entire Western alliance and deter aggression.

36 Harold Macmillan
STATEMENT IN THE HOUSE OF COMMONS
(1 November 1960)

. . . The United States has made a significant advance in deterrent power. The first Polaris missile-firing submarine, the
'George Washington', will become operational before long. I
am told that it will be quickly followed by other vessels now
nearing completion. A new and flexible element will thereby be
added to the strategic nuclear deterrent. There would be operational advantage and to that extent the deterrent would be
strengthened if sheltered anchorage on this side of the Atlantic
were available for a submarine depot ship and a floating dock.
This Her Majesty's Government have undertaken to provide.

These facilities would be used by United States submarines
on routine patrol in peace time. The anchorage will be provided
in the Holy Loch in the Clyde, and the depot ship should be
established there during February of next year. The floating
dock will follow later. Supporting facilities will be provided by
the Royal Navy. The United States naval authorities in London
and the Admiralty will co-ordinate routine measures to govern
the operation of the United States submarines so as to prevent
the risk of any difficulties arising from mutual interference be-

tween United Kingdom and United States submarine or anti-submarine forces. Such matters must cover routeing, arrival and departure notices.

Stringent safety precautions will be adopted to prevent any risk to health or safety in normal conditions. Among other local arrangements, a liaison committee will be set up to ensure the fullest possible consultation with local authorities and interests concerned . . .

The House will realise that it is impossible to make an agreement exactly on all fours with the bomber base agreement. The deployment and use in periods of emergency of the submarine depot ship and associated facilities in the United Kingdom will be a matter of joint consultation between the two Governments. Individual submarines will only visit the United Kingdom between patrols, which may last for a considerable period at a time. Their home port and refitting base will still be on the other side of the Atlantic.

As regards general control, therefore, we shall continue to rely on the close co-operation and understanding which exist between us and the United States in all these defence matters and which President Eisenhower has recently reaffirmed.

Wherever these submarines may be, I am perfectly satisfied that no decision to use these missiles will ever be taken without the fullest possible previous consultation, and, of course, it is worth recalling that these mechanisms have a greater degree of flexibility than perhaps some of the present methods of launching the deterrent. We therefore felt it right to conclude this agreement. It is in the tradition of Anglo-American co-operation in joint defence established in peace time more than twelve years ago and carried on by successive British Governments.

Like the agreement on the United States bomber bases in this country, it will serve and strengthen the whole N.A.T.O. alliance. Naturally, my Cabinet colleagues and I gave grave thought to this matter. At first sight, the addition of these facilities might seem to bring added anxiety, but, on reflection, I hope that the House will feel, as we have, that this new arrangement does not add to the risks to which we are all inevitably exposed in this nuclear age.

In any case, to have refused these facilities would not have been in the spirit of the Western Alliance, and refusal would not have given us more power or more security. It would not have reduced our real involvement. Even taking the narrow view of self-interest alone, I believe that the more we are involved with the whole great complex of the modern deterrent the more effective our voice becomes in its world-wide control . . .

SOURCE: House of Commons Debates, vol 629, coll 37–8

PART NINE

The Kennedy Years

After the stagnation of American policy in Eisenhower's final year, the British Government looked forward to new initiatives under his energetic young successor.

Macmillan especially regarded it as his duty to assure the continuity of policy. He emphasised frequently during 1960 that the 'great issue' of the rest of the century was the direction that the uncommitted peoples of the world would take, especially since at that time the United States was still regarded with considerable suspicion for its 'militaristic' policies.

When Kennedy arrived in the White House, Macmillan was quick to seize the chance to play the role of the elder knowledgeable statesman. He penned his December letter to the President-elect with considerable care. 'It must not be pompous, or lecturing, or too radical,' he reflected. He drew on his long experience to discuss what he considered the main issues facing the world. The letter marked the beginning of a remarkable friendship between the two statesmen which, despite their evident differences in age, temperament, and experience, lasted as long as Macmillan remained in Downing Street.

37 Harold Macmillan
LETTER TO PRESIDENT KENNEDY
(19 December 1960)

I was very glad to receive from Ambassador Caccia an account of his talk with you last Thursday. I need not tell you how glad

I would be to accept your invitation to a meeting at your convenience. As you have probably realised, I have refrained from making any proposal to you myself because I know how heavily you must be engaged during these weeks. Apart from anything that Khrushchev may confront us with, I have only one fixed period in early 1961 when I must be in London. That is in the first half of March, when I shall either be preparing for or conducting the Commonwealth Prime Ministers' Meeting which ends on 17 March. I could therefore go to Washington at any other time that suits you.

Now for the subjects. There is indeed plenty to talk about, and as I have just read the collection of your speeches called *The Strategy of Peace* I am looking forward with special pleasure to discussion of some of these things. If I may say so, I much sympathise with your approach and your determination to put the immense strength of your position and of your country behind a new effort to face the problems of the second half of this century.

I have in mind my deep conviction that the policies and institutions which have served the Free World well since the war are now inadequate if we are to meet the challenge of Communism. I believe this to be particularly true in the economic field. But there are also military and political aspects of this challenging situation which cause me great concern. It is up to us now to rethink urgently and radically. The effects and policies of the various countries making up what one might generally call the Western Alliance are, I believe, not properly adjusted to the realities of the 1960s.

I think the first and most important subject is what is going to happen to us unless we can show that our modern free society— the new form of capitalism—can run in a way that makes the fullest use of our resources and results in a steady expansion of our economic strength. Therefore the problem of money, the problem of its proper use in each of the Western countries, and of securing that there is sufficient credit available to keep all our countries working to the full extent of the potential available, is really the prime question of all. If we fail in this Communism will triumph, not by war, or even subversion, but by seeming to be a better way of bringing people material comforts. In other words, if we were to fall back into anything like the recession or crisis that we had between the wars, with large-scale unemployment of men and machines, I think we would have lost the hand. Of course, things are not as bad as that, but there are great dangers facing us. For one reason or another, I believe the total credit available is either not sufficient or improperly used and this makes it necessary to reconsider the whole basis on which it stands.

This leads on from the question of maintaining confidence in a free society in our own countries, to that of spreading it to the uncommitted countries. Of course, I am anxious that we should do all we can to give aid in a direct form. That in our case depends largely upon being able to maintain full production without falling into either inflation or a balance of payments crisis. In other words, our capacity to help is tied up to the world solution of the first problem. Secondly, important as direct aid is—the financing of public works and public health and so forth —probably the most immediate way to help the undeveloped countries is the rise in the value of world commodities following on the maximisation of production by the advanced countries. It is worth recalling that the price of commodities has fallen eight or nine per cent in recent years. Therefore despite all that we have tried to do in direct help, more producing power has been taken away from the primary producers by the fall in commodity values than we have been able to give back to them in aid. In a country like ours these so-called favourable terms of trade help us in the short but not in the long term, either in exports, or in the sense of doing our duty by the undeveloped countries and stabilising their position.

The next set of questions seems to me to be disarmament, and especially the Geneva Test Agreement. I believe that if we could bring the Geneva talks to a satisfactory and early solution we would have made a very big step forward. I hope the Russians still attach importance to this; they certainly did when we began, but of course it has dragged on and become tremendously technical and almost academic. I expect you have much the same feelings about this.

Next there is the immense problem of disarmament. I still cannot quite make out whether Khrushchev has misunderstood or misrepresented what we have been trying to say to him. Perhaps you may be able to make him realise that we do really want disarmament in the sense of reduction of conventional and unconventional weapons, and control and inspection, as a single operation. He tries to pretend that we want only control and not disarmament. We ought really to try to agree on a scheme which will hold the imagination of the world and at the same time be realistic. At the present the Russians have got much of the propaganda advantage. This must be corrected. All the same I have a feeling that our failure to agree with the Russians comes from a complex of reasons. In the first place, they are perhaps incredulous that the West will ever agree to disarm. In the second, they shrink from any form of inspection which will make inroads upon their closely controlled society. But we must force this issue into the open.

Well, this is enough, perhaps too much; and I would only add this. We all realise here that the leadership in the Western World must come today largely from the United States. But although the United Kingdom's power in the world is relatively so much less than yours, I believe that our special ties with every continent and the new relationships which we have built up since the war in transforming the old Empire into the new Commonwealth, give us the opportunity of being of real and important service to the cause of freedom. I am sure that the fundamental interests of our two countries are identical and that, when our policies are harmonised, they stand a better chance of success. I can assure you that we in this country will not shrink from sacrifice, nor I believe have we lost our power to think and act imaginatively in the great crisis of our time.

I am sorry to inflict all this on you when you have so much to think about. But I felt it would be easier to give you some of my thoughts before we met for they are matters on which I have brooded much.

I await our first meeting with great eagerness.

SOURCE: Harold Macmillan. *Pointing the Way* (1972), 309–12

THE UNITED STATES AND THE
EUROPEAN COMMUNITY

In the latter part of 1960, the British Government began with reservations to pay increasing attention to the political and economic implications of entry into the rapidly developing European Common Market.

In his lecture at the Massachusetts Institute of Technology, on 7 April 1961, Harold Macmillan warned of the 'canker' that the continued economic division of Europe would represent. At the same time the British Government realised the effect that a strong Common Market would have on Britain's shaky position as a world power.

But initially there was little reaction on the part of the Six to the tentative overture from Britain. Indeed, until a meeting with a French delegation in February 1961, the British themselves appeared to believe they would be able to negotiate an agreement with the European Economic Community without accepting full membership.

The Kennedy administration took the view, which was developed by Vice-President Lyndon Johnson in a speech marking the tenth anniversary of the establishment of NATO's military headquarters (SHAPE) in Paris that the best course should be full British membership in the Common Market.

38 Vice-President Lyndon Johnson
SPEECH ON THE UNITED STATES AND THE
EUROPEAN COMMUNITY (6 April 1961)

I am happy to bring to you from the people and the Government a message which is as absolutely determined and meaningful as it is simple to state. That message is that the United States is resolved to do everything within its power—and I

F

emphasize the word 'everything'—to enhance the strength and unity of the North Atlantic Community.

This message reflects the basic purpose of our foreign policy: to maintain an environment in which free societies can survive and flourish. By free societies we mean those in which the consent of the governed plays an important role.

It is essential to this environment that it be spacious. It is essential, too, that within it there should exist the will and power to protect it against enemies and the opportunity for all to develop and to pursue happiness as they see it, within the limits of ability and willingness to work.

No single nation has enough influence and power to maintain this spacious environment of freedom. The coalition of the peoples and nations of Western Europe and North America is indispensable to this end. Without their power—the resultant of population, resources, technology, and will—it cannot be preserved.

To the United States it is of prime importance to maintain and strengthen the coalition, both its cohesion and power within the Atlantic area and its capacity for constructive action outside that area.

If that cohesion and capacity are to be enhanced, vigorous measures will be required in the political, military, and economic fields.

In the political field it is to discover and act on the most basic of the various Alliance interests that are at stake and thus increase the Alliance's capacity to influence events in the world at large constructively.

Progress toward an integrated European community will help to enhance that capacity and thus to strengthen the Atlantic Community. A more cohesive and powerful Europe within a developing Atlantic Community is needed to undertake the large tasks which lie ahead. The essentially national and loosely coordinated efforts of the past will no longer suffice.

Our end goal—'that remote and ideal object' of which Lord Acton spoke, 'which captivates the imagination by its splendor and the reason by its simplicity'—should be a true Atlantic Community in which common institutions will increasingly be developed to meet common problems.

The burgeoning demands of the less developed countries no less than the growth of Soviet power dictate that a more tightly knit community eventually be achieved. In progressing toward such a community we can regain the sense of forward movement and imaginative thinking which has characterized the Alliance in its most creative periods. In the long run such progress may well prove to be indispensable if our ultimate goal of a free and orderly world community is to be achieved . . .

SOURCE: US Department of State Bulletin (6 April 1961)

Kennedy was swift to arrange for Macmillan to be the first foreign leader to visit the White House—somewhat to the irritation of the German Chancellor Adenauer, who had hoped he would be so honoured.

At their meeting, between 3 and 5 April, Macmillan found that the President and he shared much the same views on policy towards the Common Market and disarmament. But he had little success in his appeal for an expansion of international monetary reserves to improve the flow of world trade.

Macmillan, however, in his important speech at MIT on 7 April, again emphasised the need to strengthen the economy and the economic organisation of the West. He also created a brief flurry of excitement by appearing to endorse the idea of a NATO deterrent, saying 'we must find a way of meeting the legitimate feelings of our European allies'. He later insisted that he was thinking only of France and the United States and not of any other countries.

In his speech the Prime Minister delivered a timely warning about the dangers of the continued economic divisions in Europe. The consequences of these, he said, 'are only just beginning to make themselves felt in the political field'.

39 Harold Macmillan
SPEECH AT THE MASSACHUSETTS INSTITUTE
OF TECHNOLOGY (7 April 1961)

. . . Meanwhile we must face facts as they are. We must first
achieve some unity of political purpose and method in the
Western Alliance. Let us start with our two countries. Three
years ago, after a visit to Washington, I spoke at Johns Hopkins
University. I will only quote one phrase that I used, I said:
'Whether we like it or not—and I do like it—the destinies of the
English-speaking world are inextricably intertwined'. At that
time I was speaking in the presence of your President—my old
friend and comrade President Eisenhower—whose life for
twenty years was devoted to the joint purposes of your country
and of mine.

Before coming to Johns Hopkins I had spoken also at De
Pauw University in my mother's State of Indiana. There I
declared my belief that if the progress of humanity was to continue, this word 'interdependence' must be the keynote of the
second half of the twentieth century. I want tonight to consider
with you what this belief means and how we can translate it into
effective action. No easy task—for it calls for something even
more rare than intelligence—it calls for decision and resolution.
Now I have come to meet and take counsel with a new President
at the beginning of his term of office.

In his inaugural address the President used these words: 'My
fellow citizens of the world, ask not what America will do for
you but what together we can do for the freedom of men.' This
noble phrase certainly matched the level of events, and it has
set the pattern for our talks together. In the same spirit let us
look realistically and objectively at the state of the Free World
to-day. How have we been getting on since 1958? To be frank,
we have been doing fairly well but not well enough.

The vital centre of the Free World's resistance, our Western
Alliance, is no better organised, whether in the field of defence,
economics or political relations. If we have broadly held our

own we have gained no ground. When I speak of the Free World, I mean the whole non-Communist world. There are of course many groupings of nations outside the Sino-Soviet *bloc*. Some of these are economic, some political, some cultural and some defensive. But the core of the Free World is our Western Alliance, primarily the Atlantic Community. On its strength and vitality all depends. For if we can organise ourselves in imaginative partnership at the centre, the effects of our unity will spread through all the world. Three years ago your President and I declared for interdependence. To-day I say interdependence is not enough. We need unity—a wider unity, transcending traditional barriers; unity of purpose, of method, of organisation.

First, defence. Our Alliance will only be united if it is secure against aggression. Otherwise it can have no life or strength. There are two roads to security. The best, the cheapest, and the most sensible and the only one by which political man could match the successes of scientific man, is disarmament—comprehensive and effective; the only sure guarantee of peace. I do not speak of course of some mere paper treaty not commanding real confidence. I mean genuine disarmament, secured by effective controls—not a sham but a reality. Some day we may reach this goal, which, up to now, like a mirage in the desert, always seems to recede the nearer we approach it. Certainly we shall persevere, for the prize is supreme. It is the banishment of fear.

Even if we did not want disarmament on moral grounds, we certainly need it on economic grounds. The cost of defence is a specially heavy burden on Britain and America—whether we think of it in terms of men, money or resources. It weighs upon both our economies partly by our huge internal expenditure and partly by the direct cost in foreign exchange. All this puts a serious strain on our balance of payments. We in Britain spend overseas on defence about $620 millions a year. Of this $210 millions goes across the Exchanges in NATO. The rest we use in the cause of peace throughout the world. The United States are faced with the same problems at home and abroad.

Meanwhile, until disarmament comes the Free World must be secure and united.

Nor, in this age of missiles, must we overlook our conventional forces. Our task is to keep them mobile, hard-hitting and up-to-date. Our military alliances all round the world are not aggressive or offensive. Their purpose is to see that little wars and adventures do not turn into great disasters. We must maintain these Alliances. They are permanent facts in modern life. But since unity is as important as security we must try to share the burden more efficiently. Surely it is illogical that our teams of military planners, scientists and technicians should waste any of their efforts duplicating work and projects. Of course co-operation is not easy. Everyone is in favour of it in principle. In practice they find it rather a nuisance. All the vested interests work the other way. Nevertheless it is a technical not a political problem which it should be in our power to solve.

Standing behind these conventional forces is the great weight of the Western nuclear deterrent power. This guarantees our security but here the implications of unity are more obscure and controversial. The first essential is that the deterrent should deter; this is self-evident and overriding. Secondly, an effective deterrent should not be wasteful. Of course in recent years the relative advantage of the West has greatly diminished. We cannot afford to be too weak either in weapons or in means of delivery. All the same it is almost as important not to try to be too strong. The calculation is not an easy one to make. For as the armament of democracy will never be used aggressively, it may need to be larger than that of a potential aggressor. The very size of the area which we have to protect dictates some dispersal, and perhaps duplication. Yet we cannot afford waste. Moreover, we must take care lest by building up our own security we perpetuate and encourage a nuclear arms race. That is one reason why I so earnestly hope for a successful outcome of the present negotiations in Geneva. The United States and Britain will do all we can to make this agreement with Russia to end nuclear tests.

But of course a Tests ban in itself will not give us nuclear disarmament. Meanwhile, the balance of priorities must be carefully weighed. The nuclear deterrent must take account of our necessarily defensive strategy. It must be effective and not wasteful.

If then our Western deterrent is both credible and efficient, what more do we need? May I suggest to you a third element. Although the nuclear deterrent gives us security, it is not yet so organised as to contribute fully to our unity. All of us here know that America and Britain, who at present control the Western deterrent, regard themselves as trustees for the Free World. I think sometimes we are a little smug about this. It is rather like the trustees of a private fortune, of whom the beneficiary once observed: 'They may be my trustees, but I am not sure whether they trust me.' . . .

In attacking all these problems in the field of defence we have the advantage of the new and fertile mind of a young and forceful President. In the spirit of partnership we must review the burdens and responsibilities. Some of these are uneven. This could be tolerated in the early years after the war with a shattered Europe to protect. But now, in the 1960s, we must look again at our system if it is to endure. In the same way the question of nuclear power is fundamental. Its organisation is an issue on which the unity of the Atlantic Community may stand or fall. These questions in my view cannot be evaded. They must be faced.

So far I have spoken of unity in the context of our military alliances. Is this enough? Surely not—and for this simple reason. Happily the present struggle in the world is not primarily a military one. The real test will not be on the battlefield but in the market place. It is now almost 15 years since the main structure of our present system for world trade and payments was designed. That was in the heyday of the East-West war alliance. The founders of GATT, the signatories of Bretton Woods and all the architects of our post-war system could not forsee the full economic effects of the great divide. World

economic unity would have been hard enough to achieve in a
world of 19th century nation States; it became impossible as the
full effect of the Sino-Soviet system mainfested itself. At the
same time a new economic force has appeared in the world. The
second Industrial Revolution has already swept through our
developed economies. It is still only in its early stages and I am
sorry to have to tell this audience that it is largely your fault.
For this revolution is of a scientific and technological character.
And these technical developments overleap national frontiers.
They require for their effective exploitation even larger economic units. I readily admit that in spite of these new factors
our international trading and financial arrangements have
somehow or another managed to carry a great increase in world
production and trade. But no wonder they are now beginning
to creak and groan. For they are really an old model. Sooner or
later they will have to be traded in. There are now three main
problems to be resolved. The first is how to maximise world
trade. This is essential to the prosperity of developed and undeveloped countries alike. Secondly, how are we best to organise assistance and capital to build up the less developed
countries? Our common humanity cries out to us to help here,
and our economic interest in new markets encourages us and
finally political necessity compels us. Lastly how are we to
finance an ever increasing volume of trade and aid? If our
monetary arrangements are bad, or outmoded, we shall not
succeed. We shall stagnate instead of expand. And Capitalism
must expand or perish. Even Marx knew that . . .

SOURCE: The Prime Minister's office, press release

THE GRAND DESIGN

*In the face of the rising strength of the European Common Market as the
major trade competitor of the United States, the Kennedy administration
evolved its own new-policy which became known as the 'grand design'.*

*Walt W. Rostow, who at the time was the President's personal
adviser on economic affairs, defined the strategy of the 'grand design'.*

The United States, he said, faced the consequences of the revolution in technology, leading to an uncontrolled arms race; the revolution of modernisation in the developing countries; the revival of economic strength in Europe and Japan, and the political revolution in the new nations.

American strategy, he argued, had to operate in five different dimensions: to strengthen the bonds of association in the industrialised free world; to support the independence and integrity of nations undergoing industrialisation; to build the north-south link between the developed and the less developed world; to create a 'stable military environment'; and to search for 'areas of overlapping interest' in its relations with the communist world.

The President's economic advisers were concerned at the implication of the relative stagnation of the American economy compared with the apparent dynamism of the European Community. This dynamism would only be increased, it was felt, if Britain entered the Community. They feared that the Community might turn into a 'rich man's club', which would become defensive in a tariff war against the United States; and that negotiations over such matters as Berlin might be impeded.

George Ball, the US Under Secretary of State, proposed that massive tariff reductions with the European Community should be negotiated—a move that would require the presidential power to be considerably increased under the new trade act.

Ball's position ran counter to that of Christian Herter, the former US Secretary of State, who envisaged an 'Atlantic community' rather than a purely European one.

By deciding to make Ball's trade expansion proposals one of the major elements of the 1962 session of Congress, Kennedy staked his prestige and that of his administration on the success of Britain's application to enter the Common Market. Without British entry the Trade Expansion Act would be largely irrelevant. Moreover, he assumed that the European Economic Community would rapidly transform itself into a cohesive political community—and also that it would continue to subordinate itself to the United States in defence matters.

The first expression of the new policy, was in the State of the Union message on 11 January 1962. Despite the administration's best efforts

*the Trade Expansion Bill did not become law until October 1962. In
the intervening period the assumptions on which it was based had become increasingly irrelevant. Kennedy had failed, in his enthusiasm for
the 'grand design', to take account of the aims and power of President de
Gaulle.*

40 President Kennedy
EXTRACT FROM THE STATE OF THE
UNION ADDRESS (11 January 1962)

. . . But the Atlantic Community is no longer concerned with
purely military aims. As its common undertakings grow at an
ever-increasing pace, we are, and increasingly will be, partners
in aid, trade, defense, diplomacy, and monetary affairs.

The emergence of the new Europe is being matched by the
emergence of new ties across the Atlantic. It is a matter of un-
dramatic daily cooperation in hundreds of workaday tasks: of
currencies kept in effective relation, of development loans
meshed together, of standardized weapons, and concerted
diplomatic positions. The Atlantic Community grows, not like
a volcanic mountain, by one mighty explosion, but like a coral
reef, from the accumulating activity of all.

Thus, we in the free world are moving steadily toward unity
and cooperation, in the teeth of that old Bolshevik prophecy,
and at the very time when extraordinary rumbles of discord can
be heard across the Iron Curtain. It is not free societies which
bear within them the seeds of inevitable disunity.

On one special problem, of great concern to our friends, and
to us, I am proud to give the Congress an encouraging report.
Our efforts to safeguard the dollar are progressing. In the 11
months preceding last February 1, we suffered a net loss of
nearly $2 billion in gold. In the 11 months that followed, the
loss was just over half a billion dollars. And our deficit in our
basic transactions with the rest of the world—trade, defense,
foreign aid, and capital, excluding volatile short-term flows—
has been reduced from $2 billion for 1960 to about one-third

that amount for 1961. Speculative fever against the dollar is ending—and confidence in the dollar has been restored.

We did not—and could not—achieve these gains through import restrictions, troop withdrawals, exchange controls, dollar devaluation or choking off domestic recovery. We acted not in panic but in perspective. But the problem is not yet solved. Persistently large deficits would endanger our economic growth and our military and defense commitments abroad. Our goal must be a reasonable equilibrium in our balance of payments. With the cooperation of the Congress, business, labor, and our major allies, that goal can be reached.

We shall continue to attract foreign tourists and investments to our shores, to seek increased military purchases here by our allies, to maximize foreign aid procurement from American firms, to urge increased aid from other fortunate nations to the less fortunate, to seek tax laws which do not favor investment in other industrialized nations or tax havens, and to urge co-ordination of allied fiscal and monetary policies so as to discourage large and disturbing capital movements.

Above all, if we are to pay for our commitments abroad, we must expand our exports. Our businessmen must be export-conscious and export competitive. Our tax policies must spur modernization of our plants—our wage and price gains must be consistent with productivity to hold the line on prices—our export credit and promotion campaigns for American industries must continue to expand.

But the greatest challenge of all is posed by the growth of the European Common Market. Assuming the accession of the United Kingdom, there will arise across the Atlantic a trading partner behind a single external tariff similar to ours with an economy which nearly equals our own. Will we in this country adapt our thinking to these new prospects and patterns—or will we wait until events have passed us by?

This is the year to decide. The Reciprocal Trade Act is expiring. We need a new law—a wholly new approach—a bold new instrument of American trade policy. Our decision could well affect the unity of the West, the cause of the Cold War, and the economic growth of our Nation for a generation to come.

If we move decisively, our factories and farms can increase their sales to their richest, fastest-growing market. Our exports will increase. Our balance of payments position will improve. And we will have forged across the Atlantic a trading partnership with vast resources for freedom.

If, on the other hand, we hang back in deference to local economic pressures, we will find ourselves cut off from our major allies. Industries—and I believe this is most vital—industries will move their plants and jobs and capital inside the walls of the Common Market, and jobs, therefore, will be lost here in the United States if they cannot otherwise compete for its consumers. Our farm surpluses—our balance of trade, as you all know, to Europe, the Common Market, in farm products, is nearly three or four to one in our favour, amounting to one of the best earners of dollars in our balance of payments structure, and without entrance to this Market, without the ability to enter it, our farm surpluses will pile up in the Middle West, tobacco in the South, and other commodities, which have gone through Western Europe for 15 years. Our balance of payments position will worsen. Our consumers will lack a wider choice of goods at lower prices. And millions of American workers— whose jobs depend on the sale or the transportation or the distribution of exports or imports, or whose jobs will be endangered by the movement of our capital to Europe, or whose jobs can be maintained only in an expanding economy—these millions of workers in your home States and mine will see their real interests sacrificed.

Members of the Congress: The United States did not rise to greatness by waiting for others to lead. This Nation is the world's foremost manufacturer, farmer, banker, consumer, and exporter. The Common Market is moving ahead at an economic growth rate twice ours. The Communist economic offensive is under way. The opportunity is ours—the initiative is up to us—and I believe that 1962 is the time . . .

SOURCE: White House Documents (11 January 1962)

NUCLEAR DISARMAMENT

The disarmament negotiations had been broken off on 21 December 1961 following the resumption of Soviet nuclear testing. The generally strained atmosphere had been intensified during the latter half of 1961 by the closure of the border between West and East Berlin and the erection of the Berlin Wall.

At Bermuda in December, Macmillan argued for the postponement of Western nuclear testing until there had been a summit conference. Such a conference had been one of the prime aims of his foreign policy. Ideally he would have liked to initiate regular summit conferences, not least because these were an opportunity to preserve Britain's dwindling influence in the world.

Although Macmillan was able to persuade Kennedy to make one last attempt to seek a conference, the President was doubtful about the value of this, he feared the outcome of another inconclusive session like that at Vienna. Instead he suggested that a new disarmament initiative should be taken, which could substitute for a summit conference.

The two leaders sent off a joint note to Khrushchev on 7 February 1962 proposing such a meeting. It suggested that a gathering of the foreign ministers of Britain, the United States and the Soviet Union could be held at the opening of the Geneva Disarmament Conference in March.

The foreign ministers, it was said, could work out a programme of general or complete disarmament which could serve as the basis for a treaty; ascertain the widest measure of disarmament that might be possible; and isolate and identify measures that could be put into effect immediately.

At the same time Britain and the United States announced that preparations for beginning nuclear tests at Christmas Island were under way.

In his reply, Khrushchev suggested a summit meeting of the heads of all the eighteen nations represented at Geneva. This proposal alarmed Kennedy and Macmillan who were disturbed at the idea of a massive circus of heads of state. Macmillan wisely prevailed on the President to accept a reply which re-emphasised that the foreign ministers of the three nations should confer first and a possible meeting of heads of government be delayed until further progress had been made.

The idea of a meeting of foreign ministers was dismissed by Khrushchev, who again articulated the Soviet position that 'control before disarmament . . . we regard as espionage'.

In March Kennedy announced publicly that he was prepared to go forward with a new round of nuclear tests. His decision had been communicated to Macmillan on 27 February, then delayed to allow his saddened ally a brief period in which to prepare his reactions.

Atmospheric testing was resumed in April 1962.

41 Harold Macmillan and President Kennedy
JOINT LETTER TO CHAIRMAN KHRUSHCHEV
(7 February 1962)

We are taking the unusual step of addressing this message to you in order to express our own views, as well as to solicit yours, on what we can jointly do to increase the prospects of success at the new disarmament negotiations which will begin in Geneva in March.

We are convinced that a supreme effort must be made and the three of us must accept a common measure of personal obligation to seek every avenue to restrain and reverse the mounting arms race. Unless some means can be found to make at least a start in controlling the quickening arms competition, events may take their own course and erupt in a disaster which will afflict all peoples, those of the Soviet Union as well as of the United Kingdom and United States.

Disarmament negotiations in the past have been sporadic and frequently interrupted. Indeed, there has been no sustained effort to come to grips with this problem at the conference table since the three months of meetings ending in June of 1960, over a year and a half ago. Before that, no real negotiations on the problem of general disarmament had taken place since negotiations came to an end in September 1957.

It should be clear to all of us that we can no longer afford to take a passive view of these negotiations. They must not be allowed to drift into failure. Accordingly, we propose that we three accept a personal responsibility for directing the part to be played by our representatives in the forthcoming talks, and that we agree beforehand that our representatives will remain at the conference table until concrete results have been achieved, however long this may take.

We propose that our negotiators seek progress on three levels. First, they should be instructed to work out a programme of general and complete disarmament which could serve as the basis for the negotiation of an implementing treaty or treaties. Our negotiators could thus build upon the common ground which was found in the bilateral talks between the United States and the USSR which took place this summer, and which were reflected in the statement of agreed principles of September 20, 1961. Secondly, our negotiators should attempt to ascertain the widest measure of disarmament which would be implemented at the earliest possible time while still continuing their maximum efforts to reach agreement on those other aspects which present more difficulty. Thirdly, our negotiators should try to isolate and identify initial measures of disarmament which could, if put into effect without delay, materially improve international security and the prospects for further disarmament progress. We do not believe that these triple objectives need conflict with one another and an equal measure of urgency should be attached to each.

As a symbol of the importance which we jointly attach to these negotiations, we propose that we be represented at the outset of the disarmament conference by the Foreign Ministers of our three countries, who would declare their readiness to return to participate personally in the negotiations as the progress made by our permament representatives warrants. We assume, in this case, the Foreign Ministers of other States as well will wish to attend. The status and progress of the conference should, in addition, be the subject of more frequent communications among the three of us. In order to give impetus to the opening of the disarmament negotiations, we could consider having the Foreign Ministers of our three countries convene at Geneva in advance of the opening of the conference to concert our plans.

At this time in our history, disarmament is the most urgent and the most complex issue we face. The threatening nature of modern armaments is so appalling that we cannot regard this problem as a routine one or as an issue which may be useful primarily for the scoring of propaganda victories. The failure in the nuclear test conference, which looked so hopeful and to the success of which we attached such a high priority in the spring of 1961, constitutes a discouraging background for our new efforts. However, we must be resolved to overcome this recent setback, with its immediate consequences, and forego fruitless attempts to apportion blame. Our renewed effort must be to seek and find ways in which the competition between us, which will surely persist for the foreseeable future, can be pursued on a less dangerous level. We must view the forthcoming disarmament meetings as an opportunity and a challenge which time and history may not once again allow us.

We would welcome an early expression of your views.

SOURCE: Command Papers 1694. *Documents relating to Disarmament and to the Establishment of the 18-Nation Committee* (HMSO, 1962), 19

THE CUBAN MISSILE CRISIS

It is a mark of Britain's diminished influence with the United States that the greatest crisis of the postwar years should have developed, come to a peak and been resolved quite independently of any influence that the British Government might have wielded.

When Kennedy announced the measures he would take to force the withdrawal of Soviet missiles from Cuba, he encountered considerable suspicion and criticism in Britain, far more than in Europe.

Macmillan telephoned his support to the President on 23 October. He

*still tended, however, to think in terms of a new summit meeting as the
best way of tackling the crisis. The Labour Party's National Executive
Committee, on the other hand, promptly called the blockade a measure of
'doubtful legality', while Bertrand Russell, the philosopher, penned his
congratulations to Khrushchev praising him for his restraint.*

*Worried at the critical reaction in Britain, Sir David Ormsby-Gore,
the British Ambassador in Washington, persuaded Kennedy to release
photographs of the Soviet missile sites. The next evening Lord Home, the
Foreign Secretary, used the photographs during a television speech to win
public opinion over to support of the United States.*

*In his statement on 25 October, Macmillan confined himself to the
bare statement of the facts, while not saying what, if anything, Britain
might be prepared to do. Characteristically, he still spoke of the possibility of eventually moving 'into a wider field of negotiation'—a summit
conference—to resolve the crisis.*

42 Harold Macmillan
STATEMENT TO THE HOUSE OF COMMONS
(25 October 1962)

On Monday, 22nd October, President Kennedy, in a personal
message and through the United States Ambassador in London,
made clear to me his deep concern about the Soviet development of Cuba as a formidable base for offensive ballistic missiles.
It is, of course, true that the United States authorities had known
for some time of the location of a number of surface-to-air
missile sites in Cuba; but these missiles, even though carrying
nuclear warheads, may be regarded as of a defensive nature.

Very recently, however, a number of medium-range ballistic
—or ground-to-ground—missile sites have been definitely
identified in Cuba. Reports from all American intelligence
sources confirm that at least 30 missiles are already present in
Cuba. Such missiles, with their range of over 1,000 miles, could
reach a large area of the United States, including Washington
and nearly the whole of Central America and the Caribbean
including the Panama Canal. In addition, sites for intermediate

range ballistic missiles with an operational range of 2,200 nautical miles have been identified. Further sites for both types of missiles are being constructed. All these missiles are designed to carry, and must be presumed to carry, nuclear bombs. In addition, Russia has supplied Cuba with IL28 aircraft, of which over 20 have been definitely identified. These bombers are, of course, offensive and not defensive weapons.

Neither the Soviet Union nor the Cuban Government appear to have denied these facts. In addition, it is believed that there are at least 5,000 Soviet military technicians already on the island.

These facts, which are fully established on the basis of the evidence provided, serious though they are in themselves, took on a more sinister character because of the previous history of this affair. The House may recall that, on 4th and 13th September, President Kennedy issued solemn warnings about the build-up of offensive weapons in Cuba and that on 11th September the official Soviet news agency, Tass, said:

> the armaments and military equipment sent to Cuba are dessigned exclusively for defensive purposes

and added:

> there is no need for the Soviet Union to shift its weapons . . . for a retaliatory blow to any other country, for instance, Cuba.

That amounted to an official disclaimer by the Soviet Government. In addition, as recently as 18th October, Mr. Gromyko, the Soviet Foreign Minister, explicitly speaking on the instructions of his Government, assured President Kennedy in person that Soviet assistance to Cuba was of a purely defensive character. At that very moment, circumstantial evidence to the contrary was accumulating.

In view of the President's pledge that the United States would take measures to oppose the creation of offensive military power in Cuba, the Russian action, contrary to their categorical assurances, in developing this power can only be regarded as a deliberate adventure designed to test the ability and determination of the United States. The President, no doubt, formed the view, and, in my judgment, rightly, that to have accepted this would throw doubt on America's pledges in all parts of the world and expose the entire free world to a new series of perils.

The House is well aware of the action so far taken by the President of the United States in this situation, both in the area of Cuba itself, and in the Security Council of the United Nations. As regards the area of Cuba, the measures announced in the President's proclamation are designed to meet a situation that is without precedent. Moreover, it cannot be said that these measures are extreme: indeed, they are studiously moderate in that the President has only declared certain limited types of war materiel, not even all armaments, to be prohibited. The armaments specified are these: surface-to-surface missiles, bomber aircraft, bombs, air-to-surface rockets, and guided missiles, together with their war-heads and equipment. None of the categories specified in the President's proclamation could honestly be described as defensive.

In the Security Council, the United States representative has made a strong appeal for a resolution which calls for the dismantling and withdrawal from Cuba of all nuclear missiles and offensive weapons and for international supervision of this process by a United Nations Observer Corps. The resolution also urgently recommends that the United States and the Soviet Union should confer promptly on measures to remove the existing threat to the security of the western hemisphere and the peace of the world, and to report thereon to the Security Council.

As the House knows, Sir Patrick Dean, speaking on behalf of Her Majesty's Government, gave his support to this resolution. I understand that the discussion in the Security Council has been adjourned until 4 p.m. New York time today, that is, 9 p.m. London time.

Meanwhile, as the House will have heard, the Acting Secretary-General, U Thant, has addressed a message in identical terms to President Kennedy and Chairman Khrushchev. He had also sent, I am informed, a message to the Cuban Government. U Thant's proposal is that there should be a voluntary suspension on behalf of the Russians of all arms shipments to Cuba, and, at the same time, a suspension of the quarantine measures involving the search of ships. His appeal to the Cuban Government adds the suggestion that the construction and development of the military facilities and installations should be suspended, all these measures to last for a period of two to three weeks in order to give time for the parties concerned to meet and discuss with a view to finding a peaceful solution of the problem.

I am not yet in a position to inform the House of any replies from any of the three Governments to whom the Acting Secretary-General has addressed his messages. The British Government are, of course, concerned that this new threat to security should be dealt with as rapidly as possible and will add their support to any measures which genuinely lead to that end. They trust also that, based upon some alleviation of the present state of tension, it might be possible to move into a wider field of negotiation. Nevertheless, I think what has happened in the last few weeks must confirm our view that in these grave matters we cannot rest upon mere words and promises. These need, if they are to restore confidence, to be independently verified and confirmed.

SOURCE: House of Commons Debates 1962, coll 1053-6

PART TEN

The Skybolt Confrontation

The Cuban crisis had revealed the impotence of Britain in the face of the two super-powers, but it was Dean Acheson, the former US Secretary of State in the Truman administration, who rubbed home the uncomfortable facts about the sharp decline in Britain's influence in the world.

Acheson's West Point speech received little immediate attention in the United States, but in Britain, where many people undoubtedly felt he spoke for the current administration, it created a storm. The part of the speech in which he castigated Britain was reported in all the papers and the matter was raised in the House of Commons. It received considerably more attention than it deserved; however, this was a mark of Britain's lingering sensitivity towards any slight delivered from across the Atlantic.

Later, during the final years before his death, Acheson was to renew his criticisms of British policy in a series of statements supporting Rhodesia's unilateral declaration of independence. By this time, the British Government had become more inured to the former US Secretary of State's eccentric interventions in world affairs.

43 Dean Acheson
EXTRACT FROM A SPEECH AT WEST POINT
(5 December 1962)

. . . Great Britain has lost an Empire and has not yet found a role. The attempt to play a separate power role—that is, a role apart from Europe, a role based on a 'special relationship' with the United States, a role based on being the head of a 'Commonwealth' which has no political structure, or unity, or strength and enjoys a fragile and precarious economic relationship by means of the sterling area and preferences in the British market—this role is about to be played out.

Great Britain, attempting to work alone and be a broker between the United States and Russia, has seemed to conduct a policy as weak as its military power. Her Majesty's Government is now attempting, wisely in my opinion, to re-enter Europe, from which it was banished at the time of the Plantagenets, and the battle seems about as hard fought as those of an earlier day.

SOURCE: *New York Times* (6 December 1962)

As if the Cuban crisis and Acheson's scathing onslaught were not enough, at the end of 1962 Britain was trapped in a full-scale defence crisis following the abrupt collapse of the weapon which had been regarded as the future mainstay of the Royal Air Force.

From the beginning, the Skybolt programme—initially agreed by Eisenhower and Macmillan at Camp David in 1960 as part of the understanding under which the Americans received Holy Loch and the Fylingdales early warning station—had had its problems. The first five test launches failed, development costs doubled and the date at which the system would come into operation slipped from 1965 to 1967.

When, during 1962, Robert McNamara, the US Defense Secretary, decided that the programme should be scrapped, it had already cost the United States $400 million and Britain $30 million.

The United States considered that the scrapping of Skybolt might lead to a squabble with its own air force, but would not affect its deterrent strength. Both Polaris and Minuteman were well on the way to deployment and were likely to prove more effective weapons than the untried and increasingly costly Skybolt.

The cancellation of Skybolt made perfect sense to McNamara. His cold equations did not take into account British sensitivities or the future of Britain's nuclear deterrent. Anyway, many in the United States felt the British deterrent should fade away.

Even before the Nassau Conference, the United States declared that Skybolt was a failure, which the British regarded as a clear act of bad faith. The United States did not at first realise that the problem was almost entirely a political one and was surprised by the strength of the British reaction.

Once Kennedy realised the peculiar political aspects of the situation, he decided that, rather than let Britain sink, he was obliged to help with an alternative to save the face of the Conservative government. Another crucial element in the debate was the friendship the President felt for Macmillan and for Sir David Ormsby-Gore, the British Ambassador.

The fact that the United States Defense Department had already announced that Skybolt was a failure meant it would be impossible for the Kennedy administration to persuade the British to take over the further development of the missile on their own.

As a result the decision was hastily taken of providing Polaris to Britain, to be fitted with British warheads and mounted in British submarines that had still to be constructed. At the same time the President sent a letter to President de Gaulle offering him Polaris on the same terms that it was being provided to Britain. Needless to say, his well-intended gesture only served to provoke the French President's wrath. In effect, through the Nassau agreement, the United States helped Britain to preserve its small nuclear deterrent for political reasons at the very time it was publicly committed to curbing nuclear proliferation internationally. De Gaulle was convinced that Britain was committed to an Atlantic rather than a European alignment. Nassau gave him the pretext he needed to veto Britain's application to enter the Common Market.

Nassau, however, marked the final flourish of the special relationship. Despite the shock of de Gaulle's veto the following January, Britain's commitment to an eventual entry into Europe had by now become inevitable.

ANGLO-AMERICAN NEGOTIATIONS ON NUCLEAR MISSILE DELIVERY SYSTEMS

44A Robert McNamara and Peter Thorneycroft
FINAL COMMUNIQUE, LONDON (12 December 1962)

There have been full and frank talks on defence questions of mutual interest between the Honourable Robert S. McNamara, United States Secretary of Defence, and the Right Honourable Peter Thorneycroft, Minister of Defence.

The two Ministers, who will be attending the NATO Council Meeting in Paris later this week, gave special attention to the Skybolt Missile Programme, which has been under review within the United States Administration. No decision was taken on the future of Skybolt, on which discussions will continue.

SOURCE: US Information Service Press Release (12 December 1962)

44B Peter Thorneycroft
STATEMENT TO THE HOUSE OF COMMONS
(17 December 1962)

With permission, I should like to make a statement on my recent talks with Mr. McNamara in London on 11th December.

The principal subject discussed was, as the House knows, the future of the Skybolt missile. We have, of course, known from the outset of our association with the United States Government on this weapon that it constituted a formidable development problem. We knew of various difficulties that had arisen, and of the steps that were being taken to surmount them. Such difficulties, of course, were not unexpected, nor are they unusual even in simpler missiles.

However, when I visited the United States in September of this year, the situation was that while the increase in costs was causing concern, I was assured that American plans assumed delivery of Skybolt. It was not until the beginning of November that Mr. McNamara, while assuring me that no decision would be taken without the fullest consultation, informed me that the future of the weapon was under review. This consultation was carried a further stage last week, and will be continued between the Prime Minister and the President in the Bahamas.

From the point of view of the United States, the weapon is proving more expensive than originally estimated; secondly it looks as though it will be late and possibly not as efficient and reliable as had at first been hoped; and, thirdly, alternative weapon systems available to the United States Government have proved relatively more successful.

I have stressed throughout my talks with Mr. McNamara the serious consequences for the United Kingdom of a cancellation of this project, and I can assure the House that the United States Government can be in no doubt on that aspect of the matter. The discussions have, naturally, included the possibility that the United States Government might provide us with alternatives to Skybolt of which the most important is Polaris, but I would stress that no decisions either on Skybolt or on possible alternatives to it have been taken.

Since discussions between our two Governments have not been completed, I am sure that the House will accept that I cannot say any more at the present time. Indeed, as the Prime Minister said last week, it would not be in the interests of the country to do so.

Apart from Skybolt, my meeting with Mr. McNamara gave us an opportunity for informal and confidential discussion of a number of matters of joint concern to the two Governments.

SOURCE: House of Commons Debates 669, coll 893–4

44C President Kennedy and Harold Macmillan
JOINT STATEMENT, NASSAU (21 December 1962)

The President and the Prime Minister met in Nassau from

December 18th to December 21st. They were accompanied by the Secretary of Defense, Mr. McNamara, and the Under Secretary of State, Mr. Ball, and by the Foreign Secretary, Lord Home, the Minister of Defense, Mr. Thorneycroft and the Secretary of State for Commonwealth Relations and Colonies, Mr. Sandys.

The President and the Prime Minister discussed a wide range of topics. They reviewed the state of East-West relations in the aftermath of the October crisis in Cuba, and joined in the hope that a satisfactory resolution of this crisis might open the way to the settlement of other problems outstanding between the West and the Soviet Union.

In particular, they reviewed the present state of the negotiations for a treaty ending nuclear tests, and reaffirmed their intent to seek agreement on this issue with the U.S.S.R., in the hope that this agreement would lead on to successful negotiations on wider issues of disarmament.

As regards Berlin, they reaffirmed their interest in arriving at a solid and enduring settlement which would insure that Berlin remains free and viable.

The Chinese Communist attack on India was discussed with special consideration being given to the way in which the two governments might assist the Government of India to counter this aggression. Defense problems of the sub-continent were reviewed. The Prime Minister and the President are hopeful that the common interests of Pakistan and India in the security of the subcontinent would lead to a reconciliation of Indian-Pakistan differences. To this end, they expressed their gratification at the statesmanship shown by President Ayub and Prime Minister Nehru in agreeing to renew their efforts to resolve their differences at this crucial moment.

The two leaders discussed the current state of affairs in the Congo, and agreed to continue their efforts for an equitable integration of this troubled country. They expressed support for Mr. Spaak's proposal for a fair division of revenues and noted with concern the dangers of further discord in the Congo.

The Prime Minister informed the President of the present state of negotiations for U.K. membership in the Common Market. The President reaffirmed the interest of the United States in an early and successful outcome.

The President and the Prime Minister also discussed in considerable detail policy on advanced nuclear weapons systems and considered a variety of approaches. The result of this discussion is set out in the attached statement.

Statement on Nuclear Defense Systems

1. The President and the Prime Minister reviewed the development program for the Skybolt missile. The President explained that it was no longer expected that this very complex weapons system would be completed within the cost estimate or the time scale which were projected when the program was begun.

2. The President informed the Prime Minister that for this reason and because of the availability to the United States of alternative weapons systems, he had decided to cancel plans for the production of Skybolt for use by the United States. Nevertheless, recognizing the importance of the Skybolt program for the United Kingdom, and recalling that the purpose of the offer of Skybolt to the United Kingdom in 1960 had been to assist in improving and extending the effective life of the British V-bombers, the President expressed his readiness to continue the development of the missile as a joint enterprise between the United States and the United Kingdom, with each country bearing equal shares of the future cost of completing development, after which the United Kingdom would be able to place a production order to meet its requirements.

3. While recognizing the value of this offer, the Prime Minister decided, after full consideration, not to avail himself of it because of doubts that had been expressed about the prospects of success for this weapons system and because of uncertainty regarding date of completion and final cost of the program.

4. As a possible alternative the President suggested that the Royal Air Force might use the Hound Dog missile. The Prime Minister responded that in the light of the technical difficulties he was unable to accept this suggestion.

5. The Prime Minister then turned to the possibility of provision of the Polaris missile to the United Kingdom by the United States. After careful review, the President and the Prime Minister agreed that a decision on Polaris must be considered in the widest context both of the future defense of the Atlantic Alliance and of the safety of the whole Free World. They reached the conclusion that this issue created an opportunity for the development of new and closer arrangements for the organization and control of strategic Western defense and that such arrangements in turn could make a major contribution to political cohesion among the nations of the Alliance.

6. The Prime Minister suggested and the President agreed, that for the immediate future a start could be made by subscribing to NATO some part of the forces already in existence. This could include allocations from United States Strategic Forces, from United Kingdom Bomber Command, and from tactical nuclear forces now held in Europe. Such forces would be assigned as part of a NATO nuclear force and targeted in accordance with NATO plans.

7. Returning to Polaris the President and the Prime Minister agreed that the purpose of their two governments with respect to the provision of the Polaris missiles must be the development of a multilateral NATO nuclear force in the closest consultation with other NATO allies. They will use their best endeavours to this end.

8. Accordingly, the President and the Prime Minister agreed that the U.S. will make available on a continuing basis Polaris missiles (less warheads) for British submarines. The U.S. will also study the feasibility of making available certain support facilities for such submarines. The U.K. Government will construct the submarines in which these weapons will be placed and they will also provide the nuclear warheads for the Polaris

missiles. British forces developed under this plan will be assigned and targeted in the same way as the forces described in paragraph 6.

These forces, and at least equal U.S. forces, would be made available for inclusion in a NATO multilateral nuclear force. The Prime Minister made it clear that except where H.M.G. may decide that supreme national interests are at stake, these British forces will be used for the purposes of international defense of the Western Alliance in all circumstances.

9. The President and the Prime Minister are convinced that this new plan will strengthen the nuclear defense of the Western Alliance. In strategic terms this defense is indivisible, and it is their conviction that in all ordinary circumstances of crisis or danger, it is this very unity which is the best protection of the West.

10. The President and the Prime Minister agreed that in addition to having a nuclear shield it is important to have a non-nuclear sword. For this purpose they agreed on the importance of increasing the effectiveness of their conventional forces on a worldwide basis.

SOURCE: Public Papers of the President, 1962, 908–10

44D President Kennedy
PRESS INTERVIEW, PALM BEACH
(31 December 1962)

The President [in reply to a question concerning the pact of Nassau and the problems facing him in connection with it]. Well, I think it would seem to me that if anybody bothered to read the pact in detail —we made several offers to the British. First, the British position on it has been, I know, somewhat critical. In the first place, we did offer the Skybolt. We offered a 50–50 split in finishing the Skybolt, even though we, ourselves, weren't going to buy any, and the British could have bought them. So I don't think it can

be charged that the United States was in any way attempting
to make a political decision rather than a technical one.

The fact is this administration put a lot of money into Skybolt.
We increased the funds substantially after 1961 in an effort to
finish it successfully. We speeded up the program. As I say, at
Nassau we offered to go 50–50 in completing the research even
though we were not going to buy it, so that the British would
not lack its own deterrent if it chose to exercise that option. So
that was one of the choices.

The other was, of course, the Hound Dog, which presented
technical problems for the British, and the third was the Polaris.
I think that the British selected the Polaris option, first, because
of the technical problems connected with Skybolt and, secondly,
because Polaris offers a hope of being an effective deterrent for
a much longer period than Skybolt, through the seventies.

In addition, I do find it peculiar that these people who say
that we are trying to phase out the manned bombers and have
an over-reliance on missiles, when the Skybolt is the most complicated missile of them all—to read that point of view, you
would think that Skybolt was a gravity bomb rather than a
missile which is going to fly itself from a movable base 1,000
miles. So Skybolt is the top of the art of missilery.

You are almost going around a full circle to use the Skybolt.
What you are joining together is a weapon which time is dealing
some blows to, which is the bomber, and you are joining the
most sophisticated missile and putting them together.

It seemed to us with our other alternatives we were better off
to put our money some place else. But in any case, I felt that the
offer we made to the British was in keeping with both our
technical and moral obligations to them, and I think that the
arrangement we made was in the best interest of the United
States, Britain, and the alliance, because the British will have
their deterrent. It will be independent in moments of great
national peril, which is really the only time you consider using
nuclear weapons anyway. It will serve as a basis for a multi-
national force or multilateral force.

It may be that that will not develop. There are technical problems connected with it. . . .

Our whole policy has been against the diversion of resources towards independent national deterrents. We think it doesn't make strategic sense, and we think it really would cost the Europeans a great deal of money.

We have been putting in, as has been said before—we are spending perhaps $15 billion this year for our nuclear deterrent, which is as much as the budget of all of Europe combined for all its forces. To begin to have these national deterrents which will amount to a fraction of our deterrent really seems to me to be a waste of resources and to take resources away from the buildup of other forces which I think are more vitally needed.

So we have the problem of whether—on the other hand, there is the desire of Europe for a European deterrent or greater control over the deterrent. The question really would be whether a deterrent composed of a multinational force made up of the British, the Americans, and French elements, whether they would satisfy the desires of other Europeans to have a greater control over the use of nuclear weapons.

We have proposed to satisfy the others, the multilateral force, or multilateral elements of this force. This is a matter of concern, of course, to several other countries in Europe beside France. I think this is one of the great problems of the alliance in 1963, whether the alliance will begin to fragment into national deterrents which will cost great sums of money, and cause political and strategic imbalances, or whether it will be possible for us to work out some arrangements which will give Europe a greater degree and feeling of security.

There is always the argument in Europe that the United States might leave Europe, which is, of course, in my opinion, fallacious, because the United States can never leave Europe. We are too much bound together. If we left Europe, Europe would be more exposed to the Communists. It is just that until the United States is ready to give up its struggle, we are not going to leave Europe. So we are not going to leave Europe.

But, nevertheless, there are those who argue that we are going to leave Europe, or that this complete control over the nuclear weapons gives the United States too great a voice in the destiny of Europe. Therefore, we are attempting to lessen that feeling of overdependence by this multinational proposal and the root of it is the Nassau agreement, or the seed of it. Whether it is going to flower or not, we ought to be able to tell in 1963. It will depend partly, as I say, on the political decisions, the technical decisions, of the French and ourselves.

This isn't just a French problem, but it is our own and the British, and also the response of the other members of NATO. In order to provide greater cohesion in the alliance, we don't want to have a situation develop which provides less cohesion.

I would say it will take a good many weeks, possibly months, to work this out. It isn't something that the French or anyone else can give an answer to of yes or no.

Q: Sir, can you foresee any situation in which that phrase 'in the supreme national interest' might have any practical application, or why it was included in the pact?

The President: Because I don't think the British wanted to put the kind of investment we are talking about into the development of Polaris, which would cost them a good deal of money, unless they felt there might come an occasion, conceivably, where the British would be alone and would need this force. They wanted to feel free to have it. It is difficult to conceive of such a situation. I suppose they might argue that Suez might have been isolated, although as a practical matter I don't think they were then, in the nuclear sense, but they might if they were threatened with a bombardment of their island. They might feel they wanted to have the capacity to respond, or at least say they had the capacity, and if there was an attack, to respond.

We hope the situation will not come where they are isolated that way again. But I think they are conscious of that history. That doesn't mean where they threatened to use nuclear weapons against Nasser, but where they were threatened with a nuclear attack by the Soviets, they might not have felt they had sufficient means to respond. This is when there was a division in the alliance. So I think that is probably in their minds . . .

SOURCE: Public Papers of the President, 1962, 913–15

THE POLARIS AGREEMENT
Under the terms of the Polaris Agreement reached at Nassau, the British would buy Polaris missiles from the United States. Britain would build the nuclear warheads and the nuclear submarines for the system. The weapons were pledged to NATO from the beginning. However, the commitment to NATO contained an emergency escape clause which would allow Britain to withdraw its submarines at a time of supreme national danger. Through this clause, which could only be invoked under almost inconceivable circumstances. Britain retained the substance of national independence.

45 Governments of the US and the UK POLARIS SALES AGREEMENT (6 April 1963)

The Government of the United States of America and the Government of the United Kingdom of Great Britain and Northern Ireland, recalling and affirming the 'Statement on Nuclear Defense Systems' included in the joint communique issued on December 21, 1962 by the President of the United States of America and the Prime Minister of Her Majesty's Government in the United Kingdom of Great Britain and Northern Ireland;

Have agreed as follows:

Article I

1. The Government of the United States shall provide and the Government of the United Kingdom shall purchase from the Government of the United States Polaris missiles (less warheads), equipment, and supporting services in accordance with the terms and conditions of this Agreement.

G

2. This Agreement shall be subject to the understandings concerning British submarines equipped with Polaris missiles (referred to in paragraphs 8 and 9 of the Nassau 'Statement on Nuclear Defense systems') agreed by the President of the United States arid the Prime Minister of the United Kingdom at their meeting held in the Bahamas between December 18 and December 21, 1962.

Article II

1. In recognition of the complexity of the effort provided for in this agreement and the need for close coordination between the contracting Governments in giving effect to its terms, the two Governments shall promptly establish the organizational machinery provided for in the following paragraphs of this Article.

2. The Department of Defense, acting through the Department of the Navy, and the Admiralty, or such other agency as the Government of the United Kingdom shall designate, will be the Executive Agencies of their respective Governments in carrying out the terms of this Agreement. Appropriate representatives of the Executive Agencies are authorized to enter into such technical arrangements, consistent with this Agreement, as may be necessary.

3. A Project Officer will be designated by each Government's Executive Agency with direct responsibility and authority for the management of the activities of that Government under this Agreement. Each Project Officer will designate liaison representatives, in such numbers as may be agreed, who will be authorized to act on his behalf in capacities specified in technical arrangements and who will be attached to the Office of the other Project Officer.

4. A Joint Steering Task Group will be established by the Project Officers to advise them, *inter alia*, concerning the development of new or modified equipment to meet specific requirements of the Government of the United Kingdom, and concerning interfaces between the equipment provided by the

two Governments respectively. The Joint Steering Task Group will comprise the Project Officers (or their representatives), and principal liaison representatives, and may include selected leaders from among the scientists, industrialists and government executives of the United States and of the United Kingdom. The Joint Steering Task Group will meet approximately every three months alternatively in the United Kingdom and in the United States under the chairmanship of the resident Project Officer.

Article III

1. The Government of the United States (acting through its Executive Agency) shall provide, pursuant to Article I of this Agreement: Polaris missiles (less warheads), equipment, and supporting services of such types and marks and in such quantities as the Government of the United Kingdom may from time to time require, and in configurations and in accordance with delivery programs or time tables to be agreed between the Project Officers. In the first instance the missiles, equipment, and supporting services provided by the Government of the United States shall be sufficient to meet the requirements of a program drawn up by the Government of the United Kingdom and communicated to the Government of the United States prior to the entry into force of this Agreement . . .

SOURCE: US Department of State Bulletin (14 January 1963)

THE TEST BAN TREATY

After many months of stalling, the Soviet Government finally responded to Western overtures by making a serious attempt to control the swift expansion of nuclear armaments.

The Partial Nuclear Test Ban Treaty, which was signed in Moscow on 5 August 1963 and ultimately subscribed to by more than a hundred governments, did not impose a complete halt to the testing of nuclear weapons or lead to immediate disarmament. While the testing of nuclear weapons in the atmosphere was renounced, the signatories reserved the right to carry on testing underground, so long as radioactivity was not allowed to leak across national borders. The United States emphasised that it would continue to conduct underground testing—most recently as part of its programme to develop multiple warheads and an anti-missile system—until acceptable methods of verification had been developed.

The refusal of France and China to subscribe to the treaty has always been its major omission. But, as Kennedy said, the treaty did represent 'the first concrete result of eighteen years of effort by the United States to impose limits on the nuclear arms race'.

Robert McNamara, the US Defense Secretary, went to considerable lengths in the Senate hearings on ratification of the treaty to emphasise that it represented no weakening of American military power. The Senate finally ratified the agreement on 24 September.

46 Governments of the US, UK and USSR
TEST BAN TREATY (5 August 1963)

TREATY
banning nuclear weapon tests
in the atmosphere, in outer
space and under water

The Governments of the United States of America, the United Kingdom of Great Britain and Northern Ireland, and the Union of Soviet Socialist Republics, hereinafter referred to as the 'Original Parties',

Proclaiming as their principal aim the speediest possible achievement of an agreement on general and complete disarmament under strict international control in accordance with the objectives of the United Nations which would put an end to the armaments race and eliminate the incentive to production and testing of all kinds of weapons, including nuclear weapons,

Seeking to achieve the discontinuance of all test explosions of nuclear weapons for all time, determined to continue negotiations to this end, and desiring to put an end to the contamination of man's environment by radioactive substances,

Have agreed as follows:

Article I

1. Each of the Parties to this Treaty undertakes to prohibit, to prevent, and not to carry out any nuclear weapon test explosion, or any other nuclear explosion, at any place under its jurisdiction or control:

(a) in the atmosphere; beyond its limits, including outer space; or underwater, including territorial waters high seas; or

(b) in any other environment if such explosion causes radioactive debris to be present outside the territorial limits of the State under whose jurisdiction or control such explosion is conducted. It is understood in this connection that the provisions of this subparagraph are without prejudice to the conclusion of a treaty resulting in the permanent banning of all nuclear test explosions, including all such explosions underground, the conclusion of which, as the Parties have stated in the Preamble to this Treaty, they seek to achieve.

2. Each of the Parties to this Treaty undertakes furthermore to refrain from causing, encouraging, or in any way participating in, the carrying out of any nuclear weapon test explosion, or any other nuclear explosion, anywhere which would take place in any of the environments described, or have the effect referred to, in paragraph 1 of this Article . . .

SOURCE: US Department of State. *Treaties and Other International Acts Series*, 5433 (5 August 1963)

THE MULTI-LATERAL FORCE

The ill-judged multi-lateral force concept came as the latest in a long series of proposals designed to increase the nuclear strength of the NATO alliance without giving ultimate control of nuclear weapons to the Europeans.

In December 1957 the decision was taken to establish stocks of nuclear weapons in Europe.

In 1959 General Lauris Norstad, the then Supreme Allied Com-

mander, Europe, proposed a formula for giving NATO its own land-based medium-range missiles under a 'two-key' system of joint American-European control of the firing system. This idea was rejected the following year by Eisenhower.

In December 1960, Christian Herter, the US Secretary of State, made a formal offer to commit a number of Polaris submarines to NATO. He accompanied this by a proposal for a seaborne missile force manned by multi-national crews.

In 1961 this concept was embraced in its essentials by Kennedy and germinated as the multi-lateral force.

One element of the Nassau plan was for the creation of a special nuclear force within NATO. At the beginning this was not defined in much detail, though it was apparently intended to include the new British Polaris missiles, along with at least equal American forces.

In contrast to the British concept of a multi-national force, which would have excluded the Germans, the United States envisaged a highly integrated undertaking in which national identities would have been submerged.

Originally conceived as a fleet of mixed-manned Polaris submarines, the Kennedy administration developed the idea into a concept of a fleet of about twenty-five surface ships carrying eight missiles apiece.

Not surprisingly, West Germany was much attracted to the idea, although it mistrusted the American belief that the United States should retain its veto on the use of the missiles.

Britain, on the other hand, all along had reservations. Having just acquired Polarises of her own, provided Holy Loch for the Americans and assigned her V-bombers to NATO, Britain felt she had contributed enough to the allied effort. Lord Home said that Britain would provide men and facilities to the Multi-Lateral Force—or MLF, as it swiftly came to be known—but would stay clear of full participation. The recollection of the Skybolt fiasco was also a sober reminder of the possible penalties of entering into too close an agreement with the United States.

After the British general election of 1964, Harold Wilson, the new Prime Minister, told the House of Commons that MLF would add 'nothing to Western strength, is likely to cause a dissipation of effort within the alliance, and may add to the difficulties of east-west agreement.'

At about the same time, President Lyndon Johnson embarked on his own review of the MLF concept and began to back away from his initial support for the scheme.

At a meeting between Wilson and Johnson, 7–9 December 1964, it became plain from the communiqué that, while MLF and the British counterproposals for a separate 'Atlantic nuclear force', a NATO nuclear command over a fleet of surface ships, the existing land-based missiles in Europe and the V-bombers, had been discussed, neither of the alternatives had been endorsed.

By the end of the year the United States indicated that, while it was not yet prepared to abandon MLF, it was willing to consider modifications and alternatives. This position was the prelude to the abandonment and slow death of the whole impractical scheme.

47 President Johnson and Harold Wilson
JOINT STATEMENT (8 December 1964)

THE PRESIDENT of the United States and the Prime Minister of the United Kingdom met in Washington 7th December to 9th December. They were assisted by Secretary of State Rusk, Secretary of Defense McNamara and Under Secretary of State Ball and by the Foreign Secretary, Mr. Gordon Walker and the Secretary of State for Defence, Mr. Healey.

In the course of a wide ranging exchange of views, the President and the Prime Minister reviewed the current international situation in light of the responsibilities which their countries carry for maintaining, together with their allies and friends, peace and stability throughout the world. They reaffirmed their determination to support the peacekeeping operations of the United Nations and to do all in their power to strengthen the systems of regional alliance in Europe, the Middle East and the Far East to which they both contribute.

They recognized the importance of strengthening the unity of the Atlantic Alliance in its strategic nuclear defense. They discussed existing proposals for this purpose and an outline of some new proposals presented by the British Government. They agreed that the objective in this field is to cooperate in finding the arrangements which best meet the legitimate interests of all members of the Alliance, while maintaining existing safeguards on the use of nuclear weapons, and preventing their further proliferation. A number of elements of this problem were considered during this initial exchange of views as a preliminary to further discussions among interested members of the Alliance.

They also agreed on the urgency of a world-wide effort to promote the non-dissemination and non-acquisition of nuclear weapons, and of continuing Western initiatives towards arms control and disarmament. They recognized the increasing need for initiatives of this kind in light of the recent detonation of a Chinese nuclear device.

The President and the Prime Minister reaffirmed their determination to continue to contribute to the maintenance of peace and stability in the Middle East and the Far East. In this connection they recognized the particular importance of the military effort which both their countries are making in support of legitimate Governments in South East Asia, particularly in Malaysia and South Vietnam, which seek to maintain their independence and to resist subversion.

They recognized also that a nation's defense policy must be based on a sound economy. The President and the Prime Minister, while determined that their countries should continue to play their full parts in the world-wide peacekeeping effort, affirmed their conviction that the burden of defense should be shared more equitably among the countries of the free world.

They agreed also on the need for improvement in the balance of payments and in the productivity and competitive position of both their economies in order to ensure the underlying economic strength which is essential for fulfilling their heavy international responsibilities. In this connection they arranged to explore in detail the possibilities of closer cooperation between their two countries in defense research and development and in weapons production.

The President and the Prime Minister reaffirmed their belief in the importance of close allied cooperation in international affairs. They agreed that this meeting was only the first stage in their consultation in which the matters that they had discussed would need to be examined in greater detail. They looked forward, too, to continuing discussions at all levels both within the Alliance and in wider international negotiations in pursuit of nuclear and conventional disarmament and all measures to reduce world tension.

SOURCE: White House Documents (8 December 1964)

PART ELEVEN

Towards a New Alliance

As chairman of the Foreign Relations Committee, Senator William Fulbright, an Arkansas Democrat who blends Southern charm with the acuity of a former Rhodes scholar, has watched over the foreign policies of successive administrations with a sharply critical eye. In recent years he has become one of the most outspoken critics of United States involvement in areas around the world, arguing for a withdrawal of the American presence and even an extensive cutback in US foreign aid commitments.

48 Senator William Fulbright
THE SPECIAL RELATIONSHIP

In the eighteenth century the western world was conscious of its common civilisation. America was linked to England politically, and to Europe as well as England by powerful bonds of commerce and culture. There were accepted rules and principles of international behavior, and even the frequent dynastic and colonial wars that were fought were limited conflicts for limited purposes that did not seek to overturn the existing order of nations and societies.

There followed, in the wake of the American and French revolutions and the Napoleonic wars, an age of nationalism which brought with it an emphasis on the self-centered nation and its autonomous growth. In America, nationalism took the form of self-imposed isolation from the rest of the world while we concentrated on developing the resources of the vast North-American continent. In Europe, nineteenth-century nationalism was at first a unifying force, and one which was closely associated with democratic and humanitarian ideas; but in the last decades of the century there developed a growing divergence between democracy and nationalism as the latter became strident, aggressive, and militarist. The bonds of common civilisation were increasingly strained by the rise of militant nationalism. In the twentieth century these bonds were shattered and western civilisation all but destroyed itself in the ferocity of two world wars. Only the United States, drawn reluctantly from its isolation into the vortex of conflict, emerged from these great trials strong and intact.

The convulsions of the world wars had three immediate consequences: first, Western Europe emerged physically and spiritually exhausted, its economy shattered and its peoples demoralised; secondly, Russia emerged as a virile and ambitious power, posing a new danger for the West with a world policy of aggressive totalitarianism; thirdly, the nationalism which had all but consumed the West spread through Asia, Africa and Latin America, resulting in the rapid disintegration of the old western empires.

During the immediate postwar years, the United States, as the only remaining centre of strength in the western world, bore the full burden of defending the West against the new communist imperialism. With our monopoly of atomic weapons and our vast economic power, we were able to stem the tide of communist expansions and to provide the material resources for beginning the reconstruction of western community. American leadership, through the Marshall Plan and the formation of the NATO alliance, carried Europe through the immediate crisis of the postwar years and enabled the European nations to begin to rebuild their shattered economies.

Through its aid and support for Western Europe, the United States moved to rejoin the Atlantic community from which it had separated in the eighteenth century, while a new generation of Europeans began to reconstruct the bonds of community that had been severed by a generation of tyranny and war. A slow and painful trend towards unification thereupon took hold, going beyond reconciliation toward the possible realisation of the ancient and elusive dream of a genuine federation of Europe.

The 'grand design' for Atlantic partnership envisioned the concurrent development of two sets of relationships: an evolving federation of Europe with institutions vested with specified supernational powers and a broader set of arrangements for linking Europe and America to each other in a close military, political and economic partnership. Underlying this concept of a double pattern of relationships were three basic expectations: first, that the 'Europe of the Six' would not wish to remain exclusive but would welcome the membership of Great Britain and other western European countries; secondly, that a united Europe, whatever its composition, would not develop an exclusive nationalism of its own, but would welcome new arrangements with the United States and Canada for the common defense, the expansion of trade, and close cooperation in the field of aid to the underdeveloped countries; and thirdly, that the United States would enter into such cooperative arrangements even though they involved limited but real incursions on American sovereignty, particularly in the area of sharing responsibility for the control of nuclear weapons and delivery systems . . .

The challenge of Atlantic partnership is a challenge to the most persistent and destructive myth of the last two centuries of Western history: the myth that the modern nation-state is a spiritual organism with a sanctity that transcends the individual. In reality, the modern nation is the product of the historical evolution of human groups from their tribal beginnings to ever larger forms of social organisation, not as the result of some mystical force of history, but in response to very practicable economic, military, and political needs. Until the twentieth century the building of nations represented a broadening of human bonds, but in the modern world of peoples made inter-dependent by scientific and technological revolution, the mythology of the absolutely sovereign and self-sufficient nation delimits the bonds among men, confining them within political communities no longer capable of satisfying the requirements of security and economic growth . . .

The concept of Atlantic partnership is rooted in these realities. It may indeed exceed our capacity to extend the frontiers of our loyalty, and if realised it may still fall short of the needs of the nuclear age. But the Atlantic idea represents a reasonable ac-commodation between an intolerable nationalism and an un-attainable world community, between the deeply ingrained habits that bind us to the nation state and the unprecedented dangers that must drive us eventually to seek our safety in the community of mankind.

SOURCE: Senator J. William Fulbright. *Old Myths and New Realities* (New York, 1964)

No presidential assistant since the war has won the power or inter-national renown that Henry Kissinger acquired under Richard Nixon. He skilfully opened the way for President Nixon's visits to Peking and Moscow and handled with brilliance the negotiations leading to the ceasefire which ended the Vietnam War. Kissinger's major writing, however, was done in the period before he entered the White House, when he produced such works as Nuclear Weapons and Foreign Policy. *This reappraisal of the Atlantic alliance is taken from his book,* The Troubled Partnership.

49 Dr Henry Kissinger
THE TROUBLED PARTNERSHIP

. . . Great Britain's relations to the Continent in the postwar period have been extraordinarily ambivalent. In the years im-mediately following the war, the countries of the Continent were on the verge of chaos. The quest for a modicum of stability overrode all other considerations. Great Britain alone seemed to possess a structure capable of sustaining a long-range, orderly policy. During this period, Britain could have had the leadership of Europe for the asking. It would have seemed inconceivable that Europe might exclude Britain from its community—assuming that it would ever be able to form one.

Yet it was precisely the memory of its recent isolation that prevented Britain from seizing its opportunity. Throughout Britain's history, the threats to its security had come from the Continent, which in Britain significantly is called Europe. Britain's historic policy has been to prevent the emergence of a powerful and united Continent. To promote the unity of Europe, to submerge Britain in such a structure and to substitute European for American and Commonwealth connections, all this had represented a wrench with tradition which few in Britain have been prepared to make.

The memory of the war reinforced this hesitation. The countries of the Continent had surrendered and forced Britain to fight alone. In the late forties, these countries were still wracked by internal dissension. Although Britain was geographically close to Europe, its emotional ties were to its recent ally across the sea and to the Commonwealth. Long before anyone in the Continent could even imagine excluding Britain from whatever structure might be formed, Britain had made a tentative choice against the Continent.

The more the memory of the war receded, the more apparent it became that total defeat might be more conducive to making a new start than partial victory. For Great Britain, the tremendous exertions of the war did not lead to a well-deserved respite. On the contrary, Britain was obliged to undertake another major effort to adjust to a loss of international influence—a task which was made even more difficult by the memory of the recent heroic effort. While defeat enabled the Continent to free itself from the shackles of traditional nostalgia, Britain's policy, courageous and steadfast during two difficult decades, now began to turn stagnant. Its exertions had consumed so much energy that Britain never seemed able to decide which option to pursue: close relations with the United States, a new concept of Commonwealth, or an unreserved entry into Europe. By trying to combine all three, Britain ran the risk of losing each. The roots of Britain's exclusion from the Continent go deeper than one individual's arbitrary decision.

This ambivalence has been described by some as Britain's search for identity. Rather it is that this sense of identity has been incompatible with an unreserved entry into Europe. Britain's coolness toward Europe has been a consistent feature of the postwar period ...

Britain had always considered itself primarily a world power and not a European power. Its sense of identity was bound up with relations across the sea, not across the Channel. Its emotional ties were less with Europe than with the 'special relationship' with the United States.

This relationship is difficult to define, and there is no doubt that President de Gaulle sees it as more formal than it really is. Unquestionably the enormous prestige gained by Britain during the war has played a major role. Unique ties of language and culture encourage many informal connections. Anglo-American relations would therefore be 'special' whatever the formal arrangements ...

In the sixties, this policy became less effective for a number of reasons. For one thing, the 'special relationship' has never had the same psychological significance for the United States that it did for Britain. The memory of Britain's wartime effort, despite the very great prestige gained by it, has diminished with time. As the postwar period progressed, many influential Americans have come to believe that Britain has been claiming influence out of proportion to its power. Consequently they have pressed Britain to substitute close association with Europe for special ties across the Atlantic. This school of thought has objected to giving Britain a preferential voice or even the appearance of it.

They believe that Britain should be treated as simply one or other European country that should seek its fulfilment in Europe . . .

But the 'special relationship' lasted long enough to bring about a number of illusions in Allied relationships. Where Britain tended to exaggerate its special influence in Washington, the United States may have overestimated the extent of Britain's pliability. It became an axiom of United States policy that Britain's entry into a supernational Europe would be a guarantee of Atlantic partnership. This is why Washington championed Britain's entry into the Common Market so ardently and why it was so outraged when this policy was thwarted.

SOURCE: Dr Henry J. Kissinger. *The Troubled Partnership. A Reappraisal of the Atlantic Alliance* (New York, 1964)

Caught up in the continuing and seemingly endless turmoil of the Vietnam War, President Johnson was seldom able to pay the attention to European affairs that would have been advisable. As a result, the United States' relations with the Continent were largely allowed to drift with little new initiative from Washington. Johnson's concept of the Atlantic alliance was essentially a conventional one, as is seen from this brief excerpt from a speech he gave in October 1966 to the National Conference of Editorial Writers.

50 President Johnson
ADDRESS TO THE NATIONAL CONFERENCE OF EDITORIAL WRITERS (7 October 1966)

Our first concern is to keep NATO strong, and to keep it modern and to keep it abreast of the times in which we live.

The Atlantic alliance has already proved its vitality. Together, we have faced the threats of peace which have confronted us—and we shall meet those which may confront us in the future.

Let no one doubt even for a moment the American commitment. We shall not ever unlearn the lesson of the thirties, when isolation and withdrawal were our share in the common disaster.

We are committed, and we are committed to remain firm.

But the Atlantic alliance is a living organism. It must adapt itself to the changing conditions.

Much is already being done to modernize its structures.

—We are streamlining NATO command arrangements;

—We are moving to establish a permanent nuclear planning committee;

—We are increasing the speed and certainty of supply across the Atlantic.

However, there is much more than we can do.

There is much more that we must do.

The alliance must become a forum, a forum for increasingly close consultations. These should cover the full range of joint concerns—from East-West relations to crisis management.

The Atlantic alliance is the central instrument of the entire Atlantic community. But it is not the only one. Through other institutions the nations of the Atlantic are now hard at work on constructive enterprise.

In the Kennedy Round, we are negotiating with the other free-world nations to reduce tariffs everywhere. Our goal is to free the trade of the world, to free it from arbitrary and artificial constraints.

We are engaged on the problem of international monetary reform.

We are exploring how best to develop science and technology as a common resource. Recently, the Italian Government has suggested an approach to narrowing the gap in technology between the United States and Western Europe. That proposal, we think, deserves very careful study and consideration. The United States stands ready to cooperate with all of the European nations on all aspects of this problem.

Last—and perhaps really most important—we are working

together to accelerate the growth of the developing nations. It is our common business to help the millions in these developing nations improve their standards of life, to increase their life expectancy, to increase their per capita income, to improve their health, their minds, their bodies, to, in turn, help them really fight and ultimately conquer the ancient enemies of mankind: hunger, illiteracy, ignorance, disease. The rich nations can never live as an island of plenty in a sea of poverty.

Thus, while the institutions of the Atlantic community are growing, so are the tasks that confront us multiplying.

Second among our tasks is the vigorous pursuit of further unity in the West.

To pursue that unity is neither to postpone nor to neglect for a moment our continuous search for peace in the world. There are good reasons for this:

—a united Western Europe can be our equal partner in helping to build a peaceful and just world order;

—a united Western Europe can move more confidently in peaceful initiatives toward the East;

—unity can provide a framework within which a unified Germany can be a full partner without arousing fears.

We look forward to the expansion and to the further strengthening of the European community. Of course, we realize that the obstacles are great. But perseverance has already reaped larger rewards than many of us dared hope for only a few years ago.

The outlines of the new Europe are clearly discernible. It is a stronger, it is an increasingly united but open Europe—with Great Britain a part of it—and with close ties to America.

Finally, thirdly, one great goal of a united West is to heal the wound in Europe which now cuts East from West and brother from brother.

That division must be healed peacefully. It must be healed with the consent of Eastern European countries and consent of the Soviet Union. This will happen only as East and West succeed in building a surer foundation of mutual trust.

Nothing is more important than peace. We must improve the East-West environment in order to achieve the unification of Germany in the context of a larger, peaceful, and prosperous Europe . . .

SOURCE: White House Documents (7 October 1966)

Under the impetus of Senator Jacob Javits, the liberal New York Republican, a conference was held in February 1968 on the concept of an Industrial Free Trade Area.

Those from Britain attending the conference at New York University included such well-known opponents of the Common Market as Douglas Jay MP and Hugh Fraser MP, and Frank Cousins, the trade union leader.

The conference did not envisage a closely knit federal union or a supernational organisation, so it was not of itself incompatible with the Common Market, even though many of its adherents had their reservations about the market.

As a free trade area, the proposals opposed the adoption of a common customs barrier against third countries, as was provided for under the Treaty of Rome, which established the Common Market.

Senator Javits took a cautious approach, emphasising that British entry into the Common Market might be advisable, but that it would be a good idea to investigate what the possible alternatives might be before plunging into the market.

51 Senator Jacob Javits
ADDRESS AT CONFERENCE ON AN INDUSTRIAL FREE TRADE AREA (17 February 1968)

. . . We are here to consider an Industrial Free Trade Area to include our three countries and such other industrialized and trading nations as choose to join. We meet under the auspices of a great university and draw upon the wisdom of academic experts. The issue, however, is of practical importance in consideration of urgent international economics and political questions—it is not academic at all.

When in 1965 I first addressed myself to the possibility of such an Industrial Free Trade Area, I was dealing with a theory. But time and events have caught up with us and changes in the structure of world economics and political power demand that we begin to test our theories against present realities and that we find answers to our problems before they overwhelm us.

Now what are the realities?

The nations of western Europe tend to believe that the United States has become preoccupied in Asia, and has been diverted from the maintenance of its European ties;

President de Gaulle continues to insist on French domination of the European Common Market, and shows no signs of wavering in his determination to keep Britain out of the EEC;

The pound sterling has been devoured and Britain has taken austerity measures which reduce the effectiveness of the pound as international reserve currency.

The harshest reality of all, as far as the western community of nations is concerned, is the present situation of Britain. How will its future role be affected as a leading factor in international security, diplomacy and finance? It is clear that unless some decisive steps are taken there is a real possibility of further drift and deterioration of Britain's overall economic position.

Well nigh stripped of empire, drained by two world wars, excluded from the European Economic Community, the United Kingdom cannot carry on a world role from a position of economic isolation. Because the United States, Canada and the entire western world need the strength, the wisdom and the leadership of the United Kingdom, we must work to overcome that enforced economic isolation. In my judgment, the Industrial Free Trade Area proposal is a practical and reasonable way to do it. It would not only throw the United Kingdom a lifeline in its time of distress but provides the United Kingdom Government and people with a means of getting out of economic danger through their own efforts.

The IFTA concept is important for other reasons too beyond the present plight of the United Kingdom. To me and to many others, the concept of an Industrial Free Trade Area represents the next step in the continuing effort to liberalize world trade.

Obviously, there is a great feeling of brotherhood and common heritage between the peoples of the United States, Canada and Britain. But we are not—or should not—proceed on this basis. What we are talking about here is not philanthropy; it is reality. The western world needs Britain as much as Britain needs the western world. This is an exercise in enlightened self-interest for all concerned.

I wish to emphasize that I favored—and continue to favor—the admission of the United Kingdom into the EEC, and that the free trade area idea was proposed by myself and others only as an alternative. With Britain facing no immediate prospect of EEC membership, however, I feel that the alternative of the IFTA must be considered now in more practical terms. Basic decisions designed to restore the economic health of Britain and the western world simply might be too long deferred if we await solution to British membership in the EEC, even associate membership.

Let us take the lead here today, so that it can be said in years to come that we saw an impending economic crisis in Europe and worked as valiantly as we could to head it off before it was too late. I, for one, consider it my duty to bring these studies to the attention of the highest authorities in my government and I respectfully urge those of you in a position to do likewise.

In assessing the situation which now confronts us, it is essential to bear in mind the fact that the postwar arrangements in Europe assume and depend on Britain being a major power there. Should economic factors compel Britain to withdraw from its military and political commitments in Germany and Berlin, the most unsettling and dangerous consequences would ensue. Present arrangements, which provide at least some stability, could rapidly come undone and bring on a volatile and potentially explosive situation in central Europe.

This prospect is certainly one which should give pause to the leaders of France—on whom it seems to be making no impression—and to the leaders of all western European nations. A sober realization that nothing less than the stability of Europe is involved in Britain's well being and financial situation should be the common platform from which the Atlantic community of nations—the entire Western community of nations in fact— proceeds. Nor can central Europe and the USSR be unconcerned—dislocation of the status quo in the Federal Republic of Germany and West Berlin abruptly and in response to financial stringency could create grave problems and tensions for them too.

It would be altogether too tempting a target for opponents to resist. If they took advantage of it because of the inviting target it would involve a crisis far greater than any which now faces the United States and its western allies.

Therefore, the concept of an Industrial Free Trade Area composed initially of Canada, Britain and the United States could be of vital importance . . .

SOURCE: Press release from the office of Senator Javits (17 February 1968)

Sir George Catlin, the distinguished writer and professor of political science and philosophy, has been hailed as one of the pioneers of the idea of Atlantic union. Through a long series of writings, dating back to the early days of World War II, he set out his concept of a close union between the United States and Britain as the basis for an Atlantic union.

52 Sir George Catlin
THE ATLANTIC COMMONWEALTH

One of the repeated comments of Premier Robert Schuman, along with M. Jean Monnet the true begetter of a United Europe, was that at some stage the effective development of a functional and economic integration must also force into the foreground the problem of political integration, whatever the fashion this might take.

The argument of the last chapter was that the realistic development of a Free Trade Area, including the United Kingdom, the United States, Canada, Australia and New Zealand, to which some, if not all, of the EFTA countries and indeed the Low Countries and others might adhere, was the next practical step in the sequence of GATT and the Kennedy Round, and offered the best step forward—one likely to be achieved and more realistic for the present than exclusive attention to EEC. The success, however, of even such a modest and purely economic proposal, firmly based upon free trade principles, is contingent upon the mutual trust, spirit of cooperation and even emotional dynamism in this direction of the countries involved. To emphasize this is not sentimentalism. Indeed not to emphasize it is what would show lack of political realism. Two World Wars bear testimony to the political realism of the argument.

It is at this point that any policy which can be claimed, as to its nucleus, pre-eminently to 'look Westward', ever the traditional British policy, has to confront the widespread phenomenon of 'anti-Americanism'. Most rampant on the Continent of Europe, especially in Russia and France—today less so in Russia and more so, to the point of obsession, in Gaullist France —it is not limited to Europe. As a first line of criticism, adopted by many who would strongly disclaim anti-American sentiments, it takes the shape of declaring that any Western 'free trade' or, even more, 'organic' policy is 'impossible', since the Americans themselves would never consider it. Each side 'passes the buck' to the other side; and declares, 'Let us see *their* invitation.' It is to be hoped that, in the previous pages, this dogmatism of defeat, over the entire range from immediate economic proposals to Utopian federal aspirations, has been exposed and, by recitation of the facts, killed dead. This, of course, does not mean that American and, indeed, Congressional opposition to almost any proposal one cares to mention cannot be discovered. Of course it can be. But the practical politics of leadership are not conducted on this basis.

The next line of objection is to be found in the almost hysterical fear of American hegemony. For anybody who actually prefers the pre-1914 forces of International Anarchy and Balkanization, backed up by newer forces of tribalism and chauvinism, this sentiment is perhaps natural and even logical enough. It is, however, interesting in this context that what *The Times* has properly called 'the chairmanship of the President of the United States' and his position as final authority for SACEUR, itself the determinant military factor in NATO, has so seldom been regarded as controversial by the major British professional students of military strategy or, indeed, by the British public at large. The claims by the Luce publications for 'an American century' were brief and were usually treated both with a modest scepticism and as having earlier British parallels. It can, of course, be argued that this lack of resentment was natural in Britain, being the other one of the Anglo-Saxon Powers—although, if one adds the other great Dominions there are many more than two. Anyhow it is with Anglo-American relations that we are especially preoccupied in this chapter.

There are, to begin with, objections to collaboration which come from the Left. These indeed have diminished since the thirties owing to increased disillusionment among the faithful with the social policies of the Soviet Union, themselves under constant, vigorous and even virulent attack by the People's Republic of China. There is no longer the militant confidence of a monolithic ideology. It is not so long ago that, on the Continent of Europe, the City of London was pinpointed as the very citadel of Capitalism, *Finanz-Capital*, itself regarded as ideologically monolithic. Then 'Wall Street' became the favourite target. There are few today who would or could regard the Federal Reserve Bank of America, however criticized in technical detail, as the special enemy of the British economy or of the well-being of the British working class. The 'gnomes of Zürich', instead, have become the chosen devils or even the Common Market provisions which would provide for free migration across state lines.

There remains indeed the Vietnam War, which began as a

matter of a few thousand technical advisers and has ended with
the wholesale engagement of the American army, navy and
air force—a war which, in a private letter to Vice-President
Humphrey, I ventured to describe as 'the albatross around the
neck of Anglo-American [although not American-Anzac] relations'. The thesis that America should never go to the aid of her
friends, even when (as, for that matter, in France in 1941) the
alleged official government is strongly opposed to the intervention, or the neo-isolationist argument that Asia should be left
alone to the Asians (as the Japanese said) and Europe to the
Europeans, are these dangerous in the implications which their
own proponents have probably not adequately considered. That
the United States today is, on the other extreme of argument,
primarily a Pacific power, is no less misleading.

The Administration is blamed. (There has never been a time
in America, in my memory, when the President was not being
blamed, whether for action or for inaction.) What stands out in
this issue (and has been commented upon by Nelson Rocke-
feller) is that the Americans got themselves far more deeply
involved than they had in any way at first intended; that they
were anxious for any withdrawal that could not be so represented
as an American Port Arthur or Dien Bien Phu as to upset the
world balance of power; that Hanoi had no present intention of
pressing forward to negotiation; and that Peking was chagrined
by even such moves (Russian-encouraged) towards negotiations
as Hanoi might choose to make.

It should, further, always be borne in mind that the political
critics in Congress of President Johnson's policy have often been
more conspicuous in attacking his poverty programme and plan
for 'the Great Society' than for holding the President too
'hawkish' in Vietnam. As the *New Statesman*, scarcely a pro-
Presidential organ, wrote editorially (26 April 1968): 'President
Johnson, for all his faults, has made civil rights speeches not
only to justify himself but to persuade others.' That journal's
demand has been for more social action in Britain.

The second group of objectors whose views are—to use the

Marxist terminology—'objectively' anti-American are to be found in that centre which finds its political voice in business-men and civil servants. As a broad generalization it is safe to say that in Britain anti-Americanism only flourishes on the ex-treme Left (not least in pro-Communist quarters, themselves a little behind the times) and on the extreme Right. However, many moderate businessmen will argue that American industry and the high development of American technology constitute a threat to Europe, to Britain—and to themselves. Responsible civil servants, having studied the statistics, will soberly agree with them. There could be 'economic imperialism'. There is danger of a vast 'takeover bid' . . .

Comment has already been made on American investment in Britain (usually beneficial) and in Europe. In Canada, as Mr Lester Pearson pointed out, if all American investment were withdrawn, the country would be bankrupt within six months, however distasteful this thought may be to Canadian romanti-cism and neo-nationalism (itself a divisive and not a uniting sentiment). The enthusiasts for Britain-in-the-Common-Market have praised the beneficial effects on industry of the fresh wind of competition, not to speak of free migration. But talk of fresh competition from America has been another story. The weak wished to huddle together; and some saw themselves as leaders in the huddle. The marvels of technological development would do great things for civilization and render practicable massive aid to underdeveloped countries. But to American development in practice the answer was: 'Let us set up a trip-wire and stop it.' In an international world, the correct answer, from the point of view of growth, of the wages of the worker and of the development of the industry, is not the reactionary one of pro-tectionism but, if any industrial complex is indeed more de-veloped, let us join it, share with it, develop with it. The old maxim is not without prudence: If you can't beat them, join them. The opposite plan to this has been called 'the convoy policy', where the pace of the whole is set by the most awkward and obstinate member. It is not to be commended. British industry, sometimes too traditional, requires recent American practical methods and the American market and reserves. But it is mere defeatism to suppose that British science and technology is of such a quality that it cannot hold its own, and indeed take some lead, even in the most advanced fields. The facts point this way. Jealousy is not even a profitable commercial virtue.

SOURCE: George E. G. Catlin. *The Atlantic Commonwealth* (1969)

While he was Prime Minister, Harold Wilson made some comments on the meaning of the special relationship between Britain and the United States at a press conference in Washington following his first meeting with President Johnson.

'It is first a relationship at all levels,' he said. 'President-Prime Minister meetings are essential and should be frequent. There is a good deal to be said for the growing informality which has been developed, so that they tend to be routine and not symbolising any great crisis or dramatic turn of events. It means an equally close relationship between senior British ministers and senior American cabinet officials, particularly Secretary of State, Secretary of Defence, and Secretary to the Treasury.'

Despite his adherence to the concept of the special relationship, Wilson persistently refused Johnson's pleas that Britain should participate in the Vietnam War to the extent of sending a token force. However, despite the expressed opposition of many members of the Labour Party, the Prime Minister always loyally expressed his public support for the American war policy, whatever his private reservations may have been.

Following his defeat in the 1970 elections, Wilson expanded on his views on the special relationship in an address to the University of Texas.

53 Harold Wilson
ANGLO-AMERICAN RELATIONS:
A SPECIAL CASE

Frequently I am asked, 'what about the special relationship?'

I am never quite sure what this means. I am more interested in a close relationship based on a common purpose, common objectives, and as far as can be achieved community of policy, a relationship based not on condescension or on a backward-looking nostalgia for the past, but on the ability of both parties to put forward their strength and their own unique contribution to our common purpose. Charles Lamb said in one of his essays, 'There is nothing so irrelevant as a poor relation', and if ever our relationship with you were based on that status the sooner it were ended the better: that is why the first priority in British internal policy is to build up our economic strength so that as partners—in the alliance, in Europe, and the Commonwealth—we are relevant and necessary. It is on that, not on any conception of past greatness that our standing in the world will depend. Our ability to restore the lost dynamic to Britain's economic society, to restore a sense of economic and social and moral purpose, will have far more bearing on our value as an ally than any vain nuclear posturings ...

... Our closest relationship is based to a large extent on an identity of view and purpose over a wide area of world problems. We are not seeking in the main so much to decide on Anglo-American action in particular areas, as to coordinate our influence in the acceptance of objectives and plans we have formulated in common, most frequently in consultation with our other partners—in NATO and SEATO, in various international economic organizations, above all, in the United States.

Very often on many issues our purpose is complementary, rather than identical. Britain cannot compete with American power, whether in defence terms, nuclear and conventional, or in military and industrial terms. But there are areas of the world where we have influence or a special entrée, as in other areas this is true of our very powerful neighbour.

We have little to bring to common purposes through the military value of Britain's nuclear capability. Nothing at all to contribute by the pretence of being a so-called independent nuclear power. But our nuclear experience and expertise, both in political and technical matters, means that we can make an important contribution—for example in inter-allied discussions —on the Nuclear Planning Group of NATO, on the new and more streamlined strategy for NATO and in the consultative discussions that the United States Government holds with our NATO allies about the Strategic Arms Limitation Talks (SALT) with the Soviet Union.

The areas of co-operation therefore I would define as follows. First the NATO allies. It would be unthinkable that any major new initiative within NATO whether for increasing its strength and effectiveness, or combining its power to work for a detente with the Eastern world, could be undertaken without close prior consultation between our two countries and between each of us and our NATO partners.

Second, we have an important role to play in disarmament, where again our nuclear experience has value. The main breakthrough in the 18-national Disarmament Conference took place as a result of bilateral discussions during Mr. Johnson's Presidency between Washington and Moscow; but at one of the most difficult moments, it was a British initiative which helped to bring the two sides together. We have throughout supported the United States view that the more generalized advances we all seek cannot be regarded as secure without adequate inspection. New and improving techniques for the outside detection of nuclear tests are continuously being developed, and in this context the very close—and largely unpublicised—consultations between the British Cabinet, scientific secretariat and opposite numbers in the United States can be of vital importance. As indeed can be the work of non-official scientists at such meetings as the Pugwash Conferences with similarly unofficial Soviet scientists. At the end of the day—we have perhaps not quite reached it yet—it will be a matter for combined scientific and political judgement where the balance of advantage rests, between disarmament and security, in deciding how low must be the threshold for the outside detection of nuclear tests we should regard as adequate.

Third, our co-operation is vital in economic matters, as fellow members of the International Monetary Fund and the World Bank, but also of more Atlantic groupings such as the Group of Ten, the monthly meeting of central bankers as Basle, and wider-than Atlantic organisations, such as the OECD ...

SOURCE: Speech to the University of Texas (30 April 1971), press release

PART TWELVE

A Natural Relationship

President Nixon prepared for his historic visits to Peking and Moscow during 1972 with a series of preliminary discussions with major Western leaders, opening with his sessions with President Pompidou of France in the Azores and Edward Heath, the British Prime Minister, in Bermuda.

The discussions between Nixon and Heath were described by the White House as centring on the 'middle-term future' of the world. The chief topic for consideration was the evolving relationship between the United States and the European Community, of which Britain was within little more than a year to be a full member. The leaders also reviewed the situation of South Asia in the aftermath of the Indo-Pakistan war, during which the British Government had developed strong reservations over the American policy of support for Pakistan.

In a toast to Mr Heath, President Nixon praised the enduring 'special relationship' between Britain and the United States, while observing that there were now some 'tactical differences' in the dealings of the two countries.

54 President Nixon
TOAST AT A DINNER ON BOARD
HMS GLAMORGAN, BERMUDA (20 December 1971)

I could well respond to the Prime Minister's remarks by saying, as I can, with great conviction, that I agree with every word that he has uttered. However, I think the occasion demands a bit more than that, because of its historic significance, and so it is important on such an occasion that I, on my part, state on behalf of all of our officials who are here, our appreciation for the hospitality that has been extended and our hopes for the future as that future will be affected by this meeting.

First, I think we will all agree that we could not have selected a better place in which to meet, as far as its historical significance.

The Prime Minister had some marvelous historical anecdotes with regard to Bermuda. I think the best one that our staff was able to think up was one from Mark Twain. Mark Twain once visited Bermuda, and he said to a friend at the conclusion of his visit, he said, 'You may want to go to heaven, but I would rather stay here.' So the closest thing to heaven, certainly on this earth, and this hemisphere on such an occasion like this, is Bermuda.

Then, too, the place that we are meeting, this beautiful ship, the fact that it is Her Majesty's Navy, it seems to me, that that choice must have been made, when the Prime Minister did his usual careful checking of the backgrounds of those who would be here, not only the President of the United States and his guests, the Secretary of State and the Secretary of the Treasury, were all former naval people.

But whatever the case might be, what really made me realize that he was going the extra mile in picking the place and picking this ship, was when I found that the motto of this ship is 'Aim For the Highest.' That just happens to be the motto of the Secretary of the Treasury, also.

As I was talking and reminiscing with a great deal of appreciation about the association we had during World War II, our two countries, and the friendships we developed, I was thinking of what is called that special relationship between Britain and the United States. I was thinking of how Bermuda fitted into that relationship, and the fact that we are the fourth of four very historic meetings that have been held here: 1953, Prime Minister Churchill and President Eisenhower; 1957, President Eisenhower and Prime Minister Macmillan; 1961, President Kennedy and Prime Minister Macmillan; and now Prime Minister Heath and I.

As I thought of those dates, and of the probable agendas of those meetings, I thought in terms of how much the world has changed, not simply since 1953 or since 1961, I thought of how much the world has changed, and I have tried to think in terms of that special relationship between Britain and the United States which has existed for so long and to what extent that relationship still is healthy, maturing, and also necessary.

On the one hand, it would be quite easy to gain the impression, through a superficial examination, that the relationship had not only changed, as the Prime Minister has already suggested, but that it perhaps no longer was relevant, because on the one side, with the Prime Minister's courageous leadership, Britain is now entering the European Community, and as it does, its relationship with us will be one which is, of course, new in many respects, but necessarily will affect its relationship with the United States and other countries also.

On the other hand, we find that the President of the United States will be visiting this year Peking and Moscow. So a superficial examination of those events would say, on the one hand, the British are moving to Europe, and on the other hand, the United States is moving toward Moscow and toward Peking, and, therefore, what happens to the relationship, the relationship which meant so much in 1953, in 1957, and 1961? Is it still something that can be talked about? Is it still the same?

The answer, of course, is, it is not the same. The fact that it is not the same does not mean that it is still not very necessary, and perhaps even more important than it was. I say that for this reason: We do live in a changing world. We live in a world, as we all know, in which powers that were not important just a few years ago now have become enormously important. We live in a world where there are dangers on the scene today, that

H

no one could foresee 25 years ago, at the end of World War II, or even 10 years ago in 1961.

We also live in a world where there are great opportunities, opportunities in terms of building the structure of peace which may not have existed even 5 years ago.

So, as the Prime Minister, with his colleagues, with his government, seeks to explore those opportunities in Europe, as we, in our own policies, seek to explore those opportunities for building a structure of peace, by these significant journeys to nations with which we have now and will continue to have very fundamental and profound differences of philosophy, we look again back to that relationship between the two of us, what comes home on such a day as this, if I may speak in personal terms, the 5 hours today the Prime Minister and I talked, that was really a full, far-ranging discussion. And all the diplomatic words—'a very candid,' 'straightforward,' 'frank' exchange of views—could be applied to it.

What impressed me at the conclusion of that discussion was not the fact that there were some tactical differences; but the fact that after we had discussed virtually all the problems in this complex world, in this changing world, that there are certain fundamental facts that have not changed in the relationship between Britain and the United States.

We all know we share a common language. We share the common law. But what is more important is that we have, without question, dedication to principles that are uncommon, uncommon because they are transcendent and because they are ones to which we, whatever journeys we may make in the world, whatever new initiatives we may undertake separately, they are principles to which we will always have dedication.

We know, therefore, that when we talk, we begin with a devotion to the freedom of men, a devotion to economic progress in a climate of freedom, and a devotion to building a structure of peace in which all nations may have the right to their independence without infringement by other nations, great or small.

These could be just words. They are usually spoken on such occasions as this. But I can assure you that after one of the most fruitful discussions that it has been my privilege to have since holding this office, that I can reassure you that that special relationship, special in the sense of a dedication to principles that are inalienable, indestructible, and which will be here long after all of us are gone, that that relationship is as strong now, and even more necessary now than ever before, because as the world changes, as the forces of power and the balances of power shift throughout the world, it is even more vital that these principles to which our Nation and the British people have been devoted throughout our history, that those principles be maintained, that we believe in them, that we sacrifice for them, and that we work together to see that they prevail, whatever our journeys may be, together or separately.

For that reason, I believe that this meeting has been, along with its predecessors, an historic meeting. I believe it will serve a useful purpose. I believe that it builds that kind of foundation on which our two countries can go forward together in different ways, at times, toward the same great goal of a world of peace in which people can live in freedom and have progress without infringement by other peoples.

Because of that kind of ideal, may I say that on this occasion, while it is normally the custom to, as we have, very properly, toast the Queen, we have toasted the President of the United States, I think that all of you would like to join me in a toast to our host, the Prime Minister.

SOURCE: White House Documents (27 December 1971)

By the 1970s and his second period of service as Foreign Secretary, Sir Alec Douglas-Home was probably, with Andrei Gromyko and Chou En-Lai, one of the three most experienced foreign affairs statesmen in the world.

His record in the field stretched back to the period before World War II, when he served as parliamentary private secretary to Neville Chamber-

lain. He became Secretary of State for Foreign Affairs under Harold Macmillan from 1960 to 1963, conducting relations with the Kennedy administration, and then succeeded Macmillan as prime minister.

The Pilgrim Society is an organisation dedicated to Anglo-American understanding.

55 Sir Alec Douglas-Home
ADDRESS TO THE PILGRIMS, NEW YORK
(25 September 1972)

It is always a great pleasure for me to meet the Pilgrims of the United States.

Yours is a body of the highest distinction devoted to the cause of maintaining good relations between the United States and Britain.

We are, it is true, becoming partners in Europe, but that to Britain is not exclusive. In international relations the state of marriage is not necessarily monogamous. We are far more than 'just good friends,' and will remain so.

It is one of the curses of modern communications that conflict and failure tend to be exaggerated, success to be neglected . . .

. . . As you know, we British will be joining the European Community on 1 January, 1973. This decision was not taken lightly. After a great national debate lasting many years we decided that British membership was to the advantage of the United Kingdom, Europe and the world community as a whole. We could not stay outside so dynamic an association.

Britain will bring economic strength and political experience to an already flourishing Community, which has no intention of adopting selfish, inward-looking policies.

Successive Administrations in the United States have accepted this and have supported the concept of a united Europe. I am sure that they were and are right. The existence of the Community of the Six over the past fourteen years has not damaged American economic interests. American exports to the Six have almost doubled. There has been a continuing and substantial balance of payments surplus in favor of the United States in its trade with the Six. And the greater prosperity in Europe which enlargement will promote is very much in the American economic interest.

On the political side, enlargement of the Community will strengthen the vitality of Western Europe and the Western Alliance. The concept of the 'twin pillars' is as relevant today as when it was first formulated.

But there are those who believe that British entry will nevertheless have the effect of damaging relations between Britain and the United States. We shall of course be substituting for a bilateral relationship, one with a partnership of nations. This is inevitable. As unity within Europe grows, we in Britain will be increasingly acting and thinking as a member of a team and at the end of the road there will be a need for an even wider partnership between Europe and the United States in which the relationship between Britain and America will form an integral part.

But we are not there yet. The creation of a united Europe will require a long and continuing process of adjustment by all concerned.

At every stage it will be important that full weight is given on both sides of the Atlantic to the long-term interests which the enlarged Community and the United States have in common. We have a common interest in peace and in each other's prosperity. Economic competitors we may be. But the prosperity of the Western world is indivisible, and we must not forget this fact.

We have a common interest in the reform of the international monetary system and in greater trade liberalisation.

At a time like the present of upheaval and adjustment in world-wide trade patterns, no-one is free from protectionist pressures. But the enlarged Community will be essentially dependent upon external trade and have a clear interest in the maintenance of a liberal world trading system.

H*

Community tariffs are on the average lower than those of the United States and most European countries maintain fewer non-tariff barriers to trade than does the United States.

Both the United States and Europe have a clear interest in the orderly reduction of these obstacles to trade which still remain.

We have a common interest too, in the achievement of a detente with Eastern Europe and the Soviet Union, and of course in the security of the Western world at every stage.

Speaking of security, may I just say that Europe's security is, in my view, very much America's security—and vice versa—and we should avoid getting led into the trap of trying to distinguish between them.

During this process of an evolving relationship between the enlarged Community and the United States there will inevitably be scope for misunderstandings. There may be those who will seek to foster or exaggerate differences, genuine or imaginary.

You will remember Talleyrand's reply when informed that the Prussian Ambassador had died—'I wonder what he did that for?'

Good relations between Britain and the United States and a proper understanding of each other's aspirations will therefore in the years to come be perhaps of greater importance than before.

We are friends now. We must keep it that way.

SOURCE: British Information Services Press Release (25 September 1972)

A convinced advocate of entry into the Common Market, Roy Jenkins held strong beliefs which led him to oppose the leadership of the Labour Party during late 1971 and then a few months later to resign from the shadow cabinet. In 1972, during a series of three lectures at Yale University—later published under the title Afternoon on the Potomac?—*Mr Jenkins reflected on the consequences of America's swift rise to undisputed world leadership after World War II and the effect that this had on Britain's position. The only solution he saw was the emergence of a new European community, including Britain, which would be able to deal with the United States on the basis of some equality. The United States, for its part, would have to appreciate, as Britain did before it, that there are limits to its power to influence events in both the political and economic fields. When the United States realised this, it would still be able to exercise a considerable influence in international affairs.*

56 Roy Jenkins
LECTURE ON ANGLO-AMERICAN RELATIONSHIPS, YALE UNIVERSITY (1972)

The European political debate in Britain over the past twenty-five years has at last been about whether our relations with the countries of the Continent should be more akin to America's with continental European countries or to their own with each other. The attitude of both the Attlee Government and the postwar Churchill Government, which between them spanned the crucial decade from 1945–55, was firmly in favour of an American-style relationship. Ernest Bevin, Foreign Secretary in the Attlee Government, was a key architect of NATO, but kept Britain out of the European Coal and Steel Community. Eden, again Foreign Secretary in the second Churchill Government, which was formed in 1951, committed British troops to Germany for the rest of the century but tried to encourage the creation of a European army without British participation and tragically declined to be represented at the Messina Conference which led directly to the Treaty of Rome. These were the days, much more than in the twenties and thirties, when we saw ourselves at the meeting point of three circles: the Commonwealth, the North Atlantic, and the European.

This view of ourselves was fortified on the surface, although in reality undermined, by the position in which Britain emerged from World War II. The inheritance which Churchill bestowed on the British people in 1945 was at once glorious and thoroughly unsatisfactory. The facade of our family mansion was as splendid as it had ever been. The art treasures were still mostly in place. But the foundations were shaky, and the income attenuated. Our future was less clearly charted than that of any of the other major countries. The United States and the Soviet Union emerged with their roles as superpowers firmly under-pinned, at least for a generation. Germany, Italy, and Japan had all suffered the harsh experience of defeat; France that of occupation. Their régimes had to be constructed almost afresh. We were subject to no such brutal adjustment. But our power, so far from being built up by the war like that of America and Russia, had in fact been substantially diminished.

It took Britain some time to realise this. She did not attempt to cling to direct colonial power. Both in Asia in the forties and Africa in the fifties and early sixties Britain accepted and even forced the pace to independence. She withdrew, inevitably, occasionally jaggedly, but on the whole with good grace, from what might be described as the more selfish part of her world role. But from the more unselfish part there was for a long time no such withdrawal. Britain continued to believe that it was her duty to police large parts of the world, to defend her former dependencies, and to maintain a network of military commit-ments which, in extent if not in intensity, was barely approached by the superpowers, let alone by her power equals. In this way, not for unworthy motives, she tried to cling to a precarious position as the third of the great powers.

So long as this was so we remained wedded to the 'American' as opposed to the 'European' approach to our relations with Europe. But gradually the attempt to maintain the third great power role became increasingly unconvincing. Economically we were not in the same league as the superpowers, and the attempt to pretend that militarily we were so produced twenty years of severe overstrain which still further exacerbated our economic weakness.

Over the same period we had to rethink our relationship with the Commonwealth. The Commonwealth exists because of the accident that all its members were until fairly recently under British rule. It has the advantage of bringing together in loose and informal but occasionally intimate association, countries almost as disparate as possible from each other in race, religion, and stages of economic or social development. It is a club which imposes few obligations and is not greatly used by the members, but which has the nearly unique distinction for a club of widening rather than narrowing the horizons of those who belong. At the same time it has the disadvantage of an almost complete lack of political or economic coherence. Try to give it this and it will almost certainly break in your hands. Neither the old, white Commonwealth, with the possible exception of the remote and overdependent New Zealand, nor the newer, coloured Commonwealth countries, most of whom have too recently achieved independence to have any wish for an early merging of their sovereignty, least of all under the leadership of the principal ex-colonial power, want any approach to a tight union. Whatever its other virtues, and they are substantial, the Commonwealth has not for some time past provided Britain with any basis for a special and satisfactory role in the world. Understandably, however, in view of our past and the superficial nexus of a strong Commonwealth which persisted in London, many were slow to recognise this.

Equally the idea of the 'special relationship' in any exclusive sense between the United States and Britain has not prospered over the past ten years, both because of its inherently unequal nature and because of a certain lack of enthusiasm, for exclusivity at any rate, on both sides of the Atlantic. Nor did attempts to give it a slightly wider and more institutional framework, under the guise of the North Atlantic Free Trade Area, prove any more successful. They simply languished for lack of interest.

Source: Roy Jenkins. *Afternoon on the Potomac?* (1972)

The position of Ambassador to Washington has invariably been the most

*prestigious and important in the British diplomatic service. The man
appointed has nearly always been one close to the prime minister and also
one who might be expected to develop warm relations with the president
in power in the White House.*

*It was significant, therefore, that Edward Heath should have chosen
Lord Cromer to represent Britain in the contacts with the Nixon White
House. A member of the renowed Baring family, descended from a long
line of bankers and imperial pro-consuls, Lord Cromer appeared ideally
fitted to represent British interests in America at a time when the
British Government was preoccupied with the process of entry into the
European Economic Community.*

*It was the subtleties of relations within the Community, the Common-
wealth and the United States to which Lord Cromer referred when he
spoke to the world branches of the English-Speaking Union in Chicago
in late 1972.*

57 Lord Cromer
ADDRESS TO ENGLISH-SPEAKING UNION
WORLD BRANCHES CONFERENCE, CHICAGO
(13 November 1972)

. . . Let me now try to apply that pragmatism to the subject
which you are to discuss this afternoon: Britain turns to
Europe: the United Kingdom, the United States, the Commonwealth and the European Economic Community. I shall try to
be brief so as not to pre-empt your later discussion.

I would straightaway take issue with the phrase 'Britain
turns to Europe'. For it implies two things, neither of which to
my mind is true. First it implies that historically we have faced
away from Europe. And secondly it suggests that, by turning to
Europe, we are turning away from our traditional relationships
with the United States and the Commonwealth.

It would be wrong to see our decision to join the European
Community as a radical break with our history. Britain has
always been a part of Europe and closely involved in European
affairs. We have fought, talked, and traded with Europe since

time immemorial. In this century alone we have fought two world wars on European soil—because what happened in Europe was our intimate and natural concern. It is true that we have historically tried to avoid what were called 'entangling alliances' with the Continent and many of you will recall the famous *Times* headline: 'Storms in Channel. Continent isolated'. But since World War II we have been allied with all the major European countries in NATO. And we have engaged in close political consultation with them in the Western European Union and the Council of Europe. Despite the enterprise of Empire, Europe has always been in the forefront of our attention as well as obviously being at our threshold.

Equally our decision to join the European Economic Community emphatically does not mean that we shall in any sense turn our backs on the United States or on the Commonwealth. Certainly there will have to be some changes in the form of our relationship with the United States. But I believe that the net effect of placing our relationship with the United States firmly in the wider context of relations between the United States and Europe will be to give a better balance to these relations and so to strengthen the bonds between us, and between the United States and Europe.

Similarly with our relationship with the Commonwealth. There is no reason why our membership of the European Community should in itself weaken that. First, our ties with the Commonwealth go very deep. They are ties of language, of kinship, of history, of cultured heritage. These, rather than Commonwealth preferences and dollar quotas for bananas, are the stuff of the Commonwealth. They will not be affected by the arrangements which we enter into under the Treaty of Rome.

Secondly—despite some attempts in the United States and elsewhere to portray the members of the European Community as a group of inward-looking protectionist gourmets—Europe is and has always been outward-looking. Our membership will strengthen that trait.

Thirdly, we are joining Europe because we want to strengthen our own economic prospects, and because we want to continue to have a major voice in world affairs. As a member of a united Europe we can be a far more effective member of the Commonwealth than we should be on our own. And we shall be better able to increase our practical contribution to Commonwealth causes.

So I would reject the implications in the phrase 'Britain turns to Europe'. I do not want to sound smug or convey the impression that nothing is going to change. Of course membership is a big step for us, of course there will be changes, whether we join the European Community or not. What we are seeking to do is to secure the best possible future for Britain: a future in which we continue to count for something. We believe that by formalising our position in Europe, by becoming members of a larger and more powerful unit, we can best make our own and Europe's influence felt.

The decision to join the EEC does not mean that our ambitions and objectives have changed. Indeed they have not. They are objectives which we share with you in the United States and in the Commonwealth. We take them into Europe with us, the better to be able to achieve them.

The United States has consistently supported the aspiration of European unity. The far-sightedness of American statesmen and the unexampled generosity of the American people after World War II raised Europe from its ruins. Since then you have given every encouragement and support to the European peoples in their efforts to draw closer together. Now you justifiably look to Europe to help you, in greater measure than before, bear the burdens which the defence of our way of life imposes. I believe that as the deepening of European cooperation progresses, so we shall indeed do more.

But while no-one doubts that the United States and Europe will be in fundamental accord, equally there is no point in pretending that there will not be some problems and difficulties to be worked out between us as the European Community develops.

Let us look very briefly at what these are likely to be. First there will be trade problems. These are the most immediate because it is in the trade field that the impact of enlargement will first be felt. I do not propose to go into any detail of this today. I will only say this. Trade between the United States and Europe has prospered enormously in the past. It has run very substantially in the United States' favour. The prospects for future expansion are limitless.

But this prospect will be denied us if either the United States or Europe turns its back on the process of liberalisation of world trade which has brought us to our present level of prosperity.

We must push ahead with removal of remaining trade barriers, both tariffs and non-tariff barriers. 1973 must see a new round of international negotiations within the GATT to achieve further liberalisation. You undoubtedly have some cause for complaint against Europe. Equally we in Europe feel that there are many ways in which the United States imposes unfair restrictions on trade. Both sides must be prepared to make concessions if we are to avoid a situation of competitive restrictions. The prosperity of each of us is increasingly dependent upon the prosperity of the other.

While trade problems may be the most immediate we shall also need to work out a new relationship on the monetary front as we in Europe move towards closer economic and monetary union. Europe will be a very powerful monetary grouping. The very constructive approach taken by the United States at the recent meeting of the IMF gives every hope that an equitable reform of the world payments system, which does not permit privileges to any one country and which takes account equally of the interests of the United States, Europe and the developing countries, can be worked out. Then thirdly there will be adjustments to be made in the political relationship between Europe and the United States.

Of course Europe does not yet act as a single body in world affairs. It may be many years before we do so. But we are making progress on the harmonisation of foreign policies. Enlargement will prove a stimulus to this, and on an increasing number of issues there will be a single European voice. This is something which I believe you in the United States will welcome.

SOURCE: British Embassy, Washington, Press Release (13 November 1972)

Andrew Shonfield's analysis of the condition of the Anglo-American alliance was based on a long career in the field of foreign affairs, first as Foreign Editor of the Financial Times *and Economic Editor of the* Observer *and then as Director of Studies and research fellow at the Royal Institute of International Affairs.*

58 Andrew Shonfield
A GRUMBLING ALLIANCE (November 1972)

In this and the next lecture I am going to talk about the European Community's relations with the rest of the world—starting with the United States. In the early days of the European Common Market, the Six managed to achieve a kind of illusion of privacy within the international system: what I mean is that they treated the often quite profound effects which the arrangements that they made with one another had on the rest of the world as if they were subsidiary matters, certainly of no particular concern to them. They behaved for much of the time rather as though they were living inside a charmed circle, bounded entirely by their own problems and preoccupations. The special circumstances of the later post-war period, when Europe finally withdrew from empire and experienced the longest uninterrupted run of prosperity ever, based on cultivating its own garden, certainly helped.

The forward march of American world power, which accompanied the European withdrawal, was another major factor. The Europeans were provided with a sure military defence through the American nuclear umbrella; and American power, abetted to a diminishing extent by the British, supplied sufficient security for the movement of world trade to guarantee Europe's requirements of vital raw materials like oil. At the same time the American dollar provided an extremely effective international medium of exchange and a common reserve currency for the Europeans. Why should the countries forming the European Community have cared very much about what happened in the world beyond Western Europe?

Meanwhile the politics of the European charmed circle led to the building-up of a network of special agreements between the Community and a number of favoured states on its southerly periphery. Many of these were Mediterranean countries; others were in Black Africa, former colonies of France and Belgium. What has now been established as a result of this is a fairly well-defined zone of client states—more or less dependent commercial partners of the Community. To American eyes, this systematic build-up of privileged trading arrangements by the Europeans, with its corollary of discrimination against the outsider, must look altogether too much like a variation of their own early federal history—a kind of commercial Monroe Doctrine for Eurafrica.

That does not make the Americans of today like it any better. On the contrary, as the design of the European construction which they helped to foster has become clearer, they have grown more indignant about it. They feel cheated on two counts. First of all, there is much less of a unified political power in the Community than they had hoped to see established. The aim of the American supporters of a United Europe was always to bring into being an effective political partner on the other side of the Atlantic who would be able to share with the United States the responsibility for major international decisions. Secondly, the United States was looking for an ally in sustaining a universal system of international trade and payments, based on a uniform set of rules accepted by all and according equal treatment to all comers. The Americans can argue fairly that they made a number of sacrifices during the early post-war period in setting up a system of this kind, which derived from the agreements reached at Bretton Woods in 1944. This was America's grand design for the post-war world. They now find that they face an invigorated Western Europe, owing its success partly to that grand design, which seems to be bent on a policy of discrimination against outsiders.

There is a certain irony in the historic reversal of roles between the two sides of the Atlantic. In the past, from the late 19th century right up to the Great Depression of the 1930s, the cult of the universal trading and financial system, with free access on equal terms to all markets, guided the international policies of Britain and a group of smaller European countries which are heavily dependent on foreign commerce. The United States for most of this time was living very much in an enclosed world of its own. It only began to break out of this in the Thirties. The habit of treating foreign trade and finance as if they were essentially matters of domestic politics took the Americans quite a long time to live down. But now, as the chief guardians of the universal order which they have helped to establish since the last war, they are faced with a Europe which is in its turn trying to use international trade to consolidate its own regional arrangements.

Recently there has been an observable sharpening of the American tone towards Europe. Behind this tone there seems to be a considered switch of policy which was spelt out in a special report for the President in 1971 by Mr Peterson, now the Secretary of Commerce, on United States international economic policy. There he makes the point that not only the content of American policies but also 'the methods of diplomacy will have to be changed.' He goes on: 'Our international negotiating stance will have to meet its trading partners with a clearer, more assertive version of new national interest. This will make us more predicable in the eyes of our trading partners.'

There are two questions that I want to explore. First, how far is the United States likely to push its new aggressive and demanding policy towards Europe? And secondly, how is the European posture towards the United States likely to develop during the 1970s in the face of this American pressure?

To make the first question concrete, is it conceivable that if the Americans continue to feel very frustrated about European behaviour, they will withdraw their military forces altogether from Western Europe? From a European point of view, the main purpose served by the American presence is to provide a visible guarantee of the military involvement of the United States in the defence of this territory. It is important that American troops should not only be about in Europe, but should also be in some clear sense in the front line—so that any attempt by the other side to invade a piece of territory or, say, to conduct a raid across the frontier in Berlin would immediately risk engaging American military forces in battle. Thus to remove American soldiers altogether from Europe would be likely to be interpreted as meaning a significant weakening of the American nuclear guarantee against the Soviet Union and its allies. It would be an extreme step to take. It is also hard to envisage the circumstances in which the United States would not wish to have some of its forces stationed on the territories of its closest military allies, who happen also to be extremely rich and economically powerful. Unless the United States ceases to be a world power, it will need to maintain substantial armed forces somewhere, and West Europe is a convenient place in which to keep some of them. The truth is that the European military establishment of the United States is a not very expensive way of maintaining the posture of a great power. Of course, the establishment need not be as big as it is now. But then a cut in this force seems likely whether the Europeans co-operate with the Americans in their economic policies or not.

There seem, therefore, to be strong reasons for thinking that the American response even to extreme friction with the European Community would fall well short of a complete military withdrawal. A more likely outcome would be some less precise but nevertheless marked change in American behaviour towards the European Community on matters on which the Europeans are themselves divided. Hitherto the American interest in furthering European integration has meant that when the member states have had deep differences, the United States has not exploited them. On the contrary, its desire to have them speak with a common voice has been the dominant motive. But there were signs during the 1971 dollar crisis that the Americans were at least contemplating the possibility of bargaining with the member countries individually, giving the favoured ones special concessions on trade. It is perhaps this kind of tactical manoeuvre which we should expect to see pursued rather more vigorously if friction grows in the future. It could, in certain circumstances, prove to be very damaging.

The answer to the second question depends on how far the differences of approach to the major issues of economic and financial policy which at present divide the United States and Europe are of a fundamental character. If, in spite of the close American military connection with Europe and the reasonable prospects of continuing European integration, I foresee a more difficult relationship between the United States and Western Europe during the period ahead, it is because of certain essential features of contemporary international economic relations. These do suggest that there are profound forces at work which are likely to make the European Community an awkward partner for the US in economic and financial affairs, which is precisely where the strength of the European Community is greatest. The United States still produces somewhat more than the combined output of the enlarged Community of nine countries, but the Nine are much more important as world traders— they are together responsible for some 40 per cent of all international trade—and they own over half of all the world's currency reserves. There is a historical tendency for the United States to see the relatively low proportion of its national income that is derived from international trade as a powerful source of bargaining strength. In a crisis where the United States is in disagreement with the rest of the world on some aspect of economic policy there is a standard reflex action on the part of a substantial section of American public opinion. It crows: 'In the last resort we can opt out; you can't.'

It is the visceral American reaction, recalling with satisfaction that it is, after all, only dealing with the bad Old World from which it escaped long ago. One noticed the reaction once again during the dollar crisis in 1971. In effect, the line taken by the United States Treasury was that the essential strength of the dollar reflected the overwhelming productive power of the nation, which was responsible for about one-third of the total measured output of the world; and if the Europeans didn't like the way the Americans were handling the dollar, they could either lump it or take their business elsewhere. The choice was a matter of indifference to the United States.

Now I believe this line of thought to be based on an American delusion. The Americans, in fact, lost their secluded playground some time ago. They are still playing the same sports, and the immediate landscape may look the same, but it happened to be set in the middle of a busy and populous city. The people outside are all within shouting distance all of the time. I shall not attempt to list the factors that have so greatly increased America's interdependence with the rest of the world. The most important are in any case political and psychological. The United States is a world power, exercising authority and influence on a scale that is probably larger than has ever been done before. It cannot both be and do that, and opt out . . .

Back in the Twenties President Coolidge said: 'The business of the United States is business.' He summed up an important strand in American thinking—which is that governments do best when they simply provide the opportunity for the forces of private commerce to assert themselves. By the same token one might say today: 'The business of the European Community is politics and social welfare.' Again, the Americans, who tend to see this European venture as an exercise in classic New World federalism, designed to liberate the forces of private enterprise

from the interference of national states, are going to be dis-
appointed. For the fact is this is a very interventionist Community, most active in regulating the domestic affairs of its
member countries and at the same time annoyingly deficient in
clear-cut authority when it comes to conducting its relations
with outsiders. From an American point of view this looks like a
nasty combination of busybodying at home and sloth abroad.

The new American political tactics, as they have emerged in
the 1970s, appear to be an attempt to blackmail the Europeans
into creating the collective authority which they lack by pre-
senting them with the threat of massive inaction by the United
States. The theory is that once the Europeans realise that the
leadership and initiative are no longer coming from the United
States, they will produce some leadership of their own. This
approach was much in evidence, as I have said, during the
dollar crisis of the latter part of 1971 and afterwards. The
Europeans are now being told, in effect, that they must either
put up their own substitute for the dollar system—or shut up,
and accept the monetary arrangements that are designed to
meet American convenience. I suspect that this ploy may have
long-term consequences that the Americans may find by no
means convenient. It is always risky to invite a number of
people to look for a means of agreeing among themselves by
ganging up against you. They may, after all, find one! The
Europeans are genuinely irked by certain aspects of the American dominance of the world monetary system, and I believe
that they can make their own financial arrangements much less
dependent on the dollar, while stopping far short of the creation
of a fully-fledged European monetary union.

The point is a little technical, but what I am arguing is that
the countries of the European Community could arrive at an
agreed set of restrictive rules designed to control certain transactions in dollars and to limit the use of dollars as part of their
currency reserves. In that case they would in effect reduce the
freedom of manoeuvre of all dollar-holders—and most of these
are, after all, still Americans. They could also put the American

Treasury in a very awkward position if they decided that henceforth the dollar was no longer an acceptable asset to go into their currency reserves. There are already vast quantities of spare dollars in the hands of European central banks, and it is to be expected that they will try to reduce the amount and to agree on common rules restricting the future acquisition of dollars.

Once again, there is here a built-in formula for feeding the fires of mutual resentment. For the Americans undoubtedly believe that offering the world the opportunity of converting itself to a dollar currency system was a great service performed at considerable sacrifice to themselves. They point to the fact that in the course of it they lost control over their own currency, because too many other people outside the United States were using it. The Europeans do not deny this fact, but they emphasise the very large financial advantages which the Americans have had in the process. The question, however, is not who is right, but how to find some means of mitigating the quarrel. What is clear is that the recent American tactic of treating it as if it was someone else's problem is not very promising from this point of view.

One can, I think, understand the American aim better if one sees it as part of a more general realignment of policies in the context of what may now be called the Nixon-Kissinger doctrine. This is the view that by the late Sixties the American posture in world affairs was both excessively exposed and excessively rigid. The most spectacular moves designed to reduce both exposure and rigidity have concentrated on the United States' enemies, China and Russia. But the allies have also been subjected to an effort to reformulate the terms of their bargain with the United States in such a way as to limit the degree of American involvement. The Americans tend to argue that their own bargaining position has been significantly weakened, because their allies have been able to exploit the fact that America has such a large stake in the maintenance of the international system itself. It is almost as if the United States Government felt that it, too, had to demonstrate every now and then that it could play hookey!

My point is that in practice the United States can't. It has too much at stake in the world economic and financial system to opt out. But equally, it is not inclined towards the alternative approach, which I have called the 'Community method', because that involves too great a departure from old established habits of conducting international relations. It is the complete opposite of opting out: indeed, it commits you to opt *into* a bargaining process with a lot of foreigners on almost every subject of domestic interest. One would have to be very sanguine to envisage anything more than a highly tentative approach to arrangements of this kind for some time yet. In the meanwhile, the likelihood is that the United States will grow increasingly impatient with the lack of European leadership, and that the logic of the slow and laborious process of European integration will produce a rich crop of European bargains which in one way or another hurt United States interest.

At the back of all this is the awkward but inescapable fact that the two regions facing each other now across the Atlantic are not only the most developed economically and the most practised in the sophisticated techniques of representative democracy: they are also the most pluralistic societies in the world. To make a significant decision in either of them requires an extensive and complicated process of internal bargaining with powerful interest groups, as well as widespread skills in achieving workable compromises. The upshot tends to be that when the domestic compromises have been made and either group has to move on to a further stage of negotiating with an outsider, its position has already acquired a high degree of rigidity. No doubt this is considerably worse for the European Community, whose member states are only now gradually getting to understand each other and to learn the techniques of effective compromise. But it would be wrong to underestimate the profound difficulty which a pluralistic society like the United States, with lots of pressure groups and an open democratic process, experiences in bargaining abroad about matters involving domestic interests. And this suggests the conclusion that if the Europeans were ever to appoint a President and an executive branch of government, like the Americans, they would still be an awkward lot to bargain with.

SOURCE: *The Listener* (23 November 1972)

It was fitting in view of the long and close association between Britain and the United States that Edward Heath, the British Prime Minister, was the first foreign leader to be invited to the White House in President Nixon's second term.

At the time of his visit a ceasefire in the long, debilitating and divisive war in Vietnam had just been reached. The President had declared that 1973 would be 'The Year of Europe', although there were already signs that other problems would soon prevent him from concentrating exclusively on that goal. The American economy was faltering and the nation was on the brink of its second devaluation in less than a year. It was apparent to the American people that there would be little of the 'peace dividend' that they had once expected would flow to the domestic economy with the ending of the involvement in Vietnam. Britain, too, was facing economic problems and a rash of damaging strikes. The nation had entered Europe, but any benefits from entry had yet to develop.

In an address to the National Press Club in Washington, the Prime Minister discussed the new union that would develop with British entry into Europe. Yet at the same time he appealed for continued cooperation with the United States on the basis of what he called a new 'natural relationship'.

59 Edward Heath
SPEECH AT THE NATIONAL PRESS CLUB, WASHINGTON (1 February 1973)

Last October the Leaders of the 9 Community countries met in Paris. We were not concerned to exchange smiles and platitudes. We were aiming to draw up an ambitious and imaginative programme for the future of the Community. That is what we aimed at, and that is what we achieved. The significance of that programme has not yet been fully realised.

We were not content with general principles. We set deadlines for work decision and action in many fields. We will encourage the development of industry on a European scale. We will work out European policies to protect our energy resources, to spread prosperity through the various regions, and promote improved conditions of work and employment. We aim to transform the whole complex of relations between European countries into a European union before the end of the present decade.

This will be a new type of union. That is why I myself have never used the phrase 'United States of Europe'. That phrase gives the impression that we shall simply be following in the footsteps of your own remarkable achievement in creating a nation. We are dealing with an entirely different situation. We are dealing with ancient European nations, each with its own traditions and background, each determined to retain its identity. Our intention is not to destroy that identity but to build on to it a new European dimension which will enable us to secure, by common action, benefits which would be beyond our reach as separate nations. That is what we mean by a European Community.

I am confident that the will exists to carry through the whole of this existing programme. In my own country we have come to the end of 20 years of discussion about our relationship with Europe. As you may know this discussion has cut right across Party lines. Now that the decision is taken and we are members of the Community I find that forward-looking people of all political persuasions are moving in to take advantage of the opportunities open to them in the Community.

In the foreign field we are also moving towards unity. At the Summit we agreed that the aim should be to work out common medium and long-term positions on foreign policy matters. We already have a common commercial policy and speak with one voice in international trade negotiations. More and more I hope that the European countries will act as one. This is essential now that the Community is the largest unit in world trade.

So once again Europe is on the move. Successive United States Administrations can take a big share of the credit for this. Over the years you have accepted the creation of a friendly, stable and prosperous Western Europe as a major interest of the United States. You have accepted that this will mean greater competition for your industries. It will mean an independent European voice in the world which will not always share exactly the same views which you hold. But you have thought, rightly I am sure, that this was a price well worth paying in return for the larger goal. I would like to pay tribute to the farsightedness and consistency with which the United States has helped Europe forward along this path.

The effect of these changes in Europe will be far-reaching. Just as the growth of the population and the increased industrial prosperity of the United States has led to the consolidation of her world power, so we can expect the new union in Western Europe to alter fundamentally the authority of individual Western European states in world affairs.

This position will not be used irresponsibly by the members of the Community. We made a public statement of our view in the Communique issued at the end of the Paris Summit meeting. We said then that the Nine had decided to maintain a 'constructive dialogue' with the United States, Japan, Canada and their other industrialised trade partners. By this we mean that we are ready to talk about the whole field of our relations. There are two areas in which there are serious and urgent problems—monetary reform and questions of international commercial policy. The Community and the United States have agreed to hold negotiations for the further liberalisation of international trade. Discussions on the international monetary system have already begun . . .

. . . Of course, defence is still an essential part of the relationship between the United States and Europe. We are rightly pursuing detente in discussions with the Russians and other Eastern Europeans in a number of different contexts. I hope that these discussions can achieve real progress. But until real detente has been achieved it would be foolish for the Western powers to weaken the solidarity or military power of our alliance. I think that this is common ground on both sides of the Atlantic. It is perfectly natural that you in the United States should from time to time re-examine the reasons for which you station forces in Europe. I believe that each such examination is bound to lead to the same conclusion. American forces are in Europe, not to do us a favour, but to preserve an essential American interest and to take part in the common defence of the Atlantic partnership.

It is equally natural that the American effort should be compared with the effort of your European partners. We certainly recognise that as the relative economic strength of Europe increases, so too should the share of the common defence burden which Europe bears. Already we have shown that we intend to improve our defence effort. In 1970 we carried through a billion dollar European defence improvement programme. In 1971 and 1972 there have been co-ordinated national force improvements of one billion and 1·5 billion dollars. The European allies now provide 90 per cent of NATO's ground forces in Europe, 75 per cent of her air forces and 80 per cent of her naval forces. There are 10 Western Europeans under arms for every American serviceman in Europe.

I have tried to show you how we in Britain and we in Europe see our own future and our relationship with the United States. We want to fortify the present relationship. We want to make it strong and durable, to take account of the shifts and changes of the past few years, the effect of which should not be overlooked; and to find common solutions which meet your needs and interests as well as our own. I am sure that this is the next major task we have to tackle together, and that is the main reason why I am here.

SOURCE: British Embassy, Washington, Press Release (1 February 1973)

THE YEAR OF EUROPE

The Nixon Administration had declared that 1973 would be its 'Year of Europe' and this was the theme taken up by Dr Henry Kissinger, the National Security Assistant, in a significant address to the annual meeting of the Associated Press in New York.

In his speech, which the New York Times *promptly compared to the Marshall Plan speech in its significance, Dr Kissinger called for a 'new Atlantic charter' and spoke with frankness on the developing problems as the West European nations and Japan became stronger and more independent of the United States.*

Dr Kissinger noted the widespread criticisms that Europe had pursued its economic self-interest too one-sidedly and was ignoring its wider responsibilities; also that the United States was seeking to desert Europe militarily and bypass it diplomatically.

He suggested a common discussion of common problems among the major trading nations, rather than an American plan for solving all problems. He urged the European nations that by the time President Nixon visited Europe (a visit then projected for later in 1973) 'a new Atlantic charter' should have been developed setting goals for the future.

60 Dr Henry Kissinger
ADDRESS TO THE ANNUAL MEETING OF THE ASSOCIATED PRESS (23 April 1973)

This year has been called the Year of Europe, but not because Europe was less important in 1972 or in 1969. The Alliance between the United States and Europe has been the cornerstone of all post-war foreign policy. It provided the political framework for American engagements in Europe and marked the definitive end of U.S. isolationism. It ensured the sense of security that allowed Europe to recover from the devastation of the war. It reconciled former enemies. It was the stimulus for an unprecedented endeavor in European unity and the principal means to forge the common policies that safeguarded Western security in an era of prolonged tension and confrontation. Our values, our goals and our basic interests are most closely identified with those of Europe.

1973 is the Year of Europe because the era that was shaped by decisions of a generation ago is ending. The success of those policies has produced new realities that require new approaches:

The revival of Western Europe is an established fact as is the historic success of its movement toward economic unification.

The East-West strategic military balance has shifted from American preponderance to near equality, bringing with it the necessity for a new understanding of the requirements of our common security.

Other areas of the world have grown in importance. Japan has emerged as a major power center. In many fields, 'Atlantic' solutions to be viable must include Japan.

We are in a period of relaxation of tensions. But as the rigid divisions of the past two decades diminish, new assertions of national identity and national rivalry emerge.

Problems have arisen, unforeseen a generation ago, which require new types of cooperative action. Ensuring the supply of energy for industrialized nations is an example.

These factors have produced a dramatic transformation of the psychological climate in the West—a change which is the most profound current challenge to Western statesmanship. In Europe a new generation—to whom war and its dislocations are not personal experiences—takes stability for granted. But it is less committed to the unity that made peace possible and to the effort required to maintain it. In the United States, decades of global burdens have fostered and the frustrations of the war in Southeast Asia have accentuated a reluctance to sustain global involvements on the basis of preponderant American responsibility.

Inevitably this period of transition will have its strains. There have been complaints in America that Europe ignores its wider responsibilities in pursuing economic self-interest too one-sidely and that Europe is not carrying its fair share of the burden of the common defense. There have been complaints in Europe that America is out to divide Europe economically, or to desert Europe militarily, or to bypass Europe diplomatically. Europeans appeal to the United States to accept their independence and their occasionally severe criticism of us in the name of Atlantic unity, while at the same time they ask for a veto on our independent policies—also in the name of Atlantic unity.

Our challenge is whether a unity forged by a common perception of danger can draw new purpose from shared positive aspirations.

If we permit the Atlantic partnership to atrophy, or to erode through neglect, carelessness, or mistrust, we risk what has been achieved, and we shall miss our historic opportunity for even greater achievement.

In the Forties and Fifties the task was economic reconstruction and security against the danger of attack. The West responded with courage and imagination. Today the need is to make the Atlantic relationship as dynamic a force in building a new structure of peace, less geared to crisis and more conscious of opportunities, drawing its inspirations from its goals rather than its fears. The Atlantic nations must join in a fresh act of creation, equal to that undertaken by the post-war generation of leaders of Europe and America.

This is why the President is embarking on a personal and direct approach to the leaders of Western Europe. In his discussions with the heads of government of Britain, Italy, the Federal Republic of Germany, and France, the Secretary General of NATO and other European leaders, it is the President's purpose to lay the basis for a new era of creativity in the West.

His approach will be to deal with Atlantic problems comprehensively. The political, military and economic issues in Atlantic relations are linked by reality, not by our choice nor for the tactical purpose of trading one off against the other. The solutions will not be worthy of the opportunity if left to technicians. They must be addressed at the highest level.

In 1972 the President transformed relations with our adversaries to lighten the burdens of fear and suspicion.

In 1973 we can gain the same sense of historical achievement by reinvigorating shared ideals and common purposes with our friends.

The United States proposes to its Atlantic partners that, by the time the President travels to Europe toward the end of the year, we will have worked out a new Atlantic charter setting the goals for the future—a blueprint that:

> builds on the past without becoming its prisoner,
> deals with the problems our success has created,
> creates for the Atlantic nations a new relationship in whose progress Japan can share.

We ask our friends in Europe, Canada, and ultimately Japan to join us in this effort.

This is what we mean by the Year of Europe.

The problems in Atlantic relationships are real. They have arisen in part because during the Fifties and Sixties the Atlantic community organized itself in different ways in the many different dimensions of its common enterprise.

> In economic relations, the European Community has increasingly stressed its regional personality; the United States, at the same time, must act as part of, and be responsible for a wider international trade and monetary system. We must reconcile these two perspectives.
> In our collective defense, we are still organized on the principle of unity and integration, but in radically different strategic conditions. The full implications of this change have yet to be faced.
> Diplomacy is the subject of frequent consultations, but is essentially being conducted by traditional nation states. The U.S. has global interests and responsibilities. Our European allies have regional interests. These are not

necessarily in conflict, but in the new era neither are they automatically identical.

In short, we deal with each other regionally and even competitively in economic matters, on an integrated basis in defense, and as nation states in diplomacy. When the various collective institutions were rudimentary, the potential inconsistency in their modes of operation was not a problem. But after a generation of evolution and with the new weight and strength of our allies, the various parts of the construction are not always in harmony and sometimes obstruct each other.

If we want to foster unity, we can no longer ignore these problems. The Atlantic nations must find a solution for the management of their diversity, to serve the common objectives which underlie their unity. We can no longer afford to pursue national or regional self-interest without a unifying framework. We cannot hold together if each country or region asserts its autonomy whenever it is to its benefit and invokes unity to curtail the independence of others.

We must strike a new balance between self-interest and the common interest. We must identify interests and positive values beyond security in order to engage once again the commitment of peoples and parliaments. We need a shared view of the world we seek to build . . .

SOURCE: White House Press Release (23 April 1973)

Afterword

With the growth of the European Economic Community, Britain's attitude towards the United States began to change. Caught in schizophrenic fashion between her loyalty to the now fading special relationship, her historic and sentimental ties to the Commonwealth, and her new commitment to the rapidly developing European Community, Britain finally decided to try to plunge into Europe. The United States, largely because it initially saw British entry into Europe as a means of broadening the EEC and transforming it into a more outward looking force, did nothing to hinder Britain's decision.

Indeed, the United States was hardly in a position to affect the historic move Britain was making. Exhausted by the cumulative impact of ten years of exhausting and fruitless war in Asia, with all the attendant social disruption that this created at home; faced by growing economic problems, and racked by suspicions of political wrongdoing and possible criminality at the very highest levels of government, the United States began increasingly to turn inwards on itself and withdraw to what, to many eyes, appeared to be a new isolationism.

Following Britain's eventual entry into the EEC, the 'special relationship', as it had existed for more than twenty years, came to an end, to be replaced by what Edward Heath was to call a 'natural relationship'. The term was an appropriate one. Despite the impact of the Common Market and the dissolution of imperial power, Britons and Americans remain linked by a common language and heritage, by a shared tradition of law and politics, and very often—in spite of all the *great differences between the two societies—a common way of looking at the rest of the world. Few can confidently predict how the relationship will develop in the future. Just as World War II marked the beginning of a new phase in the Anglo-American alliance, so the entry of Britain into the EEC signalled the ending of that phase and the opening of a new one.*

Bibliography

The wealth of material which either entirely or in part deals with the subject of Anglo-American relations since World War II is intimidating to anyone who embarks on a study of the period. Listed here are mainly those works which would be of interest to the general reader wishing to acquaint himself with the subject in some depth, without becoming bogged down in it. Bibliographies dealing with particular aspects of Anglo-American relations in more detail can be found in many of the works noted.

An invaluable basic year-by-year summary of events during the whole period covered by the present volume is to be found in the Royal Institute of International Affairs' *Survey of International Affairs*, which, with its accompanying volumes of *Documents on International Affairs*, is an excellent aid to any serious student. The United States equivalent is the Council on Foreign Relations' *The United States in World Affairs* and the volumes of *Documents on World Affairs* which partner this series. These are generally less comprehensive than the volumes published by the Royal Institute of International Affairs in London, but still useful. The United States Department of State *Bulletin* is a valuable compendium of all documents and speeches released by the State Department. Similarly, the continuing series of *White House Documents*, issued weekly, is the official source for presidential statements and news conferences. The official records of parliamentary debates published in *Hansard* and the documents released by the Foreign Office are, of course, the basic sources of official material in Britain. Those who wish may find comprehensive coverage of major events by going back to relevant issues of *The Times*, the *Daily Telegraph* and *The Economist* in Britain, or in the United States to the *New York Times*, the *Washington Post* and the *Los Angeles Times*, or to such journals as *Foreign Affairs*, *Business Week* and the now-defunct *Reporter*.

The memoirs of the major figures of the postwar years are worthwhile sources of information on policy and the evolution of allied strategy. Winston Churchill's *The Grand Alliance* (1950), Anthony Eden's *Full Circle* (1960), Clement Attlee's *A Prime Minister Remembers* (1961), and Harold Macmillan's *Tides of Fortune* (1969) and *Winds of Change* (1970) are all of considerable interest. In the US Harry Truman's *Memoirs* (1955), Dwight D. Eisenhower's *Mandate for Change* (1963) and Lyndon Johnson's *The Vantage Point: Perspectives on the Presidency* (1972) are to be recommended.

Other valuable sources are Arthur Schlesinger's *A Thousand Days: John F. Kennedy in the White House* (1965), Theodore Sorensen's *Kennedy* (1965), Philip Geyelin's *Lyndon B. Johnson and the World* (1966), Dean Acheson's *Present at the Creation* (1969), Louis Heren's *No Hail, No Farewell* (1970) and David Nunnerley's *President Kennedy and Britain* (1972). Also of interest for their coverage of the years immediately following the war with the growth of the Truman Doctrine and the Marshall Plan are Walter Milles (ed) *The Forrestal Diaries* (1951), George Kennan *American Diplomacy 1900–1950* (1952), Joseph M. Jones *The Fifteen Weeks* (1955) and Herbert Feis *Between War and Peace: The Potsdam Conference* (1960). For the evolution of the postwar monetary system and the British Loan of 1947 Richard Gardner's *Sterling-Dollar Diplomacy* (1969 edition) is to be highly recommended. A basically sound history of the early years of the period, which eschews controversy, is H. C. Allen's vintage *Britain and the United States* (1953).

By contrast in recent years there has been a spate of 're-visionist' interpretations designed to prove that postwar American policy was far from being as altruistic and noble as its more ardent protagonists, such as Dr Allen, maintained. The pioneer of these was William Appleman Williams *The Tragedy of American Diplomacy* (1959). Other recent authors of interest are the less revolutionary Edmund Stillman and William Pfaff, whose *Power and Impotence* (1966) is an excellent study of the bases for Eisenhower diplomacy, Stephen E. Ambrose's *Rise to Globalism* (1971), and Joyce and Gabriel Kolko's *The Limits of Power* (1972). Norman A. Graebner's *Cold War Diplomacy* (1962) provides a handy brief summary and some useful documents.

The early development of the atomic bomb is well covered in Robert Jungk's *Brighter Than a Thousand Suns* (UK edition 1958). Henry J. Kissinger in *Nuclear Weapons and Foreign Policy* (1958) expounds a considerably more hawkish view of the world than he was to do later as National Security Adviser and Secretary of State. Arnold Wolfers (ed) *Alliance Policy in the Cold War* (1959), Coral Bell *Negotiation from Strength* (1962), and David E. Lilienthal *The Atomic Energy Years 1945–50* (1964), are all interesting views of the same subject from different perspectives. Gar Alperovitz in *Atomic Diplomacy* (1965) examines the motivation behind the use of the atomic bomb from a revisionist standpoint.

The Suez venture has been well analysed in a number of comprehensive studies as well as numerous monographs which have attempted to reveal the 'inside' story of the Anglo-French-Israeli operation. Apart from Anthony Eden's own version of events in *Full Circle*, other works which are worth reading are Paul Johnson's *The Suez War* (1957), Herman Finer's *Dulles over Suez* (1964), which is highly critical of the late Secretary of State, Mary and Serge Bromberger's *Secrets of Suez* (1957) and Hugh Thomas's exemplary short *Suez* (1962).

Studies and memoirs dealing with the Anglo-American relationship abound. Among those mentioned in the text are

Senator William Fulbright's *New Myths and Old Realities* (1964), Henry Kissinger's *The Troubled Partnership* (1964), Sir George Catlin's *The Atlantic Commonwealth* (1969) and Roy Jenkins's *Afternoon on the Potomac?* (1972).

Acknowledgements

I wish to acknowledge the permission granted by the following authors and publishers to quote excerpts from their works:

Sir Anthony Eden. *Full Circle*, Cassell and Company, London; Houghton Mifflin Company, Boston, Massachusetts.

Harold Macmillan. *Riding the Storm* and *Pointing the Way*, Macmillan, London and Basingstoke.

J. W. Fulbright. *Old Myths and New Realities*, Random House, New York, and Jonathan Cape, London.

Henry Kissinger. *The Troubled Partnership* (McGraw Hill, New York, for the Council on Foreign Relations).

George E. G. Catlin. *The Atlantic Commonwealth*, Penguin Books, Harmondsworth, Middlesex (Copyright © George E. G. Catlin, 1969).

Andrew Shonfield. *Europe: Journey to an Unknown Destination*, chapter 3: 'The American Connection—A Grumbling Alliance', Penguin Books/Allen Lane, Harmondsworth, Middlesex (Copyright © Andrew Shonfield, 1972, 1973).

The Times, Printing House Square, London EC4. Leading article 'A Lack of Candour' (2 November 1956).

Roy Jenkins. *Afternoon on the Potomac?* Yale University Press, London and New Haven, Conn. (Copyright © Roy Jenkins, 1972).

Index